Island Bodies

UNIVERSITY PRESS OF FLORIDA

Florida A&M University, Tallahassee
Florida Atlantic University, Boca Raton
Florida Gulf Coast University, Ft. Myers
Florida International University, Miami
Florida State University, Tallahassee
New College of Florida, Sarasota
University of Central Florida, Orlando
University of Florida, Gainesville
University of North Florida, Jacksonville
University of South Florida, Tampa
University of West Florida, Pensacola

Island Bodies

Transgressive Sexualities
in the Caribbean Imagination

ROSAMOND S. KING

University Press of Florida
Gainesville · Tallahassee · Tampa · Boca Raton
Pensacola · Orlando · Miami · Jacksonville · Ft. Myers · Sarasota

21 20 19 18 17 16   6 5 4 3 2 1

First cloth printing, 2014
First paperback printing, 2016

Library of Congress Cataloging-in-Publication Data
King, Rosamond S. author.
Island bodies : transgressive sexualities in the Caribbean imagination / Rosamond
S. King.
pages cm
Includes bibliographical references and index.
ISBN 978-0-8130-4980-9 (cloth)
ISBN 978-0-8130-6206-8 (pbk.)
1. Homosexuality and literature—Caribbean Area. 2. Sexual minorities—Caribbean
Area. 3. Homosexuality—Caribbean Area. 4. Interracial marriage—Caribbean
Area. 5. Transgender people—Caribbean Area. 6. Homosexuality and music—
Caribbean Area. 7. Homosexuality and motion pictures—Caribbean Area.
8. Caribbean Area—Social conditions. I. Title.
PR9205.05.K56 2014
810.9'9729—dc23
2013051132

The University Press of Florida is the scholarly publishing agency for the State
University System of Florida, comprising Florida A&M University, Florida Atlantic
University, Florida Gulf Coast University, Florida International University, Florida
State University, New College of Florida, University of Central Florida, University of
Florida, University of North Florida, University of South Florida, and University of
West Florida.

University Press of Florida
15 Northwest 15th Street
Gainesville, FL 32611-2079
http://www.upf.com

For everyone who lives outside the boundaries

Contents

Preface

My interest in the topics explored in *Island Bodies* spans many years; this book was developed through research, conference presentations, journal articles, and long conversations. My academic research has also benefited, however, from my personal experiences and community work. I have long been a part of Caribbean communities in the region and its diaspora. I have spent time in Trinidad, Barbados, and Puerto Rico and have lived in or visited many other Caribglobal spaces in New York, Miami, Toronto, and elsewhere. Particularly as the cochair of the Caribbean Board of the International Resource Network, an online project which strives to connect Caribbean scholars and activists who work to document, examine, or improve the lives of sexual minorities in the region, and as a volunteer for and board member of the Audre Lorde Project, a New York City–based center for lesbian, gay, bisexual, two spirit, trans, and gender nonconforming people of color, I have had the opportunity to work on community projects related to sexuality and other issues—experiences that encourage me to link imaginative stories to lived ones. Finally, my experience as a mentor for Green Chimneys, a service center for sexual minority youth in the New York City foster care system—too many of whose children were thrown out by their Caribbean families—provided a reminder of the very real consequences of defying heteropatriarchy and conventional gender. While I do not engage in community work to serve my scholarly research, the two have certainly benefited each other in ways I did not foresee. I have written *Island Bodies* for the many academic, social, and cultural communities of which I am a part.

Acknowledgments

A scholarly book can be made manifest in many different ways. *Island Bodies* is the result of individual investigation and writing within a matrix of challenges and the support to overcome them. I appreciate the time and efforts of the entire University Press of Florida staff, in particular senior acquisitions editor Amy Gorelick for her enthusiastic support of this project, Nevil Parker for guiding it into existence, Barbara Drake for her fastidious copyediting, and the anonymous reviewers whose thoughtful comments have made this manuscript better. I thank all of the writers and artists whose work I engage, especially Ewan Atkinson, who generously agreed to have his work be reproduced in these pages.

The time and resources needed to complete this work were provided by many generous institutions and sources of support, including fellowships and awards from the Woodrow Wilson National Fellowship Foundation; PSC-CUNY (Professional Staff Congress-City University of New York); the University of Chicago Center for the Study of Race, Politics, and Culture; the Rutgers University-Newark Institute on Ethnicity, Culture, and the Modern Experience; the Ford Foundation; and the Brooklyn College New Faculty Fund. I also thank the editors and reviewers of the journals in which earlier versions of some chapters appeared.

I am fortunate to know brilliant friends and colleagues who have, over many years, helped to shape the research within this book. These include Natalie Bennett, Jafari Allen, Belinda Edmondson, Donette Francis, Angelique V. Nixon, Colin Robinson, Faith Smith, Lawrence La Fountain-Stokes, and Omise'eke Tinsley, as well as all the members of the infamous study group, including cofounders Urvashi Vaid and Kate Clinton and the members who invited me, Michael Bennett and Juan Battle. My present and past formal and informal mentors Carole Boyce Davies, Gerard Aching, Manthia Diawara, Clement A. Price, Charles Russell, Simone James Alexander, Helen Pyne-Timothy, and Dorothy Mermin have all been generous with guidance and advice. Friends and colleagues Gina Athena Ulysse,

Jasbir Puar, and Christina Hanhardt each provided information at crucial moments to help make *Island Bodies* a reality.

I received my political education at the Audre Lorde Project while I was completing my academic education elsewhere, and I am grateful to Joo-Hyun Kang and to everyone who was on the staff and board or was a volunteer when I was active there. In the scholarly world, the Caribbean Studies Association has been a reliable place to air new ideas and to learn from and argue with people who actually know the content and context of my research.

My wonderful Brooklyn College colleagues make my place of work engaging and welcoming. I cannot mention all of them here, so the names of Ellen Tremper, Tamara Mose-Brown, Vanessa Pérez-Rozario, Martha Nadell, Scott Dexter, James Davis, and Robert Viscusi will stand in for all of those at BC and CUNY.

It is inevitable that those who have known me the longest have provided me the most support in this process. My MMUF (Mellon Minority/Mays Undergraduate Fellowship) family, especially Carlos Decena, Hugo Benavides, Maurice Stevens, and all of the present and previous staff and leadership of the MMUF program and the SSRC (Social Science Research Council), have provided deep and varied support. Thanks also to my Lafayette Avenue family, especially Jonada Burson, Michelle Clarke, Delaina Gumbs, and Winsome McKoy. The staff of Arrow and Sol, as well as Drs. Lorenzo and Keil, will probably never read this book, but they kept me and my environment well enough to finish the project.

My parents, Synthia and Halifax King, have provided unwavering support, even when they were unaware of or unconvinced by the details of this work. In addition to them, a small group of people have been patiently by my side at every stage of this project, providing study buddies and study breaks, comic relief and reality checks. The friendship of Gabrielle Civil, Zetta Elliott, Madhu Kaza, Swati Khurana, and Andrea Morton continues to be invaluable.

Introduction

From the Foreign-Local to the Caribglobal

A young man in Port-au-Prince blends in with other young, urban Haitian men; he speaks Kreyòl and does not stand out in manner or appearance. But he is recognized as a foreigner when he stands in the wrong place to wait for a tap-tap; clearly he hasn't been here since before the earthquake.

Imagined in Haiti by the author, 2011

The Caribbean body has consistently been exploited for its labor, in previous centuries through slavery and indentureship, and more recently through cheap labor for multinational corporations. The Caribbean body has also consistently been used for sexual labor, through sexual access to slaves and indentured persons, and now through sexual tourism. But Caribbean people have persistently used their own bodies for pleasure as well as work. Any media perusal confirms that openly addressing sex and sexuality remains taboo in many regions around the world, both in the global North and in colonized and formerly colonized non-European societies. However, analyzing sexuality in post/neo/colonial societies such as those in the Caribbean requires recognizing that these subjects' sexual behaviors have been derogated, exaggerated, and exoticized by imperial and colonial powers and then held up by those same powers as examples of Caribbean people's inferiority and as justification of their oppression. In spite of, and perhaps because of this legacy, sex and sexuality appear and reappear in the Caribbean imagination as tools both of pleasure and politics, of oppression and liberation. These relationships are not *more* complicated than those of other regions, but they are complicated in particular ways as a result of realities such as slavery, colonization, and economies that are often reliant on tourism and debt. As this book will detail, sex is often more than "just" sex: it has a variety of functions and effects on the political, social, and economic realities of *both* island bodies—individual Caribbean bodies and Caribbean nations and cultures. *Island Bodies: Transgressive Sexualities in the Caribbean Imagination* examines portrayals of non-normative sexuality in Anglophone, Hispanophone, Francophone, and Dutch Caribbean literary and other cultural texts and experiences. The title of this book refers both to human bodies from Caribbean islands and to the islands themselves and the isolation and exotica often attributed to them in representations from within and outside of the Caribbean.[1] As a whole, *Island Bodies'* goal is to reveal and examine the sexual norms and expectations portrayed in Caribglobal literature and popular culture, and to analyze how individuals transgress these norms.

From Foreign-Local to Caribglobal

Foreign-local is a colloquial Trinidadian phrase that says exactly what it means; it refers to Trinidadians and Tobagonians (or their descendants) who do not live in the country full-time but who know enough about the place, language, and culture to qualify as *somewhat* local. The young man in the vignette cited at the beginning of the chapter might be called foreign-local. Depending on context and inflection, the term can be endearing or pejorative, much like other labels such as *Nuyorican* and *Jamerican*. *Foreign-local* insists that seeming opposites can coexist in the same body at the same time but paradoxically also insists that those opposites remain fundamentally both separate and different. The term *Caribglobal* takes the spirit of the foreign-local and shifts it into a broader and more unified concept. The Caribbean is generally understood geographically as "the island groupings of the Greater Antilles, Lesser Antilles, and the Bahamas, plus certain coastal zones of South and Central America sharing a cultural and historical relation to the island plantation societies (for example, Suriname, Guyana, Belize)" and including the political nations and territories within that space.[2] The region can be demarcated in various ways: along linguistic lines (French, Spanish, English, and Dutch, with their creoles, are the region's primary languages); along levels of sovereignty (independent nation-states and nonindependent entities such as Puerto Rico, Bonaire, and Martinique); along racial lines (territories with predominantly Afro-Caribbean populations, those with large Indo-Caribbean populations, those which are largely mestizo identified, etc.); as well as being divided by physical size or relative wealth. On the other hand, the Caribbean diaspora is typically understood as being separate from the Caribbean, limited to people and cultures in locations outside of the geographic region that have significant Caribbean populations, such as Amsterdam, Montreal, Miami, London, Toronto, and New York City.

In contrast, the concept of the Caribglobal includes the areas, experiences, and individuals within *both* the Caribbean and the Caribbean diaspora. Caribglobal also encompasses situations that complicate traditional definitions of diaspora, such as the regional migration that results in, for instance, large numbers of Haitians living in the Bahamas and the Dominican Republic, or of Dominicans living in Puerto Rico. The Caribglobal is not the same as either globalization or transnationalism, though these realities facilitate the existence of a Caribglobal public sphere. Inderpal Grewal and Caren Kaplan's insightful examination of transnationalism and globalization ("Global Identities: Theorizing Transnational Studies of Sexuality") includes a number of critiques, three of which are most relevant here. They write that transnationalism and globalization tend to have an emphasis on "labor migration [that] leaves out the other factors in the globalization of labor," tend to be used "as a synonym for *diasporic*," and tend "to signal the demise or irrelevance of the nation-state in the current phase of globalization."[3] The transnational focus on mobility is relevant to the Caribbean, but the lens too often focuses on those with the greatest mobility and the greatest access to the global North. The Caribglobal, however, is also concerned with people and phenomena that remain in and/or travel to the Caribbean. The Caribglobal also departs from many transnational frameworks' centering of the nation-state in that the former recognizes the relatively large number of territories that are semiautonomous (including Puerto Rico, Aruba, Martinique, the US Virgin Islands, Saba, and Guadeloupe). This mix of political statuses necessarily leads to particular relationships among territories (for example, subregional groupings that may or may not be official: the "Dutch Antilles," "French Antilles," Leeward Islands, "West Indies," "Small Islands," etc.) and with their more or less colonizing countries. Any transnational Caribbean phenomenon is also part of the Caribglobal, but

Caribglobal phenomena are not always transnational in the way the term is typically used. The same is true of globalization, which continues to facilitate the Caribglobal but which is not itself sufficient to explain the latter.

*   *   *

The complexity of the Caribglobal can be found in many aspects of Caribbean culture. For instance, fritters made from salted cod are found throughout the Caribbean and its diaspora; they are called *bacalaitos* in Puerto Rico, *balchi di pisca* in Aruba, *bakkeljauw* or *balletjes* in Suriname, *accra* in Trinidad and Tobago, *accras de morue* in Martinique and Guadeloupe, and *frituras de bacalao* in Cuba. Early globalization led to salted cod becoming popular in the region because of its price and its ability to keep for an extended time. Transnationalism, in part, explains the existence of these foods in the Caribbean diaspora. But the similarity of these dishes is due to their Caribbean specificity—to similar populations, similar histories, and similar cultures that exist in the region and extend to its diaspora. In the same way, other examples from culture and research found throughout *Island Bodies* reveal that many conceptualizations of and attitudes towards sexuality are Caribglobal because they exist throughout the region and function largely in the same way.

It is useful to remember that, as it exists now, the Caribbean region is itself a product of both globalization and transnationalism and that the majority of its residents can be defined as part of other diasporas. The distinctions between the Caribbean "home" and its diaspora are sometimes difficult to discern, as the following statements make clear: "By 2004, one third of Aruban residents were born abroad"; "Manhattan is a town in Puerto Rico, except that it's a couple of hours away by plane"; and many Haitians now consider their diaspora the "tenth department."[4] Certainly, millions of people stay in one place, whether out of choice or lack of choice. But even those who do not physically travel themselves are increasingly aware of cultural texts and influences from the diaspora, from other parts of the region, and indeed from the world. Furthermore, the nature of the Caribglobal, as the quotes above demonstrate, is that it does not depend on modern travel or technologies, and indeed is not exclusively a contemporary phenomenon. The region's territories share a number of cultural traits—from foods to language patterns to sexual mores—that have their origins in events that occurred well over one hundred years ago.

The Caribbean as a bounded region and the Caribbean diaspora both remain legitimate, real, and useful concepts, as do analyses that examine specific linguistic, racial, ethnic, gender, national, or other topics, or which examine only independent or nonindependent territories. A Caribglobal perspective, however, is pan-Caribbean; it recognizes and takes seriously the linguistic, ethnic, racial, cultural, political, and economic differences within these areas, yet remains convinced that there is enough shared history and experience among Caribbean people to warrant an inclusive approach. And as Raphael Dalleo writes in *Caribbean Literature and the Public Sphere*, "While the particularities of each island's development may be distinct, the various islands continue to occupy closely related positions within global power structures."[5]

Representing the full linguistic, racial, and geographic diversity of the Caribbean is notoriously difficult, and most scholars understandably choose to focus on only one part of the region. Despite this tendency, major similarities of history (including chattel slavery and colonialism), political and economic realities, and geography justify attempts at regional studies. Like others who have attempted pan-Caribbean projects, I hope *Island Bodies* speaks to, as Kamala Kempadoo describes them, "local particularities and regional generalities, as well as to relationships between the local, regional, and global."[6] In part because I was trained as a comparatist, and in part because I am both interested and invested in exploring the breadth of Caribbean experience, *Island Bodies* uses a Caribglobal approach with the hope that readers will gain some understanding of the remarkable commonalities found in Caribbean attitudes to sexuality.

Where *foreign-local* refers to individuals, *Caribglobal* can refer to both specific texts (for example, a song or a novel) and to cultural phenomena (for example, the secreto abierto or "open secret" approach to same-sex desire discussed in chapter 2) that appear where Caribbean people are, whether in or beyond the geographic region. These texts and phenomena need not appear in or be interpreted in exactly the same ways (for example, popular songs with similar messages created in different countries, languages, and musical genres, as seen in chapter 4) to function as Caribglobal.

I am not, of course, the first person to argue that "home" and diaspora have a great deal in common and can be studied in tandem. Indeed, as theories of transnationalism, cosmopolitanism, and globalization have become more popular, the flow of people, ideas, cultures, and goods can no longer be seen as flowing only in one direction. Scholar Carole Boyce Davies points out in *Black Women, Writing and Identity* that the African diaspora can be seen as paradigmatic of all of these phenomena. She argues that the African diaspora "refers to the articulation of a relational culture of African peoples, in an interactive politico-cultural pattern both within and outside of the terms of the nation-states in which they live."[7] This definition can be transposed to the Caribbean and its diaspora, which collectively comprise the Caribglobal. The work of Stuart Hall ("Minimal Selves," *Questions of Cultural Identity*) is also particularly useful because he discusses how so many of us manage to present relatively stable identities even as we recognize the numerous ways that we identify with and relate to larger psychic, cultural, and political narratives.[8] In short, the Caribbean and Caribbeanness are "not entirely fixed or closed categories"; the region and the diaspora are interdependent and mutually constitutive, even as they vex and inspire each other.[9]

The problematics of comparing artifacts and experiences from the Caribbean diaspora to those from the geographic Caribbean (though such distinctions are not always easy to make) are perhaps greater than those of addressing the region as a whole. Indeed, the challenge, especially for those educated and/or living in the global North, is to take the diaspora seriously as part of the region without privileging it and also without assuming that it is simply a poor facsimile of the "authentic" Caribbean "home." Too often, those in the diaspora "enact a violating gaze that constructs those 'back home' as 'backward,' while using the slippery language of identity politics to claim a right to do so," while those "at home" might claim greater legitimacy because they have not been "tainted" by outside ideas.[10] Indeed, if the diaspora often accrues privilege from being within global economic and political powers (and sometimes the very heart of global cultural imperialism), the geographic Caribbean can always "trump" the diaspora by claiming authenticity. In a Caribglobal approach, however, authenticity is less interesting and less useful than the combination of evolution and context. Such an approach asks questions such as, How are people and cultures in different parts of the region in conversation with each other? If a phenomenon exists in both the region and the diaspora, does it exist in the same way? And, equally important, if a phenomenon exists in one area and not another, how has it evolved in its location, and why has it *not* moved?

Caribglobal is an adjective; unlike the nouns *Caribbean* and *diaspora*, it does not exist alone but is grounded by the object it modifies, as in, for example, the "Caribglobal imagination," the "Caribglobal public sphere," the "Caribglobal circulation of popular music," and so on. As the last example indicates, the notion of the Caribglobal imagination acknowledges the fact that many aspects of Caribbean culture do not develop in nor are they consumed exclusively in one site or the other. In practical terms, *Island Bodies'* Caribglobal approach means that each chapter includes a discussion of cultural texts created or set within the geographic Caribbean and texts or experiences created within the Caribbean diaspora. In addition, every chapter includes substantive analysis of texts created in at least three different languages, often with reference to similar texts, experiences, or phenomena in at least one other language. However, since complete representation is not possible, some nuances have suffered. Unfortunately, the Dutch Caribbean is the least represented region in the book, a result primarily of this author's linguistic limitations and of the small number of Dutch Caribbean texts that have been translated into English. In *Island Bodies* this part of the region is more often addressed through the archive of events and experiences than through discrete cultural or literary texts. While I am pleased not to repeat the all-too-frequent complete omission of the Dutch Caribbean, I hope that others will take up this important work in more detail. In addition, the focus on linguistic diversity has resulted in less representation of the physically smaller islands, most of which are English-speaking. And while *Island Bodies* includes analysis of Afro- and Indo-Caribbean experiences, the region's two largest ethnic groups and the groups most visible in Caribglobal cultures, smaller ethnic groups—specifically Chinese and Arab Caribbeans—are not represented here.

Transgressive Sexuality, Desire, and Erotic Resistance

If tourists might assume that Caribbean people are hypersexual—a concept implicitly supported by any number of marketing campaigns—local conceptions tend to be rather different. Some religious and government officials have argued that Caribbean sexual mores are more conservative than those in the global North—for instance, in relationship to homosexuality and women's sexual agency. Indeed, there is a dominant fiction within the region that Caribbean families should be heterosexual and patriarchal, and that the women at least should be serially monogamous. Such sentiments persist despite a large, established literature detailing Caribbean matrifocality.[11] The persistent disconnect between scholarship and popular sentiment shows a clear preference for more conservative (and some might say more European) family structures. Nevertheless, research reveals that many Caribbean families are neither monogamous nor patriarchal and that a number of Caribbean people are not (in either behavior or identity) heterosexual. As one example, scholar M. Jacqui Alexander cites research showing that "for the last three decades the percentage of children in the Bahamas born outside of heterosexual marriage has averaged 58 percent"; similarly, research by Rafael Ramírez, Carlos Decena, and Jafari Allen demonstrates that heterosexuality is far from universal in the Caribbean.[12] These facts are also supported by the growing number of activist organizations serving and staffed in part by sexual minorities in Haiti, St. Kitts, Puerto Rico, Curaçao, Guyana, Trinidad and Tobago, Cuba, and elsewhere in the region. Despite very vocal claims that the "Western ideal of the eternally monogamous, patriarchal, heterosexual arrangement" holds in the region, Kamala Kempadoo argues that "Caribbean sexuality is characterized by diversity, in which multiple partnering relationships by both men and women, serial monogamy, informal polygamy, and same-gender and bisexual relations are commonplace."[13]

If the realities of Caribbean sexuality are so flexible (relatively speaking), then why do the region's political leaders still act as though marital, heterosexual, monogamous nuclear families are—and should be—the norm? This behavior persists in part because the practice of espousing conservative (some would say Victorian, Brahmanic, Catholic, and Mohammedian) ideals allows political and religious leaders to promote a Caribbean cultural nationalism that is markedly different from the "loose" morals perceived in the contemporary laws and popular culture of the global North.[14] At the same time, such conservative claims counteract the stereotypes of the Caribbean as a morally bankrupt, sexually wanton region. In addition, vilifying sexual transgressors—especially nonheterosexuals and nonmonogamous women—distracts the public from issues such as poverty and corruption, which actually pose a greater and more immediate threat to the well-being of the region's people. Along the same lines, a range of scholars from Michel Foucault (*History of Sexuality*) to Jacqui Alexander (*Pedagogies of Crossing*) have demonstrated that strict gender and sexual norms help the state define the ideal citizen and control society, both through the law and through official culture. As Alexander writes,

> Women's sexual agency and erotic autonomy have always been troublesome for the state. They pose a challenge to the ideology of an originary nuclear heterosexual family that perpetuates the fiction that the family is the cornerstone of society. Erotic autonomy is dangerous to the heterosexual family and to the nation.[15]

I do not think it is antithetical to Alexander's aims to expand this idea to include the erotic autonomy of men and trans people who also flout heteronormativity and other moral imperatives. *Island Bodies* examines how some of these transgressive sexualities maneuver within and/or try to change their society's heteropatriarchal and binary gender systems. Put another way, this book prioritizes two focus areas: one is the uses of the transgressive erotic (building on Audre Lorde's work) and the power of desire as a motivating force for individual fulfillment. The other area is how Caribbean societies and governments use culture and the law to restrict particular sexual desires and/or their expression. Four main sexual transgressions are examined here: unconventional genders, homosexuality, women's sexual agency, and interracial relationships. A number of considerations led to choosing these particular transgressions, primary among them an interest in studying consensual adult relationships. Another deliberate choice was to depart from the trend of exclusively examining either heterosexual or nonheterosexual experiences. As the concept of heteropatriarchy implies, hegemonies based on sexism and patriarchy and hegemonies based on heterosexism are often intimately related, if not one and the same. These choices and the Caribglobal approach led to *Island Bodies'* intervention: an argument for common attitudes towards sexuality throughout the region.

Island Bodies analyzes a range of transgressive sexualities, pointing out how they relate to each other. Some regional political and religious leaders, journalists, and activists highlight same-sex desire as being beyond the bounds of normal, acceptable behavior. Nevertheless, women's sexual agency also continues to be controversial in Caribbean cultures; although serial monogamy and having children with multiple partners are acceptable, women's public display of sexual desire and agency, such as through sexually suggestive dancing, continues to be considered beyond respectability by many. On the other hand, gender-conforming heterosexual men have few limits placed on their sexual behavior. For these men, sex with white women can be both transgressive and empowering. Such relationships demonstrate Caribbean men of color's seductive and sexual prowess and can also enact metaphoric revenge against white men for slavery, colonialism, and racism. Liaisons between white women and Caribbean men of color are transgressive for the latter when Caribbean people see these men as betraying their nation or race and when white people see those relationships as threatening existing hierarchies. Although all of these transgressions and the moral codes that refuse them are intertwined, there are, of course, significant differences in how these transgressions are treated when discovered; it is essential to recognize that erotic autonomy and even transgression do not always involve resistance to heteropatriarchal structures.

Some might wonder why this book includes a chapter addressing the experiences of trans people: those who live as, embody, and/or believe themselves to be a gender other than that assigned to them by society. While a trans state is certainly primarily concerned with gender, the reality is that because trans people do not conform to conventional gender, their sexualities are always suspect, no matter whom they desire or how they identify. As Kamala Kempadoo reminds us, "any examination of Caribbean sexuality cannot be conducted completely separate from gender."[16] Therefore, it makes a great deal of sense to include trans experiences in *Island Bodies*, alongside other sexualities that are intimately connected to gender codes and expectations. Indeed, while the actual people described in this book might or might not get along with each other if they were all in the same family or at the same party, the analysis of each transgression helps illuminate the others, and all of them reveal the heteropatriarchal codes that endeavor to govern Caribbean behavior, if not desire.

Desire and erotic resistance are necessarily intertwined in the analysis that follows. I take the notion of erotic resistance from the important "Black Atlantic, Queer Atlantic" essay by Omise'eke Tinsley, where it is used to refer to the combination of desire and rebellion during the middle passage and slavery.[17] The term *erotic resistance* also resonates with the idea of erotic autonomy, first used by Jacqui Alexander when she wrote: "Should woman be perennial daughter raised as lady, always already defined by her relationship to men? Or, should woman and citizenship signify a certain autonomy—what we might regard as erotic autonomy—and sexual agency?"[18]

This notion of erotic autonomy signifies the ability to choose the objects of one's desire and the manner in which to fulfill that desire. In the instances examined in *Island Bodies*, desire for a person deemed an "inappropriate" erotic choice, and/or the desire to express an unconventional gender, is what leads to sexual transgression. Desire, the energy that Lorde names as "the erotic," is incredibly powerful—powerful enough to lead people to behavior that might result in consequences ranging from ostracization to violence. It is important to attend to desire because too often sex is examined as though no feelings are involved. This is obvious in the example of the phrase "men who have sex with men," abbreviated as MSM, which originated in HIV/AIDS research and which has been so widely used in a variety of communities that it has arguably morphed from a label to an identity, even in places where English is not the primary language.[19] Attention to desire takes the analysis beyond sex to include feeling and affect, a term that can be understood as "the name we give to those forces" beyond cognition and emotion "that can serve to drive us toward movement, toward thought and extension."[20] The people and characters discussed throughout this book are usually *not* concerned with identity, in the sense of *naming* who or "what" they are. Instead, they choose to both acknowledge and engage desire—not only sexual desire but also a desire to become, to imagine, and to live a life beyond that proscribed for them by their society and culture.

Island Bodies' Content

Most of the popular culture and literary texts *Island Bodies* examines were created in the last forty years, a period that roughly corresponds with the establishment of Caribbean feminism as a field and a strategy, with the growth of Caribbean sexuality studies and Caribbean sexual minority activism (and with the backlash against both of these), and with the established independence or increased autonomy of most Caribbean territories. The book's focus on the 1970s to the present reveals the solidification and persistence of Caribbean sexual mores, as well as the persistent transgression by some people of those mores. The exception, transvestite carnival and festival characters that are more than one hundred years old, demonstrates the longevity of transvestism in the region.

As an interdisciplinary, comparatist project, *Island Bodies* also draws from a broad Caribglobal archive of topics and material: traditional transvestite characters and their clash with the increasingly official culture of carnivals and other festivals; both documentary and feature films; popular music; visual art; short stories, novels, and poetry; and political texts in the form of mission statements of organizations. In keeping with a Caribglobal perspective, some of this material was created in the region and some in the diaspora, and some forms are more popular in or more widely circulated in one area than another.

Including both popular culture and literature enables *Island Bodies* to examine a meaningful representation of the Caribglobal imagination through artifacts available in the public sphere. The "public sphere" includes sociocultural, political, and economic spaces—which can be physical, virtual, or psychic—as well as the structures that shape these spaces and the artifacts produced within them.[21] The genres I give the most attention to are those through which millions of people around the world glean knowledge about the Caribbean. People raised in the Caribbean will learn in school about their own territory and to some extent about the region. But because Caribbean studies is barely mentioned in classes about or discussions of U.S., European, or Canadian history, politics, or economics, most people who are not from the Caribbean learn about the region through tourism, music, or literature. Tourists typically learn less than nothing during their vacations. On the other hand, for better or for worse, people in the global North are more likely to have listened to reggae, salsa, or reggaeton than to a lecture on Caribbean history. And people both in and outside of the region are likely to turn to Caribbean literature for information as well as enlightenment, especially since it has been popularized through venues as diverse as the Feria Internacional del Libro (International Book Fair of Puerto Rico) and the Calabash, Étonnants Voyageurs (Amazing Travelers), and Bocas literary festivals, as well as Caribbean and African American college literature courses, Oprah Winfrey's book club, and awards that have been given to Caribbean writers such as the Grand Prix Littéraire de la Femme, the Casa de las Américas Prize, the FIL Literary Award in Romance Languages, and the Nobel and Pulitzer Prizes. With the prominence of these forms in the public sphere, it is important for at least some of us to discern what literature and popular culture are saying and how they are saying it. Each chapter in *Island Bodies* focuses on a different popular culture genre—the genre that exhibits enough portrayals of that sexual transgression to support a Caribglobal approach. Because this book attempts to tell different stories, it makes sense that the sites of popular culture that illuminate these groups are themselves different.

Every chapter also includes literary analysis both because of the dominance of literature in critical scholarship and because that genre is the only form in which I could find rich portrayals of each of the transgressive sexualities addressed. Literary studies is a useful tool for exploring Caribbean sexuality both because of its narrative nature and because of its worldwide circulation. The project of literary analysis and criticism cannot, by definition, factually analyze or explain the lived realities of sexuality in the Caribbean. Nevertheless, the ideas raised both in the literature and in literary criticism can be useful in the consideration of lived realities and in deconstructing social and cultural mores and hierarchies. As a product of the Caribglobal imagination, literature helps us to see some of the ways sexuality is imagined in the region and the diaspora, both as it is and was, and how it *could be.*

Form does matter, and of course written, visual, filmic, and performance texts all signify in different ways. There are also differences in the consumption of various genres, whether in intimate, private, or public spaces, and these differences will be addressed. This book explores a breadth of material that demonstrates the persistence of Caribbean heteropatriarchy and binary gender, as well as the persistence of transgressive Caribbean sexualities that present other ways of living and loving.

The book begins by discussing trans individuals who, when they cannot pass, obviously flout conventional gender, and it ends with the analysis of a transgression that largely endorses conventional gender—heterosexual interracial relationships involving Caribbean men of color. In the first chapter, "The Caribbean Trans Continuum and Backhanded Re/Presentation," I argue that this range of gender expression, which includes unconventional, indeterminate, and multiple genders, constitutes a Caribglobal *trans continuum*, with on one end those who live with a gender identity or expression that differs from that attributed to their assigned biological sex, and on the other end those who only occasionally exhibit an unconventional gender and only in contexts that are culturally sanctioned. Specifically, chapter 1 analyzes traditional transvestite carnival and other festival characters, literary portrayals of trans people on the other end of the spectrum, and three recent cases involving the trans continuum and the law. In the literary texts *Sirena Selena* (2000), by Mayra Santos-Febres, *Cereus Blooms at Night* (1996), by Shani Mootoo, and *No Telephone to Heaven* (1987), by Michelle Cliff, trans characters re-present themselves to the world as their "true" selves and genders and re-present other characters to their respective selves by delivering them to a deeper self-knowledge and awareness. Similarly, transvestite characters in the Puerto Rican Loíza festival and Trinidadian carnival provide a socially sanctioned space for exaggerated gender transgression, while reinforcing binary gender systems and stereotypes. My analysis also deconstructs Frantz Fanon's infamous footnote about trans macommères in *Black Skin, White Masks* (1967) and contrasts that passage with Caribbean trans people's self-representation in legal cases in Guyana, Cuba, and Trinidad and Tobago. In each of these instances, Caribbean cultures treat trans people in a backhanded manner, simultaneously accepting them and limiting their life possibilities.

Gender norms—specifically those for men—are also analyzed in the second chapter, "'El Secreto Abierto': Visibility, Confirmation, and Caribbean Men Who Desire Men," which explores the concept of el secreto abierto, or the open secret, in relationship to Caribbean men who desire other men. El secreto abierto is a situation in which people "know" someone is a homosexual, though the fact is not openly acknowledged. This social structure allows the individual to pursue same-sex desire but mandates discretion about that desire in speech, dress, and behavior. The chapter describes Caribglobal "unofficial official" masculine gender codes that are explicitly and implicitly taught in Caribbean families and communities. It goes on to explore what happens when same-sex desire is revealed or confirmed through an analysis of short fiction by Cuban writer Reinaldo Arenas (*The Brightest Star*, 1994), Jamaican Kei Miller ("Walking on the Tiger Road," 2006), and Puerto Rican Aldo Alvarez ("Property Values," 2001); the documentaries *Orgullo en Puerto Rico/Pride in Puerto Rico* (dir. Jorge Oliver and Irma Iranzo Berrocal, 1999), *Of Men and Gods* (Haiti, dirs. Anne Lescot and Laurence Magloire, 2002), and *Songs of Freedom* (Jamaica, dir. Phillip Pike, 2002); and visual art by Barbadian artist Ewan Atkinson. This chapter also includes a deconstruction of the myth of the Caribbean as "the most homophobic place on earth," arguing that el secreto abierto is a structure that permits, if not encourages, acceptance of homosexuality as long as discretion is observed.[22]

While in the Caribglobal public sphere hyper-visibility is associated with men who desire men, *invisibility* is the trope used most often in relationship to Caribbean women who desire women. The third chapter, "'This

Is You': 'Invisibility,' Community, and Women Who Desire Women," discusses recent activism and literature that reveal the existence of Caribbean women who desire and have sex with other women, even though they remain "near-invisible" in popular culture—implicitly acknowledged while explicitly denied. I deconstruct the myth of the invisible Caribbean lesbian; demonstrate *how* invisibility functions, that it is less a passive absence than it is an active, enforced disappearing; and reveal how some Caribbean women choose to battle their isolation and their invisibility. Specific attention is given to the organizations OCaN (the Netherlands), Grupo OREMI (Cuba), and the Women's Caucus (Trinidad), as well as to recent writing by R. Gay ("Of Ghosts and Shadows," 2003), Dionne Brand ("Hard against the Soul," 1990), Marilyn Bobes ("Someone Has to Cry," 2008), and Shani Mootoo ("Out on Main Street," 2002), set in Haiti, Trinidad, Cuba, and Toronto, respectively. The analysis shows that for women who desire women in the Caribglobal imagination, sexuality is not represented as being more important than other aspects of identity and that in fact being part of a larger Caribbean community is extremely important to these women.

Official state Caribbean narratives disavow same-sex desiring women, even as those narratives reify the heterosexual woman as a national symbol. *Island Bodies'* penultimate chapter, "'Force-Ripe': Caribbean Women's Sexual Agency," examines heterosexual and bisexual women who transgress their proscribed role. "Force-ripe" is a colloquial Caribbean phrase used to refer both to fruit picked before it is ripe and *forced* to ripen early and to girls who dress or behave as women. It is thus an appropriate phrase to use when discussing portrayals of Caribbean women's sexual agency. In the Caribglobal public sphere, music can be a symbol of nationalism as well as a vehicle for listening and dancing and is thus a productive site of inquiry. In fact, some of the most popular songs by "Queens" of Caribbean music such as Jocelyne Béroard, Ivy Queen, Alison Hinds, Drupatee, and Rihanna embrace liberal views of women's sexuality and gender relations between women and men. This chapter compares how Caribbean women in different musical genres—zouk, reggaeton, soca, chutney soca, and Top 40—uphold or flout traditional morality. Similarly, in Caribbean women's bildungsromans by Jamaica Kincaid (*Lucy*, 1990), Maryse Condé (*Heremakhonon*, 1988), and Patricia Selbert (*The House of Six Doors*, 2011), significant attention is often given to sexual maturation and sexual activity that contradict prescribed morality. Depictions of Caribglobal moral expectations of the sexualities of girls and women will be examined, as well as how young women use sex and the proclamation of desire to assert independence and as part of their transition to adulthood. The competing traditions of Caribbean women's erotic reserve and release—from Indo-Caribbean matikor to Afro-Caribbean carnival—will contextualize the contemporary music and novels.

Both Caribbean cultures and laws stipulate that the ideal Caribbean citizen is a heterosexual, gender-conforming, biological man. There are clearly fewer restrictions on the sexual behavior of heterosexual, gender-conforming men than for the subjects analyzed elsewhere in *Island Bodies*. The book's final chapter concentrates on one of the few consensual transgressions remaining for such men: interracial relationships between Caribbean men of color and white women. When portraying these relationships, the focus in Caribbean diaspora literature, such as that by Junot Díaz (*Drown*, 1997), V. S. Naipaul (*The Mimic Men*, 1967), and Dany Laferrière (*How to Make Love to a Negro without Getting Tired*, originally published in French in 1985), is not on sexual desire, but on the metaphors of revenge for slavery and racism and of the conquest of white society and white men. Contrastingly, the focus in films set within the region—*Vers le Sud/Heading South* (France, dir. Lauren Cantet, 2005) and *The Lunatic* (United States, dir. Lol Crème, 1991)—is on white women's desire to escape from boredom, responsibility, and/or patriarchy through having sex with Caribbean men. A discussion of the adoring yet racist media coverage of Dominican Porfirio Rubirosa's midcentury affairs and the marriage of Surinamese man Waldemar Nods, portrayed by journalists as an ideal love affair, provide examples of how these issues play out in the so-called real world. Here, a Caribglobal analysis explores why the portrayals set in the region and in the diaspora are strikingly divergent yet maintain heteronormative and racial ideals. The title to this last chapter is taken from a song by Bob Marley, who was the product of a mixed relationship and also had relationships with "white" women.

The conclusion of *Island Bodies* explores how the preceding chapters reveal both the limits and the possibilities of the Caribglobal imagination. It builds on and extends the ideas presented by Jamaican writer Thomas Glave and Trinidadian activist Colin Robinson, who have respectively discussed the Caribbean's "nobility of imagination" and "poverty of imagination" in relationship to nonheteronormative sexualities. The breadth of bodies and desires addressed in Caribbean music, literature, film, festivals, and activism at the end of the twentieth and the beginning of the twenty-first centuries challenges the region's gender codes and heteropatriarchy—and even insists that these structures are not the monolithic traditions many politicians and religious leaders proclaim them to be. In the end, this book argues that what island bodies look like and which other bodies they desire have been quite varied for an extremely long time; what remains is for Caribbean laws and hierarchies to catch up with the broad Caribglobal imagination.

Methodology

As my description of the Caribglobal concept implies, *Island Bodies* is fundamentally a comparatist project executed through close reading strategies. Each chapter compares phenomena as they are portrayed and experienced in different parts of the region and its diaspora, and as they are portrayed in different genres. This comparatist approach sometimes leads to perhaps unexpected uses of criticism and theory. For instance, work on how masculinity and gender codes stigmatize men who desire men is useful in the chapter on heterosexual interracial relationships. Similarly, while *loca*, a (more or less derogatory) term used to refer to men who desire men, is mentioned in chapter 2, it is also the name of a traditional transvestite carnival character in Puerto Rico discussed in chapter 1. This kind of overlapping represents more than happy accidents; it demonstrates how Caribbean heteropatriarchy, androcentrism/misogyny, and transphobia are not only interrelated but also depend on each other to maintain the heteropatriarchal status quo.

Language is another element of this book that demonstrates a comparatist approach. Close readers of *Island Bodies* will notice that I do not italicize non-English words when referring to what they represent and sometimes (for instance, el secreto abierto and macommère) will consistently use a non-English word or phrase instead of a translated equivalent. These small gestures serve as reminders of the multilingual nature of the region, as well as attempts to lose a bit less in translation. [23]

Imagination is not only a subject of analysis in *Island Bodies*; it is also a part of its methodology. By taking creative work seriously not only as art but also as theory, as ways to understand the world and the structures that attempt to govern it, I join a trajectory of scholars who insist that a deep understanding of the world in general, and of marginalized regions, people, and topics such as the Caribbean and sexuality in particular, requires, as

Tinsley writes, "listen[ing] to other kinds of theorists."[24] The benefits of products of the imagination are no less worthy because they can be difficult to quantify. The arts turn facts into a different kind of truth, a more empathetic truth, than statistics. Gloria Wekker, herself a celebrated anthropologist, wrote in 2006 that "What we have learned about black female sexuality has been culled primarily from the work of literary authors, critics, and historians. . . . The social scientific study of black female sexuality remains a gaping wound."[25] Nor is scholars' preoccupation with culture a recent phenomenon; the most canonical Caribbean theorists and social scientists took culture seriously. Examples include José Martí's and Edouard Glissant's lifelong concerns with literature; Frantz Fanon's literary analysis in *Black Skin, White Masks;* and C.L.R. James' work on cricket in *Beyond a Boundary.* Cultural and literary texts produced and consumed by the Caribbean and its diaspora not only *use* imagination, they also contribute to how Caribbean people imagine themselves as sexual subjects, community members, and citizens.

The attention to multiple motivations, perspectives, and sites of power is crucial to *Island Bodies.* This interdisciplinary, feminist approach builds on several schools of thought from within and beyond the Caribglobal imagination. For instance, years prior to the popularity of Black British Cultural Studies, itself fuelled mostly by thinkers of Caribbean descent, Black Feminist Criticism and Theory "helped to render the imagination into a social practice that utilized cultural forms precisely because of the overlapping gender, sexual, class, and racial exclusions that constituted forms of nationalism."[26] Here, Ferguson uses "imagination" to refer to texts such as literature and film. But it is also true that acts such as activism and lawsuits against the state are *imaginative,* especially when they advocate for conceiving of citizenship, the nation, or culture more broadly. Though it may go without saying, I assume that all creations and acts—including the production of scholarship—are political and so have broader implications. *Island Bodies'* expansive and interdisciplinary approach includes Jacqui Alexander's and Emilio Bejel's analyses of Caribbean laws, sociological research on Caribbean gender, and recent legal cases involving Caribbean trans people, as well as anthropological research and the mission statements of Caribglobal sexual minority activist organizations because these texts speak to each other, as well as to literary and filmic texts. As Jafari Allen writes in *¡Venceremos?* "to talk about sexuality is to talk not only about the everyday lived experience of the sexual(ualized) body and its reproduction but also about the cultures, histories, and political-economic realities of the nation (region, diaspora, globe), and the historicity, imagination, desires, and intentions of the sexual(ualized) subject."[27] My focus on transgression also means examining the rules being broken, as well as individual, social, and political investment in those hierarchies; only through such analysis can we know what is at stake. Thus, every chapter of *Island Bodies* contends with Caribglobal heteropatriarchy and conventional binary gender.

*   *   *

Island Bodies elucidates the significance of sexual behavior to the lives of Caribbean people and examines how sexuality can support or challenge Caribbean traditions of heteropatriarchy and binary gender. Within the topics examined, the individual's desire is seen as threatening—or supporting—the coherence and strength of Caribbean society and culture. Thus, this book connects transgressive sexual desires and experiences including promiscuity, homosexuality, and unconventional genders to other themes such as nationalism and diaspora. The people—real and imagined—discussed in the following pages resist being labeled as victims, be they trans people arrested for "cross-dressing," women banished for sexual agency, or men threatened because of their feminine behavior. As does groundbreaking scholar Kamala Kempadoo, I believe that Caribbean people are "neither inert nor passive" and that "Caribbean women and men who inhabit marginal sexual spaces resist, and sometimes rebel, against gendered and sexual regimes that privilege masculine heterosexual needs and desires, and actively work against dominant ideologies and practices that seek to deny their existence."[28]

My approach in *Island Bodies* assumes that sexual agency and erotic resistance are possible within the Caribglobal imagination *and* among living, breathing, desiring Caribbean people, and that our understanding of both sexual transgressions and the structures being resisted can deepen our understanding of who Caribbean people are and who and how we desire.

1

The Caribbean Trans Continuum and Backhanded Re/Presentation

Those who inhabit unconventional genders—whether deliberately or unconsciously and whether through behavior, dress, speech, or some combination of these—are often considered ineligible to be full, legitimate members of Caribbean societies. As in the global North, their sexuality is automatically suspect, and since they are far from ideal citizens, too often the state sees no need to treat them as full citizens or to protect them from others' mistreatment. This chapter argues that there is a continuum of gender-variant experience—*trans* experience—in the Caribbean, the range of which includes people who live as a gender other than that assigned to them at birth and those who perform transvestite carnival characters. Analyzing literature—Shani Mootoo's *Cereus Blooms at Night*, Michelle Cliff's *No Telephone to Heaven*, and Mayra Santos-Febres' *Sirena Selena vestida de pena*—as well as traditional characters from popular festivals in the Dominican Republic, Trinidad, and Barbados, and legal cases in Cuba, Trinidad, and Guyana, I further argue that in the Caribglobal imagination the portrayal of trans people is a backhanded one that acknowledges their existence while refusing them the possibility of full lives or citizenship.

It is important to begin by addressing the terminology that will be used throughout this chapter and by explaining why I have made particular choices. I remain both ambivalent and conflicted about the use of the term *transgender* in Caribbean contexts because it originated in and seems to remain most relevant to North American and European contexts. The term *transgender* is typically attributed to Californian Virginia Prince, who coined it in the 1970s as a distinct alternative to both *transvestite* and *transsexual*. I have chosen not to use the term *transsexual* because it is still largely understood in relationship to surgical manipulation of the body. *Transgender*, on the other hand, is currently used in the United States as both an umbrella term for any number of transgressive gender practices and as a term which refers specifically to those who claim or exhibit unconventional gender but who are neither transvestites nor transsexuals. Increasingly, individuals in the United States who self-identify as transgender are utilizing surgery and hormones to alter their biology, so it is a somewhat slippery term. But in the Caribbean such procedures are sometimes more difficult to obtain. A major exception is Cuba, where in 2007 the state agreed to cover such surgeries.[1]

Applying the term *transgender* to the Caribbean is also problematic because North Americans and Europeans have historically defined and continue to define Caribbeanness, and especially Caribbean genders and sexualities, in derogatory ways. Such definitions have named Caribbean women as masculine, vulgar, and uncouth and Caribbean men variously as hypermasculine or undermasculine (depending on their race) and as unintelligent. Furthermore, since most of the dominant world powers are located in North America and Europe, their descriptions and definitions of Caribbean sexuality are more prevalent globally than those coming from within the Caribbean region. Therefore, to use terms from these places, terms that Caribbean people have neither created nor always identified with, without paying attention to their etymologies and relationship to power seems to commit a further epistemic violence. Finally, using North American or European terms that do not resonate within the region could be seen as supporting the common Caribbean belief that unconventional genders and nonheteronormative sexualities are foreign menaces that amount to "postcolonial imperialism," as Suzanne LaFont notes in "Very Straight Sex: The Development of Sexual Morés in Jamaica."[2]

There are some indigenous terms that specifically describe unconventional genders, including *travesti, mati men, macha, manroyal, cambiada,* et cetera. Other terms such as *masisi, loca,* and *battyman* are variously used to refer to people exhibiting unconventional genders, engaging in nonheterosexual sexualities, or both. Throughout this chapter I will use the term *trans* as an umbrella term for unconventional genders, regardless of whether the individuals in question have pursued hormonal or surgical body modification. This abbreviation is appropriate because these five letters are the common prefix for various words referring to those who exhibit transgressive genders in English, Spanish (for example, *transsexual*), French (for example, *transsexuel(le)s* and *transgenres*), and Dutch (for example, *transgender* and *transseksueel*), the primary languages, with their creoles, of the Caribbean. *Trans* refers to a range of identities and the varieties of strategies people use to choose, inhabit, or express a gender other than that which society assigns to their body. *Trans* references the other words mentioned above while retaining difference, thus gesturing towards the similarities and the distinctions of unconventional gender experiences in the Caribbean and the metropoles that currently dominate gender and sexuality studies.

Conventional gender refers to the socially and culturally dominant correspondences between a specific biological body (typically the binary "female" or "male"), as defined by specific cultural contexts, and a set of behaviors, identities, and dispositions that are assigned to that biological body. Conventional gender is also a form of social control that depends on the oppression of other, unconventional genders. *Unconventional* gender is, therefore, any behavior, identity, or disposition that transgresses or threatens the heteropatriarchal order, including what I am calling trans genders. From this perspective, even a binary gender system implicitly acknowledges other genders—not only trans genders but genders that may exist in racial, ethnic, class, or other communities that are minority or marginal.

The Caribbean trans continuum includes, at one pole, people who feel that their gender is different than—or more complicated than—that assigned to them at birth and who want to be able to express the gender they feel rather than the one they were assigned. At the other pole are those who only occasionally exhibit an unconventional gender and only in contexts that are culturally sanctioned (such as carnival and other festivals). As will be discussed later, at this end of the spectrum, unconventional gender performances typically relate to an individual's identity only insofar as they reinforce the individual's conventional, heteropatriarchal gender. In between these poles are, of course, any number of behaviors and identifications, such as those who practice transvestism for erotic purposes or those who are drag/draga/travesti/travestiet performers. Of course, those at either end of this spectrum might vehemently complain about being included on a continuum with the others. Nevertheless, these very different gender performances are linked not only because they typically involve some form of transvestism but also because all are implicated in backhanded deliverance.

The reader will have noticed that I have not mentioned sexuality in relationship to the Caribbean trans continuum. Not only are gender and sexuality not the same, they also do not always correspond as one might expect, and being located on the trans continuum does not per se indicate or rule out any particular erotic choice, though gender and sexuality are often conflated in the popular imagination. Furthermore, the complexities of trans genders can challenge conventional notions of sexuality. For instance, when Cubans Ignacio Estrada (a self-identified gay man) and Wendy Iriepa (who underwent gender confirmation surgery) married in 2011, their marriage was legal and was legally a heterosexual one. However, the couple made their nuptials very public (they were covered by the BBC News, Al Jazeera, *Huffington Post*, and many other venues) and proclaimed it "a step forward for the gay community in Cuba."[3] Indeed, trans bodies—especially those that cannot pass—literally embody gender as well as sexual transgression, even if they perceive their sexuality as heterosexual.

A final important note regarding the scope of this chapter is that it focuses on "male to female" experiences of the Caribbean trans continuum. The dearth of representations of "female to male" Caribbean trans experiences in literary texts, festival characters, and other popular sites necessitated this restriction. This absence points to the insidiousness of androcentrism and patriarchy; even in a supposedly radical realm that troubles gender, the focus remains on biological men. This absence also points to the threat that biological women who exhibit trans identities pose to the stability of patriarchy. Thus, this chapter must be read with the understanding that its argument and conclusions are based on the limited available archive.[4] I hope that ongoing research by myself and others will uncover more Caribbean "female to male" lives and experiences and will enable scholars to analyze them as a group and in comparison with others in the trans continuum.

This chapter first addresses the poles of the Caribbean trans continuum, analyzing trans characters' portrayals in contemporary Caribbean literature and as traditional carnival characters, respectively. At the close of the chapter, I reconsider Fanon's (in)famous mention of Martinican trans people in *Black Skin/White Masks* (1952) and analyze the implications of several recent legal cases involving Caribbean trans individuals. The thread that connects all of these experiences and portrayals is *backhandedness*; though at first glance portrayals of Caribbean trans people may seem to be progressive, that sense is often subverted by details of the portrayals or treatment that restrict the life possibilities of all Caribbean trans people—or those of particular colors, races, and classes.

Caribbean Trans Characters in Literature

Trans individuals have appeared in several Caribbean novels, though not always as full, nuanced characters. As stated earlier, one end of the Caribbean trans continuum includes those who actively and publicly embrace a trans gender. The texts examined here all include characters who express—or want to express—a gender that differs from that assigned to them at birth. But there are also a number of Caribbean texts which explore the range of genders within this continuum, such as feminine men whose gender identity or expression differs somewhat from conventional norms but still largely aligns with their biology. These works include Faizal Deen's memoir *Land without Chocolate*, Achy Obejas's *Memory Mambo*, Shani Mootoo's *Out on Main Street*, and Hilton Als' *The Women*. In this chapter I focus on the former extreme because addressing more obviously contentious gender transgressors more readily leads to analysis of the structures and ambiguities of Caribbean binary gender. With such a small body of sociological and journalistic publications examining trans lives and experiences in the region,[5] Caribbean fiction can provide important—though necessarily limited—insight into trans experiences in the region.

The chapter title has a number of meanings embedded within it that I will briefly lay out here and to which I will return throughout the discussion. To begin, *re/presentation* refers to representations of trans people by themselves *and* by others. It also refers to revised *re*/presentations of the self as the "true" self; situations in which trans people change—override, if you will—their external presentations of their bodies to more accurately reflect their internal (their mental and emotional) selves. Finally, but no less importantly, this phrase refers to the re/presentation of the "other." In Caribbean fiction, trans characters are frequently used to re/present conventional gender, the trans person's *other*, as itself a myth fraught with contradictions.

In Caribbean fiction, trans characters are also typically portrayed as *delivering*, as being in service to, conventionally gendered men and women characters whose assigned biology corresponds with their gender expression. Trans people most often deliver these characters to safety, to a better understanding of themselves, and to their "true" destinies, feelings, or histories. This deliverance can occur physically, when a trans person actually delivers someone from bodily harm. It can also occur emotionally, when the trans character reveals or facilitates the recovery of memory, truth, or history, and it is typically manifested in some form of storytelling to the trans person or to the person being revealed but ultimately also always to the reader. Trans deliverance as the midwifing of selves and stories is sometimes, especially initially, resisted or resented by the one who is being helped. It is not incidental that deliverance also has a religious connotation. As scholars such as Tinsley have noted, people with unconventional genders are often seen as having special skills, powers, insight, or access. In some circumstances, particularly in communities that practice Santería or Voudoun, this privilege gives trans people the opportunity to spiritually deliver others.

Trans individuals also deliver other individuals—and sometimes themselves or each other—in the sense of *rebirth* to a truer incarnation or a better understanding of themselves. This linking of deliverance to trans people incorporates unconventional genders into Caribbean social orders by having them literally *serve* the dominant, conventional genders in the social hierarchy. The literature thus accepts trans characters as part of Caribbean culture but does so in a backhanded maneuver that keeps them in subservient, marginal roles.

In Caribbean literature, trans characters are also typically portrayed as tortured but benevolent angels. They suffer greatly for being trans, but despite the turmoil and danger they experience in their own lives, they reach out to help others, usually someone who is secure in a socially sanctioned gender and often someone who is in less immediate and physical danger than their trans savior. On the surface, portraying trans people as having special insight and abilities to help others may seem positive—and even progressive—because it places them in a position of power and shows them using that power to benefit others. However, as I will detail below, the deliverance is backhanded because Caribbean trans characters are also consistently kept on the margins of the texts and are deprived of their individuality. In the same way, Caribbean authors reveal little about the lives of trans individuals, even while describing in detail how trans people heal or save conventionally gendered men and women, revealing to them their forgotten or buried memories, hopes, longings, and histories. As a result, Caribbean literature generally treats trans people as not fully human (or as somewhat more than human) tools in service of "normal" men and women who *are* fully human, complete with limits *and* flaws. Representative Caribbean stories of trans deliverance, and of backhanded re/presentation include Shani Mootoo's *Cereus Blooms at Night* (1996), Michelle Cliff's *No*

Telephone to Heaven (1987), and Mayra Santos-Febres' *Sirena Selena vestida de pena* (2000). These novels were published within fifteen years of each other—and at the beginning of the twenty-first century, at a time when trans identities were being acknowledged more in the Caribbean and elsewhere, in and outside of literature and academia.[6]

Cereus Blooms at Night

The trope of trans deliverance is obvious in Shani Mootoo's celebrated novel *Cereus Blooms at Night*. While Mootoo was raised in Trinidad, *Cereus Blooms* is set on the fictional island of Lantanacamara.[7] Throughout the novel, Nurse Tyler, "the only Lantanacamaran man ever to have trained in the profession of nursing," tells Mala Ramchandin's life story, including her unintentional abandonment by her mother and sister, and the sexual abuse she suffers at the hands of her father. The first words of the novel are as follows:

> *By setting this story down, I, Tyler—that is how I am known, simply as Tyler, or if you wanted to be formal, Nurse Tyler—am placing trust in the power of the printed word to reach many people. . . . Might I add that my own intention, as the relator of this story, is not to bring notice to myself or my own plight. However, I cannot escape myself, and being a narrator who also existed on the periphery of events, I am bound to be present. I have my own laments and much to tell about myself. It is my intent, however, to refrain from inserting myself too forcefully. Forgive the lapses, for there are some, and read them with the understanding that to have erased them would have been to do the same to myself.*[8]

Tyler speaks the first and last words of the novel, framing it. His task is both to announce and to efface his own presence—yet he "cannot escape" himself and, notwithstanding the niceties and apologies, *refuses* to erase himself.[9] Indeed, he insists he is "bound"—both likely and required—to be present in the narrative. His unwillingness to erase himself from a text that will "reach many people" means that the reader cannot escape Tyler either. But it is also clear in the first pages of *Cereus Blooms* that Mala, a victim of physical and sexual abuse, a recluse, and eventually Tyler's patient, is the *true* focus of the novel. Tyler's introductory note declares that his primary purpose is as a device, as the teller, the deliverer, and the narrator of Mala's story. And while this position entails some power, it is not enough to reveal as much about his own life as he does about his ward's.

There are other instances in the novel which remind us whose story is being prioritized. For example, after being mocked by the other nurses for feminine accessorizing and behavior, Tyler says, "I am aware of the subtleties and incremental degrees in hostility—from the tight smile to the seemingly accidental shove—and I have known the gamut. But what would be the value of laying it all out before you?"[10] Tyler knows there is no value attributed to his story; while his presence facilitates the telling of Mala's story, that presence is accompanied by a backhanded maneuver that literally and metaphorically makes Tyler *stay in his place* as narrator but not join the narratives as a protagonist. The implication is that in order to relate Mala's abuse and pain, Tyler must repress his own.

The reader learns that Tyler is the only nurse willing to physically touch Mala, since the others fear her as wicked, either believing she murdered her violent father or that she is somehow contaminated by the longtime sexual abuse she suffered. But Tyler earns Mala's (and the reader's) trust as a caring, gentle nurse. He, not the other (conventionally gendered female) nurses, is willing to loosen the straps that restrain Mala when she first arrives at the home. And Tyler alone figures out that Mala refuses most of the food she is offered because she is a vegetarian. Though he was trained as a nurse and has been working at the Paradise Alms House for some time, Tyler is relegated to overseeing the upkeep and repair of the property—traditionally more "manly" activities than nursing. He is put in charge of Mala only when all others refuse to treat her. Mala comes to depend on Tyler and communicates with the world only through him.

Tyler recalls that once he realized there was some sense to be made of Mala's whispers and mutterings,

> I started to jot down everything she said, no matter how erratic her train of thought appeared to be. When she saw me awaiting her next word and writing it down as soon as she uttered it, she drew nearer. I soon got the impression that she actually began to whisper in my direction, that *I had become her witness.* She spoke rapidly and with great urgency, in a low monotone, repeating herself sometimes for hours without end. There was little doubt that I was being given a dictation, albeit without punctuation marks or subject breaks.[11]

Tyler has made Mala's mutterings readable to us. He is clearly chosen to tell her story, not only by circumstances but also by the true protagonist—Mala—herself.

Thus, notwithstanding numerous asides throughout the novel, the emphasis remains on Mala's story. We learn little of Tyler's family or childhood, outside of a few mentions of his grandmothers, and we learn even fewer details about other aspects of his life before he began working at the Alms House, save that he has never had a romantic or sexual encounter "outside the realm of [his] fertile imagination." This lack of information about his personal history and aspirations for his future—except, significantly, "to be—and be treated as—nothing more than ordinary"—serves to keep him just a bit more than an outline, in comparison to Mala's very (literally and metaphorically) fleshed out story.[12] Throughout, Tyler remains a sketch of a character; we know little about him, and most of what the reader does learn relates to his gender and sexual preferences, while he relates—*delivers*—Mala's life in great detail.

Tyler is identified as a man by himself and by others, and he wears men's clothes—albeit often with the "feminine" flairs of scarves or perfume—for most of the novel. Yet Mootoo makes it clear that Tyler is a trans person, that neither his gender identity nor, increasingly, his gender expression fit the conventional Lantanacamaran expectations of manhood and masculinity. Our first hint is the gender transgression of his career choice—the emphasis on his being "the only Lantanacamaran man ever to have trained in the profession of nursing." Another indication is how Tyler is treated by a conventional, even hypermasculine, man. Early in the novel and in Tyler's tenure at the alms house, he notices that "The home's regular yard boy, Toby, stood watching from afar, sucking his teeth and shaking his head and spitting low curses in my direction." Tyler is himself aware of his "unusual femininity" and his attraction to men and laments what he considers to be his condition—"neither properly man nor woman but some in-between, unnamed thing." His disappointment in his feminine attributes is directly linked to the fact that when these traits are not the inspiration for outright hostility (such as that from Toby), they are only grudgingly tolerated. It is this lack of acceptance that encourages him to study abroad, so that Tyler would "be somewhere where my 'perversion,' which I tried diligently as I could to shake, might either be invisible or of no consequence to people to whom my foreignness would be strange."[13] He assumes both that his unconventional gender and desires will be more accepted in the global North (named the Shivering Northern Wetlands in *Cereus Blooms*) than on the island and that any racism or xenophobia there would be preferable to heterosexism in the Caribbean. Yet while he does not describe discrimination of any kind while he is abroad, the fact that he returns to Lantanacamara implies that he prefers home to a foreign land and/or prefers gender and sexuality-based oppression to racism and ethnocentrism (perhaps combined with heterosexism). Even so, until caring for Mala, Tyler is isolated, lonely, and depressed.

His nursing profession and caring demeanor aside, the novel insists that it is precisely Tyler's "condition" as a trans person that connects him with Mala, who has long been ostracized in her community and who lived as a recluse. Tyler describes their affinity after observing the other nurses' hostility towards Mala: "I fancy that she and I shared a common reception from the rest of the world." This reception treats both of them as morally aberrant—him for his femininity, her for the stigma of her father's incest and her mother's lesbian affair. Later, he continues "we had found our own ways and fortified ourselves against the rest of the world ... [I had a] shared queerness with Miss Ramchandin."[14] Although Tyler finds comfort in an affinity with a similarly ostracized person, the linking of his innate unconventional gender to the rape and other abuse Mala suffers is clearly problematic.

Mootoo portrays a different community reaction to Otoh, the son of Mala's childhood friend and onetime love. Otoh is the other trans character in *Cereus Blooms* and the only biologically female trans character in the texts discussed here. Otoh also has a role in delivering Mala, albeit to physical safety and not emotional stability. He is born biologically female, but from childhood continuously presents as male such that everyone, including his parents, believes him to be and/or treats him as a biological male. Otoh's mother Elsie "fully expected that he (she) would outgrow the foolishness soon enough. But the child walked and ran and dressed and talked and tumbled and all but relieved himself so much like a boy that Elsie soon apparently forgot that she had ever given birth to a girl. And the father ... seemed not to remember that he had once fathered one." Indeed, Otoh is able to pass as a man to such an extent that he lies shirtless with girlfriends (he has "muscled breasts") and the nurse and doctor who delivered him "on seeing him later, marveled at their carelessness in having declared him a girl."[15] Unlike Tyler, Otoh is sure of and confident in his gender identity and expression, a reality that is surely due to his parents' support, his physical ability to pass as a man, and his community's deliberate amnesia and more or less willful ignorance of his biological sex.[16]

Like Tyler, Otoh feels an affinity to Mala, whom he knows of long before her arrival in the alms house. He explains his desire to befriend her by saying, "I felt as though she and I had things in common. She had secrets and I had secrets. Somehow I wanted to go there and take all my clothes off and say, 'Look! See? See all this? *I am different!* You can trust me, and I am showing you that you are the one person I will trust,"[17] Once, when he approaches Mala at her home, Otoh wears a dress for the first time in his adult life out of a desire to reveal his secrets, himself, to this woman. On his next attempt to see her, he arrives dressed as his father and sets off the chain of events that leads to Mala's arrival at the home.

Later, Tyler and Otoh's deliverance of Mala, which saves her from mistreatment, is revealed as inadvertently also benefiting themselves. Mala is the catalyst for Tyler to begin wearing women's clothes; she steals a nurse's uniform and some stockings for him to wear. Significantly, as he puts on a dress for the first time, his body feels as though it is physically changing. He explains, "It was as though I had suddenly become plump and less rigid. My behind felt fleshy and rounded. I had thighs, a small mound of belly, rounded full breasts and a cavernous tunnel singing between my legs. I felt more weak than excited but I was certainly excited by the possibilities trembling inside me. . . ." When his patient and friend does not acknowledge his transformation, Tyler is disappointed until he realizes that "the reason Miss Ramchandin paid me no attention was that, to her mind, the outfit was not something to either congratulate or scorn—it simply was. She was not one to manacle nature, and I sensed that she was permitting mine its freedom." At the end of this section he remarks, *"I had never felt so extremely ordinary, and I quite loved it."*[18] The donning of the dress both transforms him *and* feels extremely ordinary; in delivering Mala, he has enabled her to deliver *him* to a fuller expression of not only his gender but also of himself.

Linking Tyler and Otoh to Mala may endear the trans characters to the reader, since Mala is an innocent victim and a very sympathetic character. Unfortunately, this link between trans individuals and an incest survivor also encourages a reading of unconventional genders as aberrant. As Tyler himself describes, one may be read as victim, while the other is seen as perpetrator; he tells the reader that "it was a long time before I could differentiate between his [Mala's father's] perversion and what others called mine."[19] The implications are that Mala's father is responsible for her victimization and that some evil or unnatural force, or perhaps the devil or Tyler himself, is responsible for his unconventional gender. And in the end, if Mala is saved *by* the two trans people, they are in a sense saved *from* themselves by falling in love with each other and thus conforming to heteronormativity, both in biological gender and in gender expression.

No Telephone to Heaven

Like Tyler and Otoh in *Cereus Blooms at Night*, Harriet's function in *No Telephone to Heaven* (1987), by Michelle Cliff, is primarily to deliver the protagonist, Clare, to a deeper sense of herself, of Jamaica, and of her role in that country. Known as Harry/Harriet for most of the novel, this trans character is first introduced as the "medical officer" for a group of revolutionaries that includes Clare.[20] Through flashbacks, we learn that Clare's introduction to Harry/Harriet centers on the act of caretaking; Harry/Harriet holds and soothes Clare when the latter becomes sick after drinking too much at a party. However, Harriet's more important deliverance of Clare—who feels caught between black and white racial identities—is to a greater knowledge of the plight of poor Jamaicans, to the realities of Clare's own racial and class background, and to the violent history and hierarchies of their island. Harriet constantly encourages Clare to return to Jamaica from the United States and Europe and is also the one who provides physical and political "guided tours" of Jamaica by taking Clare to her childhood home and eventually to the revolutionary guerillas.[21]

We learn even less about Harriet in *No Telephone to Heaven* than we do about Otoh and Tyler in *Cereus Blooms*. The child of a wealthy white Jamaican and his dark maid,[22] Harry/Harriet is raised by his/her father and his wife. While at ten he/she is raped by a white policeman, Harry/Harriet is adamant that the rape "did not make me the way I am. No, darling, I was born this way, that I know. Not just sun, but sun and moon." As an adult, and before choosing to live completely as a woman, Harry/Harriet sometimes openly dresses as a woman: "Harry/Harriet in his/her Pucci bikini, his/her furry chest getting the odd stare . . . panties cradling his cock and balls." In scenes such as this he also performs a hyperbolized femininity, drawing laughter from those around him. As Harry/Harriet and Clare grow close,

Clare wonders aloud why Harry/Harriet would make such a scene. Harry/Harriet explains "is nuh what dem expect from me? Nuh mus' give dem what dem expect? Battyman trash.[23] No harm. Our people kind of narrow, poor souls. Foolish sometimes. Cyaan understand the likes of me."[24]

As in *Cereus Blooms*, the trans character and the protagonist in Cliff's novel are emotionally linked. However, in *No Telephone*, Harriet functions as an older, wiser sister who teaches Clare about the socioeconomic realities of their country and who helps her to come to terms with her mixed-race identity. Clare stumbles around the world, sometimes passing for white, sometimes embracing her blackness. All the while, Harry/Harriet writes to her, imploring her to return to Jamaica and fight for justice there. One letter is signed "I find myself closer to my choice, girlfriend. How about you? Jamaica needs her children. . . . Love & kisses, H/H."[25] Instead of linking trans genders to sexual abuse, Cliff links them to a revolutionary nationalism, indicating that trans individuals can both embody and promote radical change. Indeed, by the end of the novel, Harriet has obtained a respected leadership position among the revolutionaries, who may or may not know her biological gender.

Eventually, Harry/Harriet—now simply Harriet—succeeds in delivering Clare. Clare arrives back in Jamaica ill from a miscarriage and heartbroken; Harriet, now a nurse, delivers her friend back to physical and emotional health. The two then travel together to the country farm passed down to Clare. Though she cannot save Clare's child, Harriet midwifes Clare's first rebirth in a rural creek as a repatriated Jamaican, as well as her second as a militant revolutionary. Throughout the novel, Harriet listens to Clare's stories and fears while nurturing and encouraging her. Clare, though, is too self-involved to reciprocate this support or to ask Harriet anything about her life and appreciates her friend's attentions and intentions only slightly more than she resents them. One example of this self-centeredness is that when she returns to Jamaica, Clare calls Harriet "Harry" and is corrected: "Harriet, now, girlfriend . . . finally." The conventionally gendered woman asks, "'Then you have [had the surgery] done?'" and Harriet replies: "'No, man. Cyaan afford it. Maybe when de revolution come . . . but the choice is mine, man, is made. Harriet live and Harry be no more. . . . But, you know, darling, castration ain't de main t'ing . . . not a-tall, a-tall.'"[26] Harriet has resolved her issues and her happiness without Clare's help or support, and we do not know enough about Harriet to know what this transition entailed or whether anyone else supported her through *her* process.

In the end Harriet is a far more sympathetic character than Clare. Indeed, Cliff states that Harry/Harriet is "the most complete character in the novel," though the text itself tells a different story.[27] Omise'eke Tinsley notes that in Cliff's view, Harry/Harriet is the author's "most radical vision of decolonized gender and sexuality because s/he is imagined as the ideal, metaphorically perfect" Caribbean person.[28] And this is precisely what is problematic; a perfect metaphor cannot, by definition, be considered realistic. By idealizing the one trans character in *No Telephone*, Cliff also makes that character the least realistic, which, while not a problem for the novel per se, is emblematic of the backhanded portrayals of trans people found in multiple Caribbean novels. As Tinsley acknowledges, Harry/Harriet is a character

> whose metaphoric import is indeed unmissable but whose believability as a realistic character is consistently strained by her perfection as a symbol. Harry/Harriet makes sense not as an 'accurate' representation of the psychological and cultural complexities lived by male Caribbean women who love women but as a mythic character constructed to counter a composite of myths about male femininity and desire.[29]

The novel puts so much emphasis on Harry/Harriet's radical politics and selfless caretaking that it is no wonder we learn so little about his/her personal or interior life. This backhanded presentation of Harriet as an ideal, mythic character is similar to the portrayals of trans characters in other Caribbean novels, including *Sirena Selena*.

Sirena Selena

Mayra Santos-Febres' *Sirena Selena vestida de pena* (published in 2000 in both Spanish and English) has received an incredible amount of scholarly and critical attention. The novel swings between portraying trans characters—here the main characters—as individuals struggling to live the lives they want and as stereotypically mythical beings who deliver others by revealing their deepest desires. The Spanish title of the book—translated into

English merely as *Sirena Selena*—can be read in a variety of ways. An English translation of the Castilian would read: "Sirena Selena, dressed in sorrow" (or "in trouble"). However, in the Dominican Republic (where most of the novel is set), *vestida* is also used to refer to "cross-dressers" or "men raised as women,"[30] in which case the title would read something like: "Sirena Selena, Drag Queen of Pain," referring both to the protagonist's pain and to the pain she inflicts on others. Indeed, the title character is at once dressed in and caused pain by other characters' actions *and* is inherently "clothed" in trouble because, dressed as a travesti (a transvestite), she is given trouble by other people and is treated as a travesty.

Santos-Febres is the only author discussed here who places well-developed trans characters at the center of a novel. The character La Martha, Selena's most recent mentor, is introduced to the reader as "toda una señora"—"a real lady," albeit one who has breast implants and takes hormones to make herself "fabulous."[31] This notion of "real" as being separate from physicality can simultaneously be read as the narrator's embrace of trans identities and genders as true and not approximations *and* as the specific embrace of trans people who can pass and therefore support conventional genders and existing social hierarchies. This tension highlights the ambiguities of gender authenticity, which I address later in this chapter.

If Martha is already *real*, the protagonist, who is sometimes called by the male name Sirenito and sometimes by the female name La Sirena, is preparing to go through the world "as who he really is." What the main character believes to be his/her truth is bound up not only in gender but also in financial—if not class—status and in a desire to leave Puerto Rico. He/she repeats to him/herself: "I'm not about to live as a mere kept woman. And I'm never, never going back to the streets."[32] Sirena Selena never actually expresses the desire to be a woman; instead, she expresses the desire to live extremely well, and she recognizes that performing the role of a beautiful, glamorous, mysterious singer will bring her to that goal. It is an understandable desire for someone who has lived on the streets and who has collected cans and engaged in sex work to survive. The state has failed her, her friends can only partially support her with their own meager resources, and while La Martha does care for Selena, the older señora is also trying to exploit her.

While Serena is content to dress as a woman, La Martha strives to "fully" "reconcile herself with her own body" by having gender confirmation surgery. Without it, she is plagued with the fear that outside of el ambiente (the gay scene), she will be exposed as "an imposter" and that someone might shout, "Look at that. That is not a woman." She thinks to herself: "Having the operation isn't the same as dressing up—this was something she knew deep within herself. To be able to take off her clothes and see herself, finally, from the waist below the same as from above the waist, with tits and candy. Together. To finally be able to rest in a single body." Though Martha describes the desired operation first in terms of her own emotional well-being, the "rest" she refers to also implies a freedom from fear of exposure and physical violence in a society hostile to trans people. After the operation, she continues, "There would be no more dreams in the middle of the night of sleeping naked in a circus tent while everyone paid to look at her, the main attraction, chained to a pink post adorned with Christmas garland."[33] The understandable goal of many of the trans characters in *Sirena Selena* is to pass, to leave the maligned, marginal position of *draga* (drag queen) and *travesti* and become *toda una señora*. Martha's success in passing is, however, rare in the novel; other characters are beaten by the police and harassed at airports and often dress as men if they need to go outside of *el ambiente*, the areas where they live and work.

However, even though *Sirena Selena* refers repeatedly to the harsh realities of life for trans people, the narrative provides little additional detail regarding these characters' internal lives. Instead, much ink is spent portraying trans individuals—especially, but not only Sirena Selena—as mythical beings. This idealization starts with the very beginning of the novel:

Coconut shell, melancholy and restless, from the gods you came, sweet Selena, succulent siren of the glistening beaches; confess beneath the spotlight, *lunática*. You know the desires unleashed by urban nights. You are the memory of distant orgasms reduced to recording sessions. You and your seven soulless braids like a *selenita* bird, like a radiant bird with your insolent magnetism. You are who you are, Sirena Selena . . . and you emerge from your paper moon to sing the old songs of Lucy Favery, Sylvia Rexach, la Lupe, sybarite, dressed and adored by those who worship your face. . . . [34]

The phrase "from the gods you came" implies a polytheistic myth, whether from Santería or ancient Greece, or a generic myth portraying generic gods. Similarly, the statement "You know the desires" points to an omniscient knowing attributed to the supernatural and to a carnal knowing; Selena knows the urban nights because she worked them as a prostitute. Finally, this introduction invokes legendary bolero singers, foreshadowing Sirena Selena's own musical talent.

Sirena Selena is viewed as a mythical figure because of her amazing voice and the beautiful body that it comes from and because of the effects that the combination has on those who hear her. The narrator reveals that "So many people had told [Selena] so many things about her voice," praising its abilities to reveal the listeners' desires, even as Sirena herself only wants to use it to temporarily escape reality and to permanently escape poverty. The narrator proclaims that Sirena Selena looks "perfect to everyone who drank in her passion." Other trans individuals believe her voice sings their pain; they "never tire of telling her how a trickle of tarnished melancholy flows from the center of her chest, but it was always fresh, as old and as fresh as the perennial pain of love on the face of the earth." An admirer sighs, "Your voice smells like honey. Your mouth is a piece of fruit," conflating her voice and body as he tries to embrace her. That Sirena Selena sings well-known boleros, full of pathos and longing, only adds to her mystique. And Hugo Graubel, who decides to fall in love with her and is willing to pay for the privilege, believes Sirena Selena is a "being of fantasy" and "a magic well."[35] All of these fans and clients objectify Sirena Selena and her voice for their own purposes, supplicating themselves to her powers of deliverance while giving little to her in return.

Meanwhile, Solange, the Señora Graubel, is afraid that Sirena Selena is "bewitching" her husband. Indeed, even Solange, who recognizes Sirena Selena as her rival for Hugo's love and attention, is affected by the young trans singer, and we can see in their relationship yet another example of trans deliverance. Solange calls Selena a "freak," a "monster," and an "animal," but even full of hate she cannot escape the power of Selena's voice to deliver. The magnate's wife "Doesn't want to remember, but can't help feeling again how that voice caressed her soul, hypnotizing her too, transporting herself to a timeless place where only her dreams existed . . . [inviting her] to give in to the weight of her own desires." However, by reminding the older woman of her dreams and longings, Selena also reminds Solange of why she has those dreams. While she was still a child, Solange's father drank and gambled the family into poverty and virtually sold his daughter to the wealthy Graubels' feminine son. Solange had to learn the manners of the aristocracy, but after years in the role, "Now she is a *señora* for real. Now she has a house and forks and calla lilies and heirs. She has property in her name, has invested in jewels that she doesn't wear." If Martha becomes toda una señora without the appropriate body, Solange becomes una señora without the appropriate class background. And after Solange has settled into the role of la señora, Sirena Selena comes along, reminding her "You can never be what you want to be, not even with your elegant hairdos, or with the croissants you eat in the morning," adding that "you are rich but you suffer, there are memories embedded in your soul that you can't shake."[36] Sirena Selena delivers people to a deeper sense of self, but this trans character turns the tables; hers is a backhanded deliverance, one that is often full of painful memories and harsh truths.

While everyone else who hears Sirena Selena is similarly delivered to a transcendent, if disturbing, emotional state, only Solange resents it so strongly. What I call deliverance she calls *stealing*; she believes Sirena Selena "was stealing their sense of peace, stealing the safety her guests had come to the party with."[37] These perspectives, though, are not mutually exclusive; by "stealing" some guests' sense of peace and safety, Selena also gives back to them, *delivers* to them their greatest buried or forgotten desires.

This, in fact, is the secret of Selena's voice: it moves people in every possible human condition to remember old and forbidden desires, "distant orgasms," "old hatreds," and "lost causes." Ironically, Selena discovers her gift by accident, while trying to surpass her own fear of returning to prostitution after having been raped and badly beaten by a client. While a new client is sucking his penis, Selena—then living as a male "rent boy" called by the name Sirenito—sings not because he likes his voice or the boleros, but because they remind him of his abuela, in whose presence the young Sirenito felt safety and love. He soon learns that while his voice delivers him to emotional safety, because of its effect on others it can also bring him money and the marginal physical and financial security that cash can provide. Transforming himself into Sirena Selena, she knows that "Her voice is the only thing she has that can get her anywhere in life."[38] Sirena Selena is the agent of her audience's revelations, but once they have been delivered to a heightened emotional state, most of them forget the "otherworldly" singer. They remain consumed with themselves, and Sirena Selena must search for another audience to pay her to deliver them.

* * *

My examination of trans deliverance can be compared to Toni Morrison's objective in *Playing in the Dark*, which she describes in part as exploring "the way black people ignite critical moments of discovery or change or emphasis in literature not written by them."[39] Clearly, I am interested in how trans characters are portrayed and used as catalysts in Caribbean literature and culture, but I am less interested in (though only slightly less concerned about) the authors' personal identity than Morrison is for two reasons. First, I do not believe that a non-trans writer's gender identity *necessarily* leads to a reductive portrayal of trans people in a work of art. Secondly, less than a handful of texts portraying Caribbean trans people were written by those who publicly identify as trans, in part because gender identity is often neither as readily apparent nor as readily discussed as race.

Indeed, it is remarkable how much the trope-heavy portrayals of trans people in Caribbean literature are similar to those of black people in texts from the United States. Morrison writes that "black or colored people and symbolic figurations of blackness are markers for the benevolent and the wicked; the spiritual ... and the voluptuous; of 'sinful' but delicious sensuality coupled with demands for purity and restraint."[40] We have seen in *Sirena Selena, Cereus Blooms at Night,* and *No Telephone to Heaven* the mythical and in the characters of Sirena Selena, Harriet, and Otoh how myth is combined with "wickedness" and forbidden, but still desired, sexuality. A significant difference, however, between these collections of texts and the U.S. novels that Morrison refers to is that the Caribbean novels do not encourage restraint but instead encourage giving in to the desire, the "sin," the fear, *and* the pleasure. They imply that relationships with trans people are a way—if not *the* way—to discover one's own "true" self and that after emotional (and sometimes sexual) involvement with a trans person, "regular" people can go on to lead more self-aware, more truthful, and sometimes more gender-normative lives.

Another area in which the texts I analyze and the ones discussed in *Playing in the Dark* intersect is the recurrence of nurses within them. Tyler's and Harriet's medical careers concretize their presence in the texts as metaphorical and emotional healers. They deliver their charges back to reality, nurse them to health and/or understanding, and then deliver their stories to us. Sirena Selena can also be seen as a "nurse"—albeit a sadistic one—fulfilling a similar function but bringing her clients, her "patients," to knowledge via her singing and the pleasure and pain it causes. Her devotion to the saints also gestures towards the special powers often attributed to trans people in Santería and other Caribbean syncretic religions. Of course, just as caretaking in general is a stereotypically female trait, so is nursing a feminized and predominantly female profession. Like most "women's work," it is often an undervalued, thankless job. Writing about black nurses in white American texts, Morrison notes that

> if you are bent on dramatic gestures of self-reliance, eager to prove that you can go it alone (without complaining), a nurse who chooses or is paid to take care of you does not violate your view of yourself as a brave, silent sufferer. Needfulness does not enter the picture; asking for help is always out of the question, and the benefits that derive from the attentive, expert care do not incur emotional debt.[41]

In other words, because the caretaker is of a socially inferior status, the "patient" is not required to emotionally repay, or even acknowledge, the service performed. This is certainly the case in *No Telephone*, in which Clare resents Harriet's caretaking, and in *Sirena Selena*, in which cash and material goods are considered payment enough. Only in *Cereus Blooms* does a mutually loving and caring relationship derive from a trans person's deliverance of other individuals.

In *Cereus* and *No Telephone*, trans characters are central to the narration and plot, respectively, but are kept in the margins of the novels as minor characters. In short, even when they are telling *the* story, trans people do not get to tell *their own* story. However, in their absence, a trace of trans presence remains, looming.[42] Large and small details of conventionally gendered lives that are matter-of-factly presented remain, for trans characters, hidden. Readers often do not know whom trans people love, whom they desire, or what they think and dream of besides living unmolested in the external expression of their internal gender. In *No Telephone*, Harry/Harriet explains a self-ridiculing public performance by saying "Nuh mus' give dem what dem expect?"[43] Unfortunately, avid readers of Caribbean literature can expect trans characters to be mere sketches, devices used to flesh out and deliver conventionally gendered protagonists. The problem is not that individual authors choose to create trans characters in supporting roles. What is disconcerting is that *collectively* Caribbean authors create trans characters who serve conventionally gendered men and women without themselves being portrayed as full human beings. These are, in the end, backhanded portrayals; while readers may be tempted to applaud the mere presence of positive Caribbean trans characters in the region's literature, we should also be moved to criticize the creation of an archetypical, biologically male trans caretaker, an outline of a character who delivers the "true" protagonists to safety or knowledge and is then pushed back into the shadows.

Possibilities beyond Caribbean Binary Gender

Despite their being assigned service roles and incomplete characterizations, trans people in Caribbean fiction reveal both the rigid ideals of Caribbean gender and the possibilities beyond them. For instance, in *No Telephone* Harriet makes a crucial statement to Clare. When Clare says she feels an affinity for (then) Harry/Harriet because both she and the trans character "are neither one thing nor the other" (Clare, racially, and Harry/Harriet in relation to gender), Harry/Harriet responds: "At the moment, darling, only at the moment. . . . I mean the time will come for both of us to choose. For we will have to make the choice. Cast our lot. Cyaan live split. Not in this world."[44] Harry/Harriet chooses to become Harriet, even at the expense of her relationship with (and some of the financial support of) her wealthy family. The notion that "in this" Jamaican (and by extension the Caribbean) world one must choose between two gender or racial poles is a very important one. It is in all of the texts, though the need to choose is not stated as clearly as it is in *No Telephone*. This idea is also significantly different from those found in contemporary U.S. discourses, in which the trope of self-invention extends to "third" (and fourth and fifth) gender options and hyphenated "new" identities.[45] Interestingly, unconventional genders both provide examples of genders outside of conventional bounds *and* reveal the myth of conventional genders.

The first step in understanding how trans individuals reveal and reinforce ambiguities in Caribbean binary gender is recognizing how they deconstruct that system. Martha, Serena, Tyler, Otoh, Harriet: while all of these trans characters re/present other characters to themselves, they each also (eventually) represent themselves, their trans selves, as their *true* selves, the women and men they know and believe themselves to be. At the same time, trans characters in these Caribbean texts also re/present the idea of gender itself by deconstructing the myth of the "real woman" and the "real man." On the surface, trans expressions of gender may seem to highlight that which they are not: "authentic" or conventionally gendered men and women. But in fact trans individuals, set up by others as myths, ironically reveal "true" and "real" genders to be profound myths, even for conventionally gendered women and men. As Cuban Severo Sarduy writes, "transvestism . . . cannot be reduced to the imitation of a real, set model, since it strikes out in pursuit of an infinite unreality that is accepted as such from the start."[46] The revelation that no gender is completely set does not eliminate the profound power of binary gender ideals, but it does open up a space for the recognition of other, less conventional genders.

Cereus Blooms at Night points to the spaces between and beyond Caribbean binary gender by portraying trans characters who more fully embody positive gender stereotypes than do men and women whose biology and gender correspond. In this novel, the biologically male, male-identified characters share major moral failings that hurt the women closest to them, those whom they are traditionally expected to protect. Chandin is largely indifferent to his wife, and when she falls in love and runs off with another woman, he takes revenge by physically and sexually abusing his daughters Mala and Asha.[47] While Chandin makes others suffer because of an abundance of misdirected aggression and sexuality, Ambrose (Otoh's father) makes others suffer because of his *lack* of aggression. As a boy, instead of offering Mala protection, he runs from the bullies who taunt and attack her and her sister, marked as "indecent" because of their parents' sexual transgressions. Even worse, as an adult he runs away from the knowledge of her father's physical and sexual abuse and her eventual mental breakdown. While Ambrose sends a box of food to Mala via Otoh every week, he does not venture to her home himself, nor does he try to protect her from years of isolation and slander, nor later from the police and mob who call her a murderer, nor finally from the home to which she is confined. Significantly, Mootoo's novel avoids gender and sexual stereotypes of Indo-Caribbean men by portraying both violently aggressive and painfully meek men and by creating an Indo-Caribbean trans character, Otoh, who embodies an ideal masculinity. Nevertheless, neither conventionally gendered man protects the women he supposedly loves.

Indeed, Caribbean trans people excel in realms in which their conventionally gendered counterparts fail. Tyler is more caring and more emotionally intuitive than any of the female nurses or other male or female characters, save protagonist Mala. And Otoh takes great measures to provide Mala the protection his father was too scared and lazy to even attempt. In *Cereus Blooms at Night* and *No Telephone to Heaven,* the trans characters are also the moral centers of the novels. Otoh and Tyler's gender "transgressions" hurt no one—in fact they deliver Mala to safety—while the abuse that conventionally gendered men wreak on those around them is the true travesty. Similarly, in *No Telephone to Heaven* Harry/Harriet is the only one who can heal Clare. And in *Sirena Selena* the trans characters themselves steal and lie, but they are part of a community that ultimately tries to protect its own and, as such, are still portrayed in a better light than Graubel and Solange's father, who are willing to sell their souls or their children for their own pleasure.

Hugo's wife, Solange, a "real" conventionally gendered woman, is more sympathetic. She tries just as hard as the dragas and travestis to assume the role of ideal woman, doña, and wife. Solange's machinations and feelings of inauthenticity are due to her lower-class upbringing, which she wants to keep hidden because it is anathema to the stereotypical upper-class woman. Two quotations reveal the draga's and the doña's similar masquerades.

The first is Solange getting ready for a party:

Not a single detail can escape me, not a single detail. Instead of the Galliano it would be better to wear the Kenzo dress . . . it will soften my figure a little . . . With perfect makeup and the Hidalgo necklace-and-earrings set . . . I'll be stunning . . . The living image of elegance. Careful not to overdo the perfume, it's so concentrated . . . But that's what everyone is wearing these days.

The second is Serena in her visual transformation from male to female as she prepares for an audition:

The base was a fundamental weapon in the war declared against nature . . . More powder to avoid beads of sweat and to fix the work . . . After arduous deliberation [she chose] the long evening dress . . . the matching pearl-pink high heels . . . the eye shadow to use was definitely the Lancôme. . . . [48]

Although Solange does not see this connection with Sirena Selena, the latter does. The trans woman thinks to herself, "You can never be what you want to be . . . just like me."[49] In an interview, Santos-Febres herself twins these characters and says they are representative, explaining that all "women are transvestites . . . the transvestite constructs her identity for the same reasons that the gender she imitates does—to awaken an illusion."[50] In the novel, with Martha described as "a real lady" and Solange as "a señora for real," the "real woman" is simply the one who best succeeds in embodying that impossible ideal. As Doña Martha observes, "everything in this life requires rehearsal. Everything!" and "If you look like a professional, you are a professional. The rest is choreography and acting," performance and performativity.[51] In these texts, the binary gender ideal is something everyone aspires to and no one achieves.

Choreography and acting also imply education or training, and while previously in this chapter we have seen both biological and trans characters trying to become "real" women, a similar process happens for several boys in *Sirena Selena* who are taught or try to learn how to be "real men." When Hugo's millionaire father notices that his adolescent son has no girlfriend and is commonly identified as "that feeble white boy who looked like a girl," he arranges for a sex worker to "make sure" Hugo is a "stud." Hugo remembers that while his body responded to the woman, his mind escaped and he learned to hide his desire for other men. Also in *Sirena Selena*, two young men discuss the difference between hombres and mujeres. The older boy, the mentor, explains to Leocadio that when two men dance, the bigger one is not always the man; rather, "*El hombre* is the one who leads, the one who decides. The other one is *la mujer*, the woman." Later Leocadio muses on this lesson: the one with the money is the man, "And if he dances and the other one leads, then he's *la mujer*. But what if it was she who convinced him to dance. . . . Then who is *el hombre, la mujer?*"[52] This exchange takes place near the end of the novel and reveals that gender may not in practice be nearly as rigid as society's ideals. As these texts display the possibilities beyond binary gender, they also reveal the existence of multiple genders within Caribbean social hierarchies. As Leocadio recognizes, metaphorically speaking and depending on the circumstances, "el hombre," the person with power, could be a conventionally gendered man, a trans woman, a biological woman, or someone else entirely. And yet the binary categories of hombre/man and mujer/woman are reinforced, even for those who seem farthest from them. The literary treatment of trans individuals mirrors their backhanded portrayal in popular culture, where Caribbean trans people are visible largely in the stage entertainment of sketch comedy characters and drag performers, and via the erotic entertainment of sex workers.[53] Similarly, the transvestite carnival characters mentioned at the start of this chapter appear—and are sanctioned—only once a year, and then they perform for the entertainment of ostensibly "real" men and women.

Transvestism in Caribbean Festivals

The idea of transvestism as a Caribbean cultural tradition will seem preposterous to many, though cross-dressing has been a part of Caribbean festivals for over a century, at least, despite the absence of in-depth attention to this issue in Caribbean scholarship. Characters such as la loca (in Puerto Rico), Dame Lorraine, pis-en-lit ("wet-the-bed"), and baby doll (all of Trinidad and Tobago), Mother Sally (Barbados and Guyana), and roba la gallina ("chicken thief," Dominican Republic), as well as the mariage burlesque tradition (Martinique), are either only briefly mentioned or are completely ignored by those who chronicle these festivals. Their absence—or presence as mere passing references in official carnival advertising and documentation—is probably because carnivals and large street festivals are, along with beaches, a primary lure for important tourist income and because scantily clad women, not cross-dressed men, are used to advertise the Caribbean. In this section, I will focus on male transvestite characters found in the Festival Santiago Apóstol in Loíza Aldea, Puerto Rico, and in Barbados' Crop Over.[54] This discussion will show how carnival transvestism is a "supranational cultural practice" found in the region and that it is yet another example of backhanded Caribbean attitudes towards trans people.[55]

La loca

The Festival Santiago Apóstol de Loíza, commonly known as the Loíza Festival (it travels between the Puerto Rican towns of Loíza Aldea and Medianía), continues to be, in part, a celebration of Saint James the Apostle.[56] But it is arguably better known as a series of street parties featuring four traditional characters: the vejigante (a dragon/devil and one of Puerto Rico's national symbols), the caballero (the "gentleman"), the viejo (the "old man"), and la loca ("the crazy woman").[57] In 1956 folklorist Alegría wrote that the festival "is so old that its beginnings have been forgotten."[58] Scholars consistently (and vaguely) suggest that some kind of celebration of Saint James and his victory over the Moors has existed since about 1832, although they do not speculate as to when the four traditional carnival characters developed. The festival begins on July 24 and continues for ten days, a time-frame that corresponds with Roman Catholic celebrations of Saint James. The celebration includes prayer and recreation, but its most popular aspects consist of three street parades focused partly on three different manifestations of the saint and partly on the revelry and dancing that accompany most street festivals anywhere in the world.

Though the scholarly literature on the Loíza Festival focuses on the contested origins of the carnival and the symbolism of vejigantes and caballeros,[59] both textual research and observation reveal that the traditional loca is a man with a blackened face wearing a dress and a headscarf, with padded, if not greatly exaggerated, breasts and buttocks and who carries a broom and a large biscuit tin. Although they will dance with anyone, locas are sometimes paired with viejos. Here is Alegría's description of the loca masquerade:

> The *locas* pass along the streets of the town with brooms and cans, sweeping and cleaning the streets and porches of the houses and asking a recompense for their "work." They wear costumes of clashing colors and fit themselves with artificial busts. They do not customarily wear masks, but usually paint their faces black.[60]

While in more recent years locas are still seen carrying a broom and tin, they are less often seen sweeping and asking for money. Instead, they alternately walk along the streets, usually with a fierce expression, and dance with (or on) both male and female spectators. Comparing the festival portrayed in Alegría's 1949 film *Las fiestas de Santiago Apóstol en Loíza* and the festival I attended in 2003, generally speaking the dresses have gotten shorter, and locas now wear dresses all on their own, instead of over pants as some did in earlier decades.

It is possible that the broom and sweeping refer less to the "domesticated" woman than to the Espiritismo figure La Madama.[61] In Puerto Rican Espiritismo religious practices, La Madama is an important spirit guide through which one can garner knowledge and have deeds performed.[62] One scholar describes her this way:

> She is a bit portly, big bosomed. She wears a long dress, a kerchief around her neck, and a head tie. Her dress can be either white or red. She either holds in her hands or has tied around her waist a set of skeleton keys, and she always holds a broom. She is definitely for

sweeping bad things away (or towards others), but she is also a bringer of financial good fortune.[63]

The significant differences between La Madama and the loca are that the latter carries a tin instead of keys and often wears a short dress of any color. Given the popularity of La Madama not only in Espiritismo but also in Puerto Rican popular culture as a doll or as part of the logo for various products, it is even more surprising that links have not been made between the two figures in popular or scholarly circles.[64] La Madama is always black and very dark-skinned; she is one of the "main stereotypical spirit guides" of Espiritismo who are portrayed with specific "ethnic identities."[65] So a reference to La Madama would explain why locas paint their faces black regardless of their skin color. Furthermore, were she to physically manifest, La Madama would almost certainly be labeled, as spiritual mediums and witches often are, as *loca*—crazy.

Another interpretation is that the loca represents the male transvestite, the person who would change his apparent gender, even for one day. Of course, some traditionalists would take pains to insist that the loca is *not* a transvestite. While such individuals are surely engaged in a bit of gay panic, they are also making a subtle distinction. The traditional loca, who in Alegría's film is sometimes wearing a dress over pants, is a man trying to look like a man dressed as a woman. In contrast, the transvestite is understood to be a man trying to look like a woman, trying "to represent normative gender difference seamlessly."[66]

Indeed, it must be pointed out that *loca*, in Puerto Rican slang, refers to feminine men who are typically assumed to desire other men; it has been translated as "perhaps something akin to queen" in a North American context.[67] In Dominican Spanish, in addition to designating feminine (homosexual) men, it can refer to "all varieties of gender-dissenting male-bodied individuals, including people of trans experience."[68] And like *queen, maricon, masisi, macommère* and other terms, the inflection of *loca* can be insulting or demeaning, depending on who is using it and in what context. In the late twentieth century, there was a small but vocal group of concerned voices protesting the participation of "drag queens" in the Loíza Festival and advocating that only "traditional" locas be allowed to participate.[69] But when I was able to see and participate in the festival in 2003, there were no drag queens to be seen—or at least they were all dressed as locas.

The simultaneous meanings of "madwoman" and "feminine man" linked to the word *loca* suggest that these are the most probable contemporary interpretations of the Loíza character. Locas' performances are enjoyed well enough by female and male spectators during the Loíza festival. Nevertheless, like other traditional transvestite characters, the loca remains one of the least-discussed aspects of the festival.

Mother Sally

Although she also appears during Christmastime in Guyana (where she is sometimes called Bam-Bam Sally), Mother Sally is best known as a traditional character in the Barbados festival of Crop Over, held each August. As its name indicates, Crop Over was originally a harvest celebration and dates back to the time of slavery on the island. After a latent period in the mid-twentieth century, Crop Over was revived by the Barbados Board of Tourism "to attract more visitors in July and August, the traditional quiet months for the tourism industry."[70] Ten years later, the organizing of Crop Over was taken over by the National Cultural Foundation in order to make it "a 'people's festival.'"[71] The Mother Sally character sports exaggerated breasts and buttocks, dances provocatively (winding or "wukking up" on spectators), and often accompanies a tuk band.[72] Although I have been unable to locate any documented history of this character, one popular belief is that she is directly related to African transvestite masquerades (possibly the Nigerian Gelede) that celebrate female fertility. Those who endorse this history claim Mother Sally as an Afro-Bajan nationalist figure, while those who find that narrative suspect simply dismiss the character as vulgar. Ironically, in an essay about the Puerto Rican loca, one scholar notes that in Ireland the name Sally is associated with a character much like Barbados' Mother Sally.[73] Given the dearth of information on the origins of Crop Over, both histories are plausible; after all, large numbers of Irish were sent to Barbados in the seventeenth century, and it is now commonplace to acknowledge that Caribbean culture draws from African and European, as well as indigenous, sources.[74] It is also possible that some people emphasize Mother Sally's African origin as a way of distancing the character from foreign and contemporary transvestites.

The traditional Mother Sally has a great deal in common with Dame Lorraine, a transvestite character in Trinidad and Tobago with similarly large hips and buttocks and similar "rude" dancing and behavior, and with the Dominican Republic's roba la gallina, who dresses similarly, though her actions are different.[75] But while contemporary Dame Lorraine and roba la gallina performances are rather similar to older ones (even in the early twentieth century), Mother Sally has evolved in a very different way. Though the costume and dancing remain the same, as both casual and scholarly observers have noted, in Barbados Mother Sally is now typically performed by a woman, and she now appears almost exclusively for tourist audiences. As problematic as the original transvestite characters are, the transformed Mother Sally—a black woman with huge breasts and posterior, dancing in an aggressively sexual way with white men from the global North—is problematic in different ways, perpetuating not only sexual and racial stereotypes but also colonial ones.

Transvestite Characters, Class, and Race

So far I have explained the histories and contemporary performances of two Caribbean transvestite festival characters which are similar to others found around the region. But it is also crucial to explore the collective implications and significance of these characters. While the transvestite characters in the Loíza Festival and Crop Over, as well as those in Trinidadian, Dominican, and Martinican carnivals, each have particular characteristics, there are some significant similarities in the characters themselves and who they represent.

Over time, large carnivals and festivals have become "national industries" that affect regional economies, and, as such, "Caribbean carnivals and other such popular festivals are not simply modern phenomena with certain 'traditional vestiges,' but have turned into highly contested, representational sites of national and regional cultural identities."[76] To be sure, like all aspects of culture, Crop Over and other Caribbean festivals are dynamic and will change over time, but the nature of these changes and how they reflect other trends can be instructive. While the loca, Dame Lorraine, and roba la gallina persist in performances that continue to reflect their earliest recorded manifestations, the Mother Sally role is now performed mostly by women, and still other transvestite characters—most notably Trinidad's pis-en-lit and female transvestite jamette performers—have largely disappeared. Though it is difficult to determine precisely what led to these changes, there are some clues. For instance, the pis-en-lit gestured towards violence, and as I have written elsewhere, the Dame Lorraine is less intimidating than the pis-en-lit character, the latter being "an almost naked black man wearing a shift stained with blood."[77] Furthermore, female transvestism—the impersonation and mocking of those in power, rather than those without power—was likely very threatening to colonial elites.[78]

A look at economics provides additional cues to the evolution of Caribbean transvestite festival characters. It seems that the greater the country's dependence on tourism, the more likely it is that transvestite festival characters will be "sanitized" into more heteronormative presentations more legible to and less likely to offend foreign visitors. In 2012, tourism made up 39.4 percent of Barbados' GDP, a significant number by any measure. In contrast, during the same year tourism made up 8.4 percent of Trinidad and Tobago's GDP.[79] While Puerto Rico is also a popular vacation destination, tourism makes up only about 7 percent of its GNP, and Loíza has experienced significant challenges in earning a share of that revenue.[80] Loíza is "[k]nown for its preponderantly black population and its strong African roots," which can appeal to Puerto Rican immigrants and folklore enthusiasts but which is unlikely to interest most tourists, given that Puerto Rico's most popular attractions are beach resorts, the city of Old San Juan, and cruise ships.[81] While the festival itself is Loíza's main attraction, the traditional characters chosen as its official symbols are Santiago himself (the white, Spanish, Catholic hero who defeated the Moors and is represented by the caballero masquerade), now part of the emblem of the municipality of Loíza, and the vejigante, whose image is now "part of the large welcoming sign at the entrance to the town."[82] If Loíza is successful in increasing tourism, the blackface transvestite loca may well be one of the casualties of that success.

At the start of this chapter, I describe a Caribbean trans continuum and its two extremes—people who live as a gender other than that assigned to them at birth and those who perform transvestite carnival characters. As Ben Sifuentes-Jáuregui writes in *Transvestism, Masculinity and Latin American Literature*, "The meanings of a man putting on a dress range from a joke to a carnival to erotic 'deviance.' But *how* (or under what conditions) a man puts on a dress or what desires and instincts motivate a man to put on a dress" is a different matter, and it is crucial to analyze the distinctions.[83] When performing traditional characters in Caribbean festivals, a man in women's clothes or a woman in men's clothing is *not* trying to pass as another gender; nor is he or she trying to reflect a personal penchant for an unconventional gender or nonheteronormative sexuality. However, playing these characters has implications that go beyond the performers' identities. In fact, transvestite masqueraders are "playing out a complex drama that almost always brings with it consequences and implications related not only to gender but also to nationality, race, and class."[84] Regardless of their histories, as they are presented today, the locas, Mother Sallies, roba la gallinas, and Dame Lorraines mock not just women in general but also (and specifically) working-class black womanhood and femininity, while reinforcing heteropatriarchal masculinity.

The stereotypes of Caribbean transvestite masquerade characters are generalized because the idea of the promiscuous black woman existed even before these century-old festivals were first held. However, the image of the black woman that is mocked by these characters is also specific because both the "old-time" dress of the loca, Dame Lorraine, Mother Sally, and the roba la gallina, and the broom and tin of the loca gesture (among other meanings) towards a large, dark Afro-Caribbean woman who, because of her blackness, her femaleness, her rural location, and her working class status, is simultaneously undersexed, hypersexual, and outside of the modern world. While other traditional festival characters such as the caballero (Puerto Rico) and the kings and queens found throughout the Caribbean are dignified; while the midnight robber (Trinidad and Tobago) and Califé (Dominican Republic) are erudite; and while vejigantes (Puerto Rico) and other devils are scary, the male transvestite rather consistently portrays a poor, black, female buffoon. While the histories of these characters point to other readings, because those histories are not always widely known, and because their contexts have changed significantly, other, more readily accessible meanings take precedence.

In addition to mocking black womanhood, these performances also reinforce heteropatriarchal masculinity. In this structure, the undersexed woman begs to be sexually satisfied, the hypersexual woman must be both satisfied and controlled, the domestic woman needs a man to provide for her, and the clueless woman needs a man to think for, protect, and direct her. These interpretations are also implied by the now predominantly female Mother Sallies, but when such characters are portrayed by men deliberately *not* trying to pass as female, the men portraying these characters simultaneously get to play the mocked woman and the mocking man, without making suspect their own masculinity or power. This is an interpretation not limited to scholars; popular websites mentioning these characters make similar conclusions, as is evident through references such as "men dressing up as women . . . to signify their machismo-ness" and the "paradoxical display [by which] men show off their macho maleness by dressing up as women."[85]

Indeed, while foreigners might conflate carnival characters with other forms of transvestism and might assume that some or all of the masqueraders are homosexual, many Caribbean trans people distance themselves from the festival characters. For instance, Denise, a Martinican biological man who usually dresses as a woman, told an interviewer that during carnival, she was "in mourning," and added that she "felt that Carnival made a mockery of her, and the fact that cross-dressing only occurred during Carnival, a time of play, reinforced its unacceptability in daily life. . . . This mass spectacle only served to ridicule what was a deadly serious undertaking for Denise."[86] Denise's comments indicate that another effect of these masquerades is the mocking of both trans and same-sex desiring people.

*   *   *

Of course, common sense dictates that popular festivals are not often the place where one should seek progressive gender or racial representations. And undoubtedly it would be better for women and those who do not identify with traditional genders to be treated better in their homes, workplaces, and communities than for the loca, Mother Sally, roba la gallina, or Dame Lorraine masquerades to change or disappear (should such a choice ever be available). I would argue that information about these and other local and regional festival traditions should be taught to children and youth in schools.[87] This would create a population that preserves or evolves traditions with more of an awareness of their history, so that young people do not think that carnival characters are just creations for tourists, as some do in Barbados.[88]

Earlier I noted the importance of intentionality to the Caribbean trans continuum. Of course, the nature of a continuum is that such distinctions are not always clear; a Mother Sally or a loca can *also* be a transvestite, as some in Puerto Rico fear; and in the Dominican Republic, travestis (transvestites) in glamorous and/or scandalous contemporary attire are often

listed in the pantheon of traditional carnival characters as their own cat-
egory, separate from the roba la gallina.[89] And just as carnivals have generally existed in a space in which the unusual, perverse, reverse, and inverse
are tolerated, if not applauded, some of these festivals and carnivals create a
space in which a transvestite or drag queen *might* be able to appear openly
and remain unmolested and unafraid for a day or two. Cross-dressing par-
ody can have subversive and positive effects, opening up a space to critique
gender norms, even while it can also have backhanded, negative aspects, in
this case the ridicule of black working-class women and trans practices and
people.

Fanon's Macommères

Class and economics also figure in Fanon's in/famous quote about the
existence of unconventional genders and same-sex sexuality in the Caribbean. Fanon himself, not known for his liberal thinking regarding gender
and sexuality, continues to be "a towering figure in Africana philosophy and
twentieth-century revolutionary thought," referenced in fields as diverse as
politics, postcolonial theory, sexuality, gender, and critical race studies.[90]
While he mentions sexuality several times in his various books, here I will
focus on the one time he mentions homosexuality and unconventional
gender specifically in relationship to the Caribbean. The quote in question,
from a footnote in his 1952 *Peau noire, masques blancs* (published in English
as *Black Skin, White Masks* in 1967), reads:

> Mentionnons rapidement qu'il ne nous a pas été donné de consta-
> ter la présence manifeste de pédérastie en Martinique. Il faut y voir
> la conséquence de l'absence de l'Oedipe aux Antilles. On connaît
> en effet le schéma de l'homosexualité. Rappelons toutefois l'exis-
> tence de ce qu'on appelle là-bas "des hommes habillés en dames" ou
> "Ma Commère." Ils ont la plupart du temps une veste et une jupe.
> Mais nous restons persuadés qu'ils ont une vie sexuelle normale. Ils
> prennent le punch comme n'importe quel gaillard et ne sont pas in-
> sensibles aux charmes des femmes—marchandes de poissons, des lé-
> gumes. Par contre en Europe nous avons trouvé quelques camarades
> qui sont devenus pédérastes, toujours passifs. Mais ce n'était point

là homosexualité névrotique, c'était pour eux un expédient comme pour d'autres celui de souteneur.⁹¹

Let me observe at once that I had no opportunity to establish the overt presence of homosexuality in Martinique. This must be viewed as the absence of the Oedipus complex in the Antilles. The schema of homosexuality is well enough known. We should not overlook, however, the existence of what are called there [in Martinique] "men dressed like women" or "godmothers." Generally, they wear shirts and skirts. But I am convinced that they lead normal sex lives. They can take a punch like any "he-man" and they are not impervious to the allures of women—fish and vegetable merchants. In Europe, on the other hand, I have known several Martinicans who became homosexuals, always passive. But this was by no means a neurotic homosexuality: For them it was a means to a livelihood, as pimping is for others.

This is a fascinating passage which, though it has been quoted ad infinitum, has not as often been closely analyzed. I provide the French and the English texts for complete context and to highlight two words where the given English masks a greater complexity. In particular, I will focus here on *macommères*, poorly translated as "godmothers."⁹² While *macommère* can mean godmother or co-mother in several French and English Caribbean territories, it also has another common use, as a derogatory term which refers to a feminine man whose heterosexuality is often suspect because of his gender expression.

Although Fanon is consumed with the search for gender and sexual neuroses and pathologies, and though this passage is frequently cited as either proof of the nonexistence of same-sex desire in the Caribbean and Africa or as proof that that was Fanon's belief, there is some subtlety here. He begins the footnote by stating that he "had no opportunity to establish the overt presence of homosexuality in Martinique." This choice of words allows the reader to intuit that perhaps Fanon was aware of covert homosexuality or even overt homosexuality in his homeland that he was not privy to. Furthermore, Fanon—incredibly—expands "normal" conventional masculinity to include "men dressed like women," that is, men who wear skirts.⁹³ For Fanon, the masculine ability to "take a punch" like a man and to sexually desire women are far more important than the quirk of wearing skirts on a regular basis. And yet his diction is rather backhanded. That macommères are described in terms of *taking* a punch, not throwing one or even returning one, implies that trans women are targeted by (other) men for violence because of their supposedly inferior masculinity. Nor is Fanon's description of macommère's heterosexuality completely confident. To "not be impervious to the allures of women" is very different from having a passionate desire for women. Fanon's phrasing implies a passive, almost reluctant giving in rather than active amorous pursuit by macommères.

If his observations are accurate, in this footnote Fanon provides a rare midcentury description of Caribbean trans people. He describes macommères as wearing "une veste et une jupe," and while strictly speaking the 1967 translation of "shirts and skirts" is not incorrect, it is helpful to know that the French *veste* refers specifically to a *man's* shirt or jacket. This difference implies greater gender ambiguity than that of a man dressed completely in women's clothing. Both clothing ensembles place macommères on the trans continuum, though an outfit that is comprised entirely of clothing usually worn by women implies a desire to embody traditional femininity, whereas a man's jacket with a women's skirt implies a desire to simultaneously embrace *both* masculinity and femininity. In the latter case, "men dressed as women" becomes shorthand for men dressed in any way that does not overwhelmingly endorse conventional masculinity. Though it is not clear which sense Fanon intended, both possibilities expand traditional notions of Caribbean gender.

While Fanon acknowledges macommères' trans existence—and insists that we "must not overlook them"—he also implies that such predilections are limited to the working class. He does not comment directly on macommères' class status but does make clear that the women he believes would seduce macommères—and the women he believes they would be seduced *by*—are "fish and vegetable merchants," not teachers, or nurses, or the daughters of Martinique's elite.[94] Here is another backhanded acknowledgement of trans experience in the Caribbean; Fanon is happy to admit that macommères exist and are (for the most part) normal, but he takes pains to point out that only a certain type of man is a macommère and only a certain type of woman would be attracted to him.[95] This distinction contains trans genders within a particular, less prestigious, and less powerful part of the Martinican population.

Fanon makes another backhanded move in relationship to same-sex desire, claiming that there is *no* homosexuality within the Caribbean and that outside of the Caribbean, Antillean men engage in homosexuality only as "passive" sex workers. (He does not consider Caribbean female homosexuality or same-sex desire in or outside of the Antilles.) In his view, these men can only *become* homosexuals abroad; it is not possible for them to always already be homosexual, nor is it possible for them to become homosexuals within the region. The implications are clear: poor Antillean men, stranded in a foreign country, without resources and further hampered by racism, participate in homosex for money but take no pleasure in it. The middle- or upper-class Antillean man, Fanon implies, has both a normal gender expression and appropriate sexual desires, while working-class heterosexual Antillean "he-men" might wear skirts or work as homosexual prostitutes. Thus Fanon acknowledges homosexual *behavior* while denying same-sex *desire*. Picking up on this distinction, Diana Fuss in her oft-quoted essay argues that Fanon opens the door to nonheterosexual desire that is not labeled as—and may not in practice or conception be the same as—homosexuality in the global North. Though *Black Skin, White Masks* does create this possibility, given Fanon's conservative thoughts about black sexuality, it is unlikely that this is what he meant. While it is true that "European identity categories" may be "wholly inadequate to describe the many different consolidations, permutations, and transformations of" sexuality in the Caribbean, Fanon himself is willing to acknowledge unconventional gender but *not* to imagine indigenous nonheteronormative sexuality.[96] Of course, Fanon is not alone in this failure of the imagination; he is joined by hundreds, if not thousands, of elected and religious Caribbean officials, even as many Caribbean people exhibit greater, though quieter, acceptance of nonheteronormative sexualities.[97] More than fifty years after the publication of *Black Skin, White Masks*, we have the words and actions of Caribbean trans people (and, as will be discussed in later chapters, of same-sex-desiring Caribbean people) to refute Fanon's categorical statements. But even now, class and race often determine who is an acceptable trans Caribbean subject, as analysis of three contemporary cases will demonstrate.

Trans Treatment in Caribbean Law and Media

In 1997, mainstream press in Trinidad and Tobago (and several international outlets) reported Jowelle De Souza's successful court case. A Trinidadian trans woman who had gender confirmation surgery at the age of nineteen, De Souza won a settlement against the state of Trinidad and Tobago for unlawful arrest and police harassment *and* received sympathetic local press coverage.[98] Earlier that year, a photographer who "knew all about her past and was taking pictures of her without permission" had invaded De Souza's personal space; she pushed him away and was subsequently arrested and charged with assault.[99] While at the police station, officers "taunted her for hours about her sexuality," and she was eventually strip-searched. After this incident, De Souza brought suit against the state, and during the case she was represented by "one of Trinidad's most prominent lawyers, Lynette Maharaj," the wife of the sitting attorney general.[100] The case was eventually settled out of court, and she received a cash settlement that she donated to charity.

In August 2011, Ignacio Estrada and Wendy Iriepa, self-identified respectively as a gay man and a transsexual woman, left a Cuban courthouse after being joined in what was described as "the first wedding of its kind" in the country and perhaps the region.[101] Estrada explained that the couple purposefully married on Fidel Castro's birthday "to remind him of the atrocities he committed against the Cuban gay community."[102] The beautiful light-skinned Cubans in their wedding finery were extremely camera-ready and enthusiastically publicized their marriage. The story was picked up by the *Guardian, Huffington Post*, Reuters, Al Jazeera, and many other outlets, and videos and photographs of the couple continue to be easily found on the Internet.

More than a decade after De Souza's arrest and eventual triumph, and over a year before Estrada and Iriepa's wedding, in what has been described as "a series of crackdowns" on February 6 and 7, 2010, eight Guyanese (described variously as "transgenders," "men," and "cross-dressers" but who did not self-identify in any documents I discovered) were arrested and charged with "cross-dressing" under statute 153(1)(xlvii) of the country's Summary Jurisdiction (Offences) Act.[103] This statute makes it illegal for anyone who, "being a man, in any public way or public place, for any improper purpose, appears in female attire, or being a woman, in any public way or public place, for any improper purpose, appears in male attire."[104] They were detained over the weekend; all were strip-searched, some were denied medical treatment, and those who asked why they were being held were given no answer. On February 9 they appeared without legal consul before Chief Magistrate Melissa Robertson who, among other comments, "told the applicants that they must go to church and should give their lives to Jesus Christ," adding that they were "confused about their sexuality" and that "they are men, not women."[105] All were fined at least $7,500. Just a few weeks later, with legal representation, the support of local activists, and growing international attention, four of those arrested and the Guyana-based Society against Sexual Orientation Discrimination (SASOD) with the University of the West Indies Rights Advocacy Project filed a motion in the Guyanese High Court arguing that the law against "cross-dressing" is unconstitutional because it is "discriminatory" and that both the police and the magistrate had treated the accused improperly.[106]

One major distinction between these cases is that the Trinidadian case did not involve any law explicitly referencing gender or sexuality, while the Cuban marriage involved a law that implicitly involves sexuality and explicitly relates to gender—even though, legally, the couple did not violate that law. In contrast, the group I will call the Guyanese 4 was arrested and fined under, and are now suing to challenge, a statute that *specifically* bans public gender transgression. The language of the law is revealing; first, it insists that the individual in question must *be* a "man" or a "woman." Since the law does not provide a definition of these terms, the task of defining falls to the police responsible for enforcing the law and to the judges responsible for interpreting the law. The magistrate who heard the original case was clearly confident both in her own definitions of "man" and "woman" and in her decision that the defendants were "confused" (in the magistrate's words) about their own gender.[107] This case is thus a real-world example of the established binary gender categories.

The second important phrase in this statute is that transvestism should not occur "in any public way or public place, for any improper purpose." Accordingly, when the Guyanese 4 were in the privacy of any of their homes, getting dressed, they were not violating the law. And if their destination had been a friend's home or a house party, when they arrived there they would also not have been violating the law. If, however, their destination had been a restaurant or club that is privately owned but open to the public, it is unclear whether their mere presence there would have been illegal. Nevertheless, while walking en route to their respective destinations, the arrested Guyanese were certainly contravening the state's stated goal of preserving *public* propriety. However, if transvestism poses such a threat to the public, one wonders what the "proper purpose" of the practice might be. Perhaps stage comedy or drag performances or the act of performing Mother Sally qualify.

Statute 153(1)(xlvii) also makes reference to "male attire" and "female attire." As with other terms in the law, these are quite subjective. When is a pantsuit male and when is it female? What shape must a pair of earrings be to be categorized as female? Based even on this brief reading, it seems that the contention that statute 153(1)(xlvii) is "vague" has merit. Nevertheless, on September 6, 2013, the Guyanese Supreme Court handed down a contradictory ruling. It recognized transgender identities using that word, and it stated that it is legal "to wear the attire of the opposite sex as a matter of preference or to give expression to or to reflect his or her sexual orientation." However, the court did not provide an example of an "improper" purpose of cross-dressing—even in the case of the litigants—and upheld the Guyanese 4's original convictions.[108]

The Guyanese 4 plan to appeal, and it is certain that theirs will be a long battle, fought as much in the Guyanese public sphere as in the courts. Radost Rangelova writes that "the institution of the nation-state solidifies and fixes identities, marginalizing and excluding the transvestite who, because of her gender identification, cannot fully be accepted as a national subject because she transgresses the limits of what the nation-state deems acceptable and productive."[109] This is clearly true in Guyana, where the letter of the law explicitly vilifies "improper" gender expression and requires a fine of the offenders. It seems, however, that color, race, and class can be mitigating factors in the state's treatment of trans people around the region.

Trinidad and Tobago and Guyana share similar racial populations and a history of twentieth-century British colonialism.[110] But they also differ in many ways, including their laws regarding transvestism. While a local regulation specific to the 1895 carnival banned transvestism and in particular the pis-en-lit masquerade, Trinidad and Tobago does not appear to have any current laws against transvestism. On the other hand, Guyana's law is clearly still on the books and is selectively enforced. Keeping in mind these differences, when comparing the cases of Jowelle de Souza and the Guyanese 4, race and class again stand out as prominent factors in their treatment.

Newspaper accounts comment on Trinidadian De Souza's beauty so often that Tinsley describes journalists as "mythifying" her. Her fair-skinned femininity contributes to her ability to pass which, combined with male reporters' "documentation of their own response to [De Souza's] heterosexual desirability," work to present her as a "real woman" who "deserves" the justice she fought for.[111] While it is true that these portrayals are "simultaneously exoticizing, patronizing, supportive, and appreciative," the unspoken implication is, of course, that those less fair-skinned and less conventionally beautiful are also less deserving of justice.[112] Indeed, the Guyanese 4, still waiting and working for justice, are all of African or Indian descent. Though notions of "light" and "dark" skin vary, none of the Guyanese arrested is as fair as De Souza or the Cuban couple. Few pictures are available of the Guyanese who were arrested; those that appear on the *Starbroek News* website look more like involuntary mug shots than careful, glamorous headshots. Indeed, the Guyanese 4 have given almost no interviews, and half of those arrested chose not to continue with the case at all. While this may well be part of a legal strategy, it is a stark contrast to the many interviews and photo-ops provided by De Souza, Estrada, and Iriepa and may also be linked to the power of class.

De Souza is part of a wealthy local family and owns her own business, resources that provided her with the economic and social capital to have gender confirmation surgery and to legally fight for justice with powerhouse representation. On the other hand, those arrested in Guyana are all working class. Again, media reporting betrays bias; coverage of De Souza far more often mentions the fact that she is a *business owner* than the fact that she is a hairdresser. The implication is that she is a proprietor who makes a significant economic contribution to society. In contrast, no mention is made of the professions of the Guyanese 4, and no details are provided that might imply they "deserve" better treatment than they received.

If the Guyanese 4 were fairer or closer to stereotypical European beauty or wealthy business owners, would they have still been abused by the police and the judge? And if so, after protesting, would they have become local media darlings, as did de Souza? Would international media have been as interested in their wedding if Iriepa and Estrada were Afro-Cuban or if their wedding lacked the fairytale trappings of a fancy white dress and suit and a convertible driving slowly through the street? And if de Souza had been darker, or her manners or genealogy less "refined," would her case have ended so quickly and in her favor? We cannot, of course, know the answers to these questions, though we do know that color, race, and class often result in differing treatment no matter where one is in the world.

*   *   *

In literature, too, class, color, and race play roles in determining the life possibilities open to a Caribbean trans individual. Class is very important in Santos-Febres' novel; in fact, Selena's decision to perform as a female is bound up with a desire to gain economic security. Selena's early years were spent in a very loving and very economically poor environment, and as a teenager Sirenito chooses life on the street over the dangers of an institutional orphanage. Unlike La Martha, Selena does not dream of physically being a woman; nor does she dress in women's attire when clients are not around, as her adopted sister and best friend Valentina does. She is "delighted" to dress as a woman if fine clothes and jewelry are given to her, but not because of any overwhelming or intrinsic desire on Selena's own part. Mootoo, on the other hand, does not make Nurse Tyler's race, color, or class clear.[113] For instance, while being a nurse makes Tyler solidly middle class in education and profession, we do not know the conditions of Tyler's childhood.

In Cliff's novel, however, class and color are intertwined; her mixed-race trans character benefits from her (light) father's money (though she is denied his affection), a situation that enables her to provide free nursing services to the poor. And color is mentioned often in Sirena Selena, where the title character is described as a "criolla" with "light cinnamon-colored skin," while the other main character, Martha, is referred to as "tanned."[114] In a performance, Martha repeats the popular saying "Aquí, el que no tiene dinga, tiene mandinga," referring to the inescapability of African blood in Puerto Rican veins, irrespective of skin color. And despite this declaration, Martha herself does everything possible to preserve her pale skin, accentuating it with dyed blonde hair.[115] As elsewhere in Caribbean culture, light skin is preferred and has an implicit connection to class, a reality derived from the existence of a "colored" buffer middle class as far back as the eighteenth century.

Conclusion

In similar and different ways, Caribbean literature and popular culture fail trans people by presenting or acknowledging them in a backhanded fashion. The physical danger and social ostracization that trans people endure in literature and the resulting emotional pain described in the texts are all too real. But the "holes" in authors' portrayals of trans characters—the absence for many of a social, love, or sex life, and the almost complete absence of trans men in these narratives—do not correspond to reality. The mere presence of trans characters in Caribbean novels means that the literature is becoming more diverse. But activists and intellectuals have often pointed out that diversity and inclusion are very different; Caribbean authors deliver trans characters to their readers, but it is a backhanded deliverance. The failure to portray full trans lives keeps them marginal—reinscribing conventional heteropatriarchal gender—and avoids exploring how inclusion and acceptance of trans individuals could challenge binary Caribbean gender. Unfortunately, many of the human details and much of the possible impact of Caribbean trans lives remain largely hidden in the region's literary imagination.

If Caribbean literature gestures towards trans acceptance without allowing trans people full lives, traditional transvestite carnival and festival characters gesture towards transgressive gender while reinforcing conventional gender stereotypes. These characters mock working-class black women, trans people, and feminine men without disturbing the perception of the masquerader as a conventionally gendered heterosexual man. Found throughout the region, these backhanded portrayals are rich in symbolism, though the contemporary performances are full of troubling implications.

Caribbean territories encourage the belief that everyone is welcome to participate in the ongoing project that is the nation. Given the region's history and its relationship to tourism, inclusion is an oft-proclaimed value and one represented in many nationalist and marketing slogans (especially in the English-speaking territories) such as "Together we aspire, together we achieve" (Trinidad and Tobago), "Unified by freedom" (Netherlands Antilles), "Out of many, one people" (Jamaica), "One people, one nation, one destiny" and "Land of six peoples" (both Guyana). In practice, of course, inclusion is more difficult. The arguments of Frantz Fanon, a patriarch of Caribbean studies, become convoluted as he both embraces macommères and limits their sexual possibilities in a statement relegated to a footnote. And in Caribbean law and media, it seems that whether trans people are embraced as legitimate citizens or targeted for persecution depends on their class and color. Thus the celebrations of Jowelle De Souza as an individual and Wendy Iriepa and Ignacio Estrada as a couple are backhanded for the masses of trans people who, like the majority of Caribbean people, tend to be darker and poorer.

It is no secret that lighter, richer people tend to be treated better than darker, poorer people in most parts of the world, including the Caribbean. In the cases of both real and fictional Caribbean trans individuals, color, race, and class can mitigate a suspect (or outright despised) gender. And transvestite festival characters traditionally performed by black men are made female or erased altogether when a community seeks tourist dollars or a more general "modernity." In general, the Caribbean, it seems, prefers the transvestite end of the trans spectrum, especially when those performances mock women and otherwise reinforce heteropatriarchy. When it comes to trans people at the other end of the spectrum, however, the Caribbean prefers them fair-skinned, runway-gorgeous, and of a certain class. Indeed, while Caribbean trans people do live in the region—sometimes quite well and with communal and familial acceptance—the ability of Caribbean literature and Caribbean law to imagine trans people as full citizens is directly related to the class and color of the individuals in question. The popular Caribglobal imagination is broad enough to encompass the concept of trans genders, as the list of terms describing such individuals at the start of this chapter demonstrates. However, these concepts do not disturb binary gender or heteropatriarchal ideals, which are further reinforced by those in charge of making and enforcing legislative and economic policy.

2

"El Secreto Abierto"

Visibility, Confirmation, and Caribbean Men
Who Desire Men

Homosexuality, lesbianism, and bisexuality are tolerated as long as they are not disclosed or are negotiated strictly as an "open secret" or *secreto a voces/secreto abierto*.

La Fountain-Stokes, *Queer Ricans: Cultures and Sexualities in the Diaspora*, xvii

Lawrence La Fountain-Stokes made this comment about sexuality in Puerto Rico, but the concept of el secreto abierto, or the "open secret," exists in the rest of the Caribbean as well.[1] For instance, in reference to Suriname, Gloria Wekker notes that "It is common knowledge in Surinamese male mati circles that same-sex sexual behavior among men, even those who are married or in a steady, publicly displayed relationship with a woman, is quite common."[2] This "common knowledge," however, is not commonly discussed; for instance, the director of Suriname Men United states that in his country "only a few [nonheterosexual] men are open about their sexual orientation."[3] Similarly, David A. B. Murray notes that in Martinique "making a public statement about one's sexuality is neither a 'rite of passage' to becoming an 'out, gay' adult nor a necessary step to establish a secure sense of one's identity."[4] And in Guadeloupe, most men's "homosexual behavior stays an unspoken secret, and does not interfere with their social or daily life," observes Dolorès Pourette.[5] Anthropologist Jafari Allen repeatedly uses two other phrases learned from his Cuban interlocutors: "the dicta *no dice nada, se hace todo* (say nothing—everything is done) and *entendido, por no dicho* (in the know, but not declared homosexual)," which have similar meanings.[6]

What is el secreto abierto, the open secret? It is a situation in which many people "know" someone is a homosexual though the fact is not openly acknowledged. People "know" the "secret" without being told, through any combination of factors such as behaviors, speech, or dress. A Haitian activist states that, in reference to the sexual and erotic lives of men who desire men, "people will know. But it's just that no one talks about it."[7] El secreto abierto allows an understanding of Caribbean same-sex sexuality that is very different from the "closet" metaphor and "coming out" narrative that are dominant in Euro-America. Instead of a mandate of constant revelation, in Caribglobal communities there is a mandate of discretion, which is not (always) the same as hiding. In the tradition of el secreto abierto, the "secret" is not fully hidden, and thus explicit revelation is not necessary and could, in fact, be redundant. It can also be understood as a structure in which sexuality is "something present yet not remarked upon, something understood yet not stated, something intuited yet uncertain, something known yet not broached by either person in a given exchange."[8] Similarly, one anthropologist describes this tradition in Martinique as being focused not on hiding but "on discretion," and a Canadian journalist reported in 2007 that while she was in the Dutch Caribbean, "local activists tried to convey the importance of discretion" in relation to nonheteronormative sexuality.[9]

Northern perspectives might see el secreto abierto, at best, as politically incorrect and, at worst, as self-loathing. But, in fact, this Caribglobal tradition is one of many social realities that, as Gopinath has observed in South Asia and its diaspora, "suggest a mode of reading and 'seeing' same-sex eroticism that challenges modern epistemologies of visibility, revelation, and sexual subjectivity."[10] Like many social conventions, el secreto abierto depends on context; as Lancaster writes about Latin America, if discretion about same-sex desire is observed, then it can be "allowed, expressed, and tolerated—in certain tacitly agreed spaces."[11] As is demonstrated in this quote, another component of el secreto abierto is that it requires the community's complicity; the "secret" is both known and (relatively) tolerated by those around the individual. This facet of el secreto abierto is another difference from the "closet" structure, which requires individual, not collective, agency.

The tradition of the open secret indicates neither greater nor lesser homophobia or heterosexism in Caribglobal communities than elsewhere;

comparing the structure of el secreto abierto to that of coming out in such a way is not useful. Rather, they should be seen as different social imperatives meant to manage same-sex revelation; one insists on the right and necessity to tell, and one insists on the necessity and right "not to tell."[12] Exploring el secreto abierto's mechanisms and structure provides insight into how sexual minorities—in particular, men who desire other men—live and love in Caribbean communities. It is especially appropriate to study el secreto in relationship to Caribbean men because it relates to the trope of the visibility of Caribbean men who desire men, as opposed to the dominant trope of *invisibility* in relationship to Caribbean women who desire women.

In Guadeloupe, for instance, the "virulence of discussions about men who practice homosexuality is contrasted with the relative discretion around lesbian women," notes Pourette.[13] And between the 1960s and 1980s in Cuba, as Peña writes, "gender-transgressive homosexual men were marginalized and persecuted, but they were also culturally intelligible in a way that Cuban lesbians were not. José Quiroga has argued that Cuban male homosexuals had meanings imposed on them by the Cuban Revolution (such as that male homosexuals were a threat to the virile, masculine revolution), whereas from the point of view of the revolution Cuban lesbians were 'apparitional, nonexistent, and inconceivable.'"[14] Pourette writes that in Guadeloupe "the existence of the makòmé is not hidden. On the contrary he is an object of remarkable social attention; one talks about him, laughs about him, knows him."[15] And along with this visibility comes official scrutiny and criminalization, notes Yasmin Tambiah: "Throughout the debate [about the legislation of homosexuality in Trinidad and Tobago], it is male homosexuality that was explicitly scripted as the overt threat to institutionalized heterosexuality. Sex between women was barely discussed, and when it was, it was not with the same notion of threat and danger." Female homosex "was not perceived to be as threatening to institutionalized everyday heterosexuality as sex between men."[16] Of course, this double standard is itself sexist, since it assumes that women are not important, that they cannot be meaningful actors in the public sphere, and that their sexuality is of no consequence, all of which are stereotypes that continue to this day in the Caribbean and elsewhere.

The coexistence of el secreto abierto and a trope of visibility in reference to Caribbean men who desire men may seem curious. But men's bodies and behavior are always already visible in the Caribglobal public sphere, whereas women are traditionally expected to belong to the private sphere. This distinction, referred to in scholarship as one of house/street or casa/calle, often does not reflect reality.[17] At the same time, the *openness* of el secreto means that it is both legible and visible, even if it is unacknowledged. And men who break the terms of el secreto by flouting masculine gender codes become hypervisible in a negative way through their gender dissidence. This chapter explores how el secreto abierto is structured more by "unofficial-official" Caribbean gender codes than by sexual mores. It uses visual art to show what flouting these codes can look like and uses literature to show what can happen to Caribbean men in the aftermath of breaking those codes. Given the widespread idea (trumpeted by *Time* magazine in 2006) that the Caribbean is "the most homophobic place on earth," I address this myth and then explore the more nuanced reality of sexual minorities in the region through examining documentaries of Caribbean men who desire men, which largely portray them as agents and activists and as sometimes actually living full, happy lives.

Caribbean Gender Conformity Codes

Anthropologist Jafari Allen writes that by the late twentieth century in Cuba, "the rhetorics of homosexuality as contagion had already become part of the *unofficial official policy*."[18] Though he does not detail or unpack this phrase, its implications are clear. The rules are unofficial because they are not codified by the state in law or other official documents or policies. These same restrictions, though, function as official when state representatives endorse them publicly or when police or judicial arms of government refuse to punish those who attack transgressors. But before examining *unofficial* official codes, it is useful to briefly survey the official laws that regulate sexuality in the Caribbean region.

In most of the Caribbean, sexual intercourse between men is officially and explicitly outlawed. Puerto Rico and the U.S. Virgin Islands, Guadeloupe and Martinique, and the islands—including Aruba, Bonaire, and Curaçao—affiliated with the Kingdom of the Netherlands are exceptions.[19] Same-sex intercourse is legal in these territories because it is legal in the countries that colonize them, creating a particular "freedom" that depends upon a particular unfreedom. Similarly, in Martinique and Guadeloupe "France's legal code both affords protections and extends certain rights, like access to the PACS (the *pacte civil de solidarité*, a form of civil union that has been available to both same and opposite sex couples in France since 1999), to Martinican and Guadeloupian citizens."[20] Since 2007, Aruba, Bonaire, and Curaçao have been required to recognize same-sex marriages performed elsewhere since such unions are legal in the Netherlands; despite victories such as these, Kenneth van Emden, the director of Suriname Men United, reminds us that "stigma and discrimination are still rife . . . even though homosexuality is not prohibited under the Surinamese Constitution."[21] Among independent Caribbean nations, Cuba repealed its legal prohibitions of homosexual sex acts in 1979, while Suriname and Haiti are notable because they have no laws that mention same-sex activity, whether to prohibit or allow it.

While there are laws against sodomy (and increasingly against women's same-sex sexuality) in the Caribbean, these laws are rarely officially enforced. In Cuba, Allen observed that the "arbitrary and capricious Ley de peligrosidad (Law of dangerousness), which is still on the books and variously interpreted or ignored by police on the street, provides a sentence of up to four years of psychiatric therapy or prison for the sort of (mostly uninterrupted) campiness and *mariconeria* I witnessed and participated in on the streets of Havana and Santiago, between 1998 and 2005."[22] Instead, these laws serve as symbols of nationalism and thus as justification for vigilante actions, whether in the press, from the pulpit of a church, temple, or mosque, or, most often, in the street, where harassment and even murder have occurred. Some of these Caribbean laws share an emphasis on criminalizing public revelation as well as presumably private sex acts. As Peña writes, "Even in the severest period of enforcement . . . private homosexual expression was never the main target [in Cuba]. . . . The gravest crime was not same-sex sexual acts per se but, rather, transgressing gender norms in ways associated with male homosexuality—in other words, appearing visibly or 'obviously' gay."[23] Part of the reason the legislation of gender conformity and visible homosexuality are rarely enforced is that these laws include no specifics regarding *what* behavior is indecent or what constitutes visible homosexuality. Indeed, in Trinidad and Tobago, Cuba, and the Dominican Republic, laws reference the need to protect and enforce public decency, a concept again linked to visibility.[24] Cuba's 1979 revision of its penal code "clarified the association between *escándalo público* and homosexuals and expanded sanctions against visible homosexuality." And in Jamaica "the determination of what acts may be deemed to outrage public decency remains fluid and subject to interpretation by the court. By and large, it has been interpreted to mean any sexual intimacy . . . between men" excluding anal sex, which is prohibited under a separate provision.[25]

Laws, of course, are more than rules, even though we will see in this chapter how effective social rules can be in regulating social behavior. Laws, though, are *official* rules of the government, often revealing, in reverse, the state's concept of the ideal citizen. Regarding sexuality and gender (as in most cases), the ideal Caribbean citizen is a gender-conforming male. For instance, Peña notes that in Cuba from the 1960s to the 1980s the "intense focus of the state gaze on gender-transgressive male homosexuals and the public discourse against effeminacy and male homosexuality were explicitly tied to emerging national discourse about a new virile, masculine, Cuban nation and society."[26] Similar situations have existed throughout the Caribbean as newly independent states sought (and continue to seek) to consolidate national identities and as nonindependent territories sought to clarify their identity in relationship to and separate from their colonizers. Those who violate the law are subject to government punishment, and should the state for some reason not carry out punishment, vigilantes encouraged by those same laws might step in, as has been widely publicized in several cases in Jamaica.[27] And even when Caribbean communities accept gender nonconforming and same-sex desiring men—which happens often—"the self-consciously representative texts of black masculinist leaders never can" accept these citizens because these texts must define the ideal (male) citizen and must provide mechanisms for enforcing that ideal.[28]

The process of solidifying the concept of the ideal citizen continues to unfold in most of the Dutch Caribbean. In 2010 the Netherlands Antilles ceased to exist as an official political entity, and Aruba, Curaçao, and Sint Maarten became independent states *within* the Kingdom of the Netherlands, while Bonaire, Sint Eustatius, and Saba were named "overseas municipalities" of the Netherlands. These changes, which grant the municipalities *less* political autonomy than they were given when the Netherlands Antilles federation was created in 1954, encouraged millions of Dutch Caribbeans to consider what citizenship means and who a "real" citizen is.[29] For instance, controversy has swirled around what a Bonaire priest called the "five immoral laws" relating to "gay marriage, abortion, euthanasia, legalised drugs and legalised prostitution," which Dutch Caribbean territories have had to enforce since October 2012.[30] (The Netherlands government, anticipating "problems" integrating these laws, gave the Caribbean two years to culturally adjust to the changes.)[31] The same concerns are expressed in Curaçao through the questions "Who is a *Yu di Kòrsou* [Child of Curaçao] and who is not? What characterizes the *Yu di Kòrsou* and, by extension, what is authentic Curaçaoan culture and what is a 'good' *Yu di Kòrsou?*"[32] The Bonaire priest stated that "We don't deny that gay people exist here, but they are not looking to get married anywhere on Bonaire."[33] It seems clear that the "real" or "proper" citizen of the reconfigured Dutch territories is an (Afro-)Caribbean who, if not heterosexual, adheres to el secreto abierto, sharing in appearance if not in fact the new "(presumed) common national identit[ies]" through particular values and behavior.[34]

While the enforcement of both the legalization and the prohibition of same-gender sexuality vary in different places and times, the enforcement of gender codes is much more common, regardless of the laws in place. Indeed, in Caribglobal communities, public gender transgression is more problematic than private homosex. For example, Jafari Allen notes that in Cuba, "the 'dangerousness' and 'scandal' of male homosexuality is not men having sex with men—this is understood as fairly commonplace—but rather it is the failure to perform the strict script of masculinity and *hombría* (idealized attributes, rights, and responsibilities of manhood) that is itself classed and raced."[35] Emilio Bejel similarly concludes that "the condemnation of homoeroticism in modern Cuban society" can be linked to "a condemnation of anything that could be considered a *transgression of gender roles.*"[36]

Indeed, the codes that comprise unofficial-official policy explicitly relate more to gender conformity than to sexuality, precisely because these subjects are often seen as being intimately connected, if not inseparable. Kamala Kempadoo explains that in the Caribbean,

> heterosexuality is assumed to be a central component of gender identity in many people's lives . . . It is this powerful set of ideas and practices—that heterosexuality defines gender—that also serves as a reminder that any examination of Caribbean sexuality cannot be conducted completely separate from gender.[37]

It follows, then, that homosexuality is also seen as being intimately connected to gender. While scholars often want to separately analyze sexuality, sexual behavior, and gender, "Understanding the potential dynamism of this relationship is paramount to appreciat[ing] the way men [who desire men] transgress and remake heteronormativity in their lives."[38] So, while some in the global North may consider men who engage el secreto abierto as "backward" and self-hating, it is also possible to understand their choices as transgressive not only of heteronormative sexuality but also of unofficial-official gender, cultural, and national codes.[39]

The conceptual and legal distinctions between sexuality and gender are, however, overshadowed by colloquial understandings that lock sex and gender together into one body. Consider the following list of more or less pejorative Caribbean terms for effeminate and/or same-sex-desiring men: *maricón*, makòmé, *loca, nicht, batty bwoy*, and *boeler/buller*. What all of these terms, save the last, have in common is that they, like the laws meant to suppress them, focus at least as much on gender expression as they do on sexual behavior or desire. The definition of *maricón* (a pejorative for men who are or are perceived as gender nonconforming or desiring other men) in the 1889 Cuban *Diccionario razonado de legislación de policía* (Dictionary of police legislation) persists in Cuba today: "An effeminate and cowardly man; He who does woman's work; Men who imitate women in their mannerisms, insinuations and at time even in their dress, taking their place in the most shameless acts."[40] And in Guadeloupe, according to anthropologist Dolores Pourette, "the homosexual is labeled with the pejorative term makòmé. The makòmé is a man who usually displays feminine behavior and attributes (in his language, his clothing, and his [body language], and who [engages in homosexual acts] with masculine men, sometimes for financial compensation. The discourse claims that he is not a real man, but a man-woman. There is no feminine equivalent of makòmé."[41] Similarly, Suriname Men United links public silence around same-sex desire in that country to cultural expectations of gender performance; men who desire men "remain strictly hidden because society expects them to behave in a certain way and they don't want to be regarded with disfavour."[42] As these definitions indicate, ideal masculinity is most easily defined through its opposite—or to put it another way, masculinity is typically distinguished through the feminine man. In fact, notes Patricia Mohammed, "the most common definition of masculinity seems to be its distance from what is denoted as feminine in most cultures."[43] Antonio de Moya defines the Dominican concept of hombría as manliness or manhood consisting of "courage, determination and power, closely related to provision of resources for the family ('responsible fatherhood,' for instance)."[44] Similarly, Jafari Allen describes Cuban hombría as being "among the most prized values in the society because it is always already constitutive of honor, dignity, strength, and bravery, and it is the 'opposite' of homosexuality."[45] As many scholars point out, gender codes can vary significantly based on class, race, and location (for instance, rural and urban),[46] but the understanding of what constitutes manliness, hombría, mannelijkheden, masculinity, virilité, and machismo is broadly similar in the Caribbean and relates to dress, mannerisms, speech style, and other particularities. For instance, men wishing to appear heterosexual in Guadeloupe "must keep to a dress and body code and methods of self-expression" and must "present themselves to others as masculine," notes Pourette, who adds: "They must like sports, be 'burly' and have well-formed muscles. The whole thing is not to appear effeminate. The desire to 'be a man' and to affirm themselves as such also manifests in sexual roles."[47] Antonio de Moya observes that the "stigma against male homosexuality partially results in the perception of this role as feminine, weak and lacking power. These characteristics are understood as antagonistic to those possessed by the hegemonic, patriarchal male."[48] Masculinity (as well as femininity) can be considered "*a form of labor* coordinated through transfers of knowledge and collective evaluation and coaching."[49] As labor, adherence to gender codes for most people requires being taught, learning, and practicing.

It is not difficult to imagine what the codes of unofficial-official gender conformity require of men. They must be traditionally masculine men in attire, mannerisms, behavior, and speech. Masculinity, like femininity or Trinidadianness or Dominicanidad, is "a system of signs" and "a repertoire" that is "generally closed and insular."[50] Writing about Martinique, Murray argues that this system must not only be learned but must also "be constantly performed, maintained and proven through sexual conquests, physical and verbal contests, and an ability to create a reputation of independence and individuality."[51] If an individual will not or cannot adhere to the gender script, he is at risk of being subjected to various social sanctions, including "Social death, that is to say the exclusion and banishment from the social and family group"; in addition, he is often accused of being—if not assumed to be—a masisi, a batty bwoy, a loca, a sodomite, a makòmé, a maricón, or a homosexual.[52] Prevailing gender codes are perpetuated by families and individuals, but they are created by the political and economic ruling class and then, as Allen points out, represented to the broader population as a stable "national culture" that often carries "the force of 'nature,'" an idea that is also seen in de Moya's description of masculinity in the Dominican Republic.[53]

Similarly, Caribglobal gender codes are often taught as "a list of things not to do rather than the reverse," and one of Carlos Decena's subjects recalls injunctions "Not to play with dolls. Not to do household chores, because that was not for men. Not to dress up as women. Not to wear makeup. Things like that. That we have to hang out with men. We weren't supposed to hang out with women too much. The way we sat: we were to sit one way. Women sit in another way."[54] Just as el secreto abierto requires collective agency, "the work of socialization is collective" and is enforced and reinforced by family members, authority figures, culture, and law.[55] Information about acceptable and unacceptable behavior is not always explicitly communicated; sometimes "the process of becoming" a man relies "on transfers of knowledge about body codes through demonstration" or "explanation by analogy, imitation, and critique."[56] Not surprisingly, the level of derogation, ridicule, and verbal or physical abuse that accompanies learning gender roles is directly related to how easily the individual performs those codes. If the process works smoothly, the boy or man internalizes the codes and eventually performs hegemonic masculinity with few errors. If it does not work smoothly, the boy or man can be subjected to violence or "less spectacular exclusions" that support the existing "regime of sexualized inequality" in the region.[57]

Confirmation and Revelation in Literature

The concept of el secreto abierto, the open secret, also points to a consideration of the status of knowledge. "Knowing" someone's sexuality is not always a straightforward matter. Just as the seeming paradox of unofficial-official policies towards sexuality exists throughout the Caribbean, so too can one "know without knowing," without acknowledging knowledge of another's sexuality. A person may not admit to others that they know about someone's same-sex desire, or they may not admit such knowledge to themselves because there has been no explicit confirmation of it. Decena refers to these states as "active not knowing."[58] Among many whites in the global North, both the hegemony of the closet and the tradition of identity politics encourage revelation of same-sex identities and/or behaviors.[59] But for the most part in the Caribbean, revelation is neither expected, nor encouraged, nor rewarded. As Lawrence Chang, cofounder of the Jamaica Forum for Lesbians, All-Sexuals, and Gays (J-FLAG) explains, in Jamaica the real problem is not *being* a homosexual but *confirming* that one is a homosexual.[60] The predominant ways of confirming one's own—or someone else's—same-sex desire are through flagrant gender nonconforming behavior, a self-revealing speech act, a report from a trusted source, or the observation—en flagrante delicto—of actual erotic behavior. As will be seen in this section's literary analysis, regardless of the form it takes, revelation sometimes—but not always—has disastrous consequences for the one whose "secret" is resolved into "fact."

Because sex acts are less likely to correspond to sexual identities in the Caribbean than they are in the global North, confirmation of same-sex desire through self-revelation is the most reliable, though probably also the least likely, form of revelation in the region. Since—presuming a person is mostly gender conforming—one can generally be accepted as a full member of Caribbean society regardless of sexuality, there is little to gain and much to lose from revealing same-sex desire. Thus, *not* publicly claiming homosexuality "is a compromise most 'gai' Martinican men are willing to make in order to make sure that they do not bring any harm to themselves or their family's name. Nor is this considered by many to be a particularly debilitating compromise—the importance of maintaining family and personal reputation outweighs any advantages to publicly announcing one's homosexuality."[61] This emphasis on respect and discretion over disclosure and its consequences exists throughout the Caribbean; writing about sexual cultures in Latin America, Roger Lancaster describes a "tolerant intolerance" that proscribes "the rule not to speak as a homosexual (in public)" as a way to protect both "public 'propriety' *and* 'secret' transgressions."[62] Similarly, Decena argues that in the Dominican Republic, hegemonic, heteropatriarchal masculinity "is produced as a wholesome, ordered, *discreet*, and measured body," and activist Erin Greene notes that many members of the now-defunct Rainbow Alliance Bahamas "felt that these terms [homosexual, lesbian, transgender, etc.] were a part of being visible that they were unwilling to engage."[63]

While revelation of same-sex desire can result in acceptance, it can also lead to shunning,[64] social death, physical violence, and the entire range of small slights and major catastrophes in between. And adhering to el secreto abierto—with "the often quiet compliance with the heteronormative models of citizenship and social organization that were introduced at and have been institutionalized since the beginning of colonization of the Caribbean"—does not always prevent these outcomes.[65] All too often, someone forgets a line of the gender script and betrays him or herself. Caribbean literature provides numerous examples of such scenarios, most involving revelation through gender nonconforming traits or behavior. These examples are found largely in short stories; with the exception of several well-studied texts from the Spanish Caribbean, there is a dearth of full-length novels with a (male or female) same-sex desiring protagonist.

Part of the collection *The Fear of Stones*, Kei Miller's "Walking on the Tiger Road" is a story told from the dual perspectives of a mother and a son; the mother, Miss Mary, reminisces about their lives and her hopes for a reunion while the son, Mark, journeys back to Jamaica from the United States to surprise his mother after many years. Miss Mary remembers that, as a child and a teenager, her son's "woman's ways" and his tendency to "swinging the hips, him wrist dem flapping like any woman" made his sexuality suspect in their village, though Miss Mary herself blames this behavior on the absence of Mark's father and the boy's subsequent lack of a male role model.[66] The very notion that Mark's comportment requires an explanation confirms that although she loves her son very much, Miss Mary also wishes he behaved more like the majority of men in her community. That community's "strong suspicion" about Mark's sexual predilections develops into "bona fide fact" after his abrupt—and unexplained—departure from the island, rumored to have been triggered by Mark's impending trial for having been caught in the act of "buggery."[67]

When Mark returns to Jamaica many years later, he again fails to exhibit an "appropriate" gender performance, this time in the face of a direct accusation. A young man calls out to Mark, "So is you dem say a battyman?" Instead of delivering a quick retort or laughing off the question, Mark is seized with fear; he "had never felt comfortable with the language of macho Jamaican men, with their gesticulations or their mannerisms. *Mark was being asked to perform, and suddenly he had stage fright.*" Mark's weak response is to ask Idle Bwoy, who had called out to the returnee and whose name identifies him as a kind of local everyman, "'What kinda question that?'"— *while resting a hand on the other man's thigh.*"[68] Idle Bwoy interprets the touch as a reverse accusation, an identification of his own sexual predilections, and he responds by kicking Mark to the ground. As other men gather, Mark makes a second choice that is outside of the male gender code of his community: he refuses to defend himself, to perform at all, and he simply walks away. This refusal to participate in male community and competition seals Mark's fate, as his silence is correctly understood as an admission of same-sex desire. The men follow Mark along the road, stoning him from behind until he is within view of his mother's home. The story ends with his collapse, and while Mark's survival is unclear, it is clear that "his kind" is still not welcome in the village.

Famed Cuban author Reinaldo Arenas' novella *The Brightest Star* (its original title in Spanish is *Arturo, la estrella más brillante*) also portrays a young man betrayed by his gender-nonconforming comportment, this time in a prison setting in Cuba. Unlike Mark in "Walking on the Tiger Road," Arturo must become *more* feminine to remain safe. At first, Arturo distances himself from the other prisoners, whom he describes as having "endless, stupid conversations, with their exaggerated, effeminate, affected, artificial, false, gross, grotesque gesturings and posturings."[69] Arturo (like the author's friend Nelson Rodríguez Leyva, to whom the novella is dedicated, and like Arenas himself) is taken to a Unidades Militares para Ayudar a la Producción (Military Units to Aid Production [UMAP]) camp after being picked out during a "roundup" following an opera performance.[70] The reasons given in the novella for the arrest of several young men are "that one young man's hair was too long, or that another wore clothes of a certain cut or (most fatal) exhibited certain telling traits, had certain 'mannerisms.'"[71] As is seen in other Caribbean countries and fictions,[72] the *certain* clothes, traits, and mannerisms are all related to gender performance, and in Arenas' case are clear enough to deprive people of their liberty but amorphous enough that they cannot be clearly defined.

In the nightmare of the camp, Arturo retreats to a life of the mind, abused by the soldiers and by the other inmates, who correctly perceive that he feels he is superior to them. Eventually (and ironically), he realizes that his introversion and indifference is incendiary to the other inmates, and in order to have some peace, he learns "to cackle and howl with laughter like any ordinary queen, to sing, pose, shadow his eyes and dye his hair" while still retreating into his own imagination when he can.[73] In the confines of the camp, the social rules are different from those outside, and the men imprisoned for sexual and gender indiscretions must perform their "crime" over and over again so the guards can be justified in their degradation of the prisoners. Though Arturo's gender nonconformity and presumed homosexuality are the cause of his arrest, the cause of his death is his commitment to his own intellectual and aesthetic thought, which he holds on to despite the dehumanizing circumstances of the camp.

In both Miller and Arenas' fiction, men are punished for what Decena describes as "the degree to which our bodies speak in ways we cannot fully control."[74] Despite efforts to perform hegemonic masculinity, the men's bodies betray them and exhibit behaviors for which other men condemn them to violence or imprisonment. Significantly, in both texts some of the men who persecute the protagonists themselves desire other men, implying that both self-loathing and self-preservation can be powerful motivators for regulating adherence to gender codes within the self as well as within others. Still, even within strict Caribbean gender codes, there are individuals who are able to transgress with few or no negative ramifications, often because their position in society shields them from punishment.

The Shield of Class

Class can sometimes protect those who are gender nonconforming, as in the cases of Cuban Alberto Guevara and Jamaican Rex Nettleford. In his memoir *Before Night Falls* (published in Spanish as *Antes que anochezca*), Arenas writes that Guevara, "whose scandalous homosexual life was well known all over, especially in Havana . . . never had to face the consequences of [his] behavior, while others had to pay such a high price."[75] Nettleford, a former dancer with some feminine qualities who neither married nor was romantically linked to any women, was never publicly chastised or punished for his gender expression or real or perceived sexuality, presumably because of his prominence as the Chancellor of the University of the West Indies' Kingston campus, his class, and his political connections. Larry Chang said his father told him: "if you are going to be a gay man in Jamaica, you have to be like Rex Nettleford—you have to be untouchable in every way."[76] Chang disregarded this advice and became one of the first openly gay activists in Jamaica.

The documentary *Of Men and Gods*, which focuses on feminine same-sex desiring men in Haiti in the 1990s (discussed in detail in this chapter) shows that there, class as well as status within Voudoun can prevent or mitigate public punishment for gender nonconforming behavior or same-sex desire. To most of those interviewed in the film, "remaking the gender and sexuality that dominant heteropatriarchy" assigns to them "is *natural*, not to mention *lwa*-like."[77] For instance, Innocente, one of the film's subjects, says, "I have a man's body but a woman's style" and describes being verbally abused and "called masisi"[78] when dressing femininely or as a woman. But Innocente also notes: "Since I've become a houngan, they've stopped. Now they come knocking on my door, asking me to call the loas, to give them a remedy for this and that. This is the kind of respect I've found in voodoo."[79] To Innocente's community, the power to call upon Voudoun's gods and provide other religious services mitigates Innocente's gender identity and sexual behavior. Fritzner, the only traditionally masculine man interviewed at length in the film, is also a houngan, a Voudoun priest. In his own words, Fritzner's gender presentation, class, and community position enable him to sexually do as (and whom) he likes without fear: "I'm a father and I've been a masisi for a long time now. I do it in an honest way, at home. I have a house, a land, I'm a grown up. If I feel like caressing a man I do it." For these self-described masisi, being a community leader has resulted in respect, an elevated reputation, and, it seems, greater acceptance of their gender expression or same-sex desire. As with Nettleford, Guevara, Chang, and others, class and community standing can enable individuals to flout gender codes, though they are typically still expected to maintain el secreto abierto. In *Of Men and Gods*, Innocente talks a great deal about gender expression but rarely mentions the type of people Innocente is attracted to, while Fritzner emphasizes that his honesty about his sexuality is confined to his home. Similarly, Arenas' language, that Guevara's "scandalous" life *was known* all over Havana, rather than that he *made it known*, implies adherence to el secreto abierto, and the consistent silence around and invisibility of Nettleford's private life are a paradigmatic example of el secreto abierto. Chang was punished for his visibility and activism with threats that eventually led to his receiving political asylum in the United States.[80]

Of course, revelation does not always yield negative results. Aldo Alvarez's "Property Values" is a counterexample. In this humorous short story set in Puerto Rico's elite society, a woman who discovers a man (and his partner's) homosexuality attempts to ostracize them, but it backfires because the rest of the community—including his mother—is supportive. Dean's mother describes his tastes as "extravagant and specific" when she asks Claudia, a real estate agent, to help her son find a home in Puerto

Rico.[81] Dean himself leans more towards openness than to secretiveness, mentioning Mark as his "partner," which Claudia interprets as "friend." Later she chastises herself: "'Partner?' 'Antiques?' 'Upstate New York?' Dead giveaways."[82] When she sees the visibly sick Dean and notices "how they touched, casually flaunting their desire for each other," Claudia is horrified: "Dean had homosexual AIDS. And he'd brought his fornicator with him!"[83] Claudia makes assumptions not only about Mark but also about his mother, assuming that she despises her son and his sexuality as much as the realtor does. She even tries to smear both mother and son by gossiping about his illness to others. But in a turn probably more unusual in Caribbean literature than in Caribbean life, Dean's mother and her social circle already know of both his sexuality and his health condition, and their support is symbolized by a meeting they organize to put on an AIDS benefit. It is the ignorant and biased realtor Claudia who is shamed and ostracized, not the same-sex-desiring Dean. One of the interesting aspects of this story is that the Caribbean community maintains el secreto abierto, and all are portrayed as *already knowing* the nature of Dean and Mark's relationship. The reader is not privy to scenes of their revelation; in other words, we do not know whether they have always been supportive, from the moment of discovery, or whether they had to go through a process to become accepting. Nevertheless, "Property Values" is a positive portrayal of an overwhelmingly supportive upper-class Caribbean community.

Confirmation and Revelation in Art

Because it can involve viewing the human body, visual art can also be a productive site of analysis regarding notions of el secreto abierto and the confirmation or revelation of same-sex desire, even though few explicitly homoerotic Caribbean images exist. Indeed, "the forms through which same sex desires are articulated are just as important as what is said," as Tara Atluri notes, and this is even more true when very little, or nothing at all, *is* said, or when the communication does not actually use speech.[84] As scholar Rudi Bleys writes about visual art in Latin America, the "expression of 'gay' content can be direct and intentional, through narrative disclosure or iconographic content. Often, however, it remains hidden underneath the artist's apparent adoption of publicly available representational tropes and can be revealed only after close scrutiny."[85] The level of scrutiny needed actually depends on how easily one can read the clues—whether the viewer can recognize and interpret the narrative or iconography. Nevertheless, this is the visual equivalent of el secreto abierto, and as we have seen throughout this chapter in anthropological and literary texts, as well as in documentary film, the tropes that signal same-sex desire are typically those of gender nonconformity and same-sex erotic contact.

*   *   *

Barbadian Ewan Atkinson's artwork also engages el secreto, both breaking and upholding its imperatives through images for which a homoerotic reading is only one of several possible interpretations. Atkinson is an inventive artist who largely produces series of aesthetically and conceptually related works. Although much of his work is relevant to this chapter, I will examine in depth one piece from his 2007 *Fiction* series. According to Atkinson's own description on his website, the *Fiction* series' drawings and catalogue

> served as an introduction to a project that involved the mapping of a fictional 'neighbourhood space' and the characters that inhabit it. The narratives are driven or generated by interactions between characters and by each character's relationship with their environment. The characters themselves are derived from personal and family histories, Barbadian folk culture and global popular culture.[86]

The images of this neighborhood feature a variety of images, from aerial views and abstract shapes to animals, detailed images of people (including characters he names Little Girl Blue, Businessman, Starman, the Couple, etc.), and hybrid characters. The drawings share an expansive and starkly white background and most include tiny colored dots and other fine details.

Paradise Terrace and a Mouthful of Water, a mixed-media piece that is now part of the permanent collection of the National Art Gallery of Barbados, is one of the works in the *Fiction* series that shows what can be interpreted as homoeroticism. On the left side of the image, the Couple, two men, are kissing; one has his hand on the other's chest, either caressing him or pushing him away. The men are dressed identically and thus could be the same person multiplied, or twins, or lovers who are dressed like each other. While the viewer's own thoughts and feelings will affect their interpretation, the fact that the men are named the Couple and several visual details of the drawing point to a nuanced interpretation.

Ewan Atkinson, *Paradise Terrace and a Mouthful of Water*, 2007. Mixed media on paper, 14" × 17". By permission of Ewan Atkinson.

On the right of the drawing is a kind of carnivalesque minotaur, similar to those named in another drawing as Dogs. The figure's legs seemingly belong to a man because of their muscularity and hairiness; the bent leg in *Paradise Terrace* implies a coy pose, a hint at gender nonconformity. The figure itself is clearly linked to the Dogs in another drawing in the series, but in *Paradise Terrace* the figure has more detailed and animated features and seems to combine Barbadian folk culture (specifically the steel donkey character) and a gender nonconforming man. While the figure could be seen as masked, as hiding sexuality, I think that considering it in the context of el secreto abierto is helpful here; the fey pose is clearly visible, so the gender nonconformity is actually *not* completely hidden. Furthermore, rather than seeing the mask as hiding the figure, I see the figure as an integrated, hybrid character that, like many real Caribbean people, combines gender nonconformity and Caribbeanness in one body without explicitly naming an identity; after all, one cannot speak with a mouth full of water.

The "water" coming out of the figure's mouth can easily be linked to the Caribbean sea and comes from the blue that dominates the masked head's interior. And because the water shoots over the couple, instead of at them, it is protecting or perhaps even baptizing them. On the other hand, a mostly dark circle hovers over the couple, which could signal danger or partial disapproval. The couple is standing on a defined square, a terrace which can represent domesticity or confinement, but this representation is ambivalent, not absolute, because there are no walls; the fence is flimsy—representing demarcation more than effective confinement or protection—and the fence only appears on one side of the rectangle. Contrastingly, the carnivalesque figure is confined neither by domesticity nor space, though a landscape (rectangles that can be read as buildings) is enclosed within it. In a gesture reminiscent of el secreto abierto, the more hidden figure has more freedom; the masked character is not bounded by lines and is physically larger than the couple. At the same time, the figure is partially masked, and rainbow lines hide the figure's mouth, again symbolizing silenced or controlled speech, as is mandated by el secreto's strictures. But the stream includes many colors—enough, in fact, to resemble a straightened-out rainbow, the now international symbol both of diversity and of nonheterosexuality. Significantly, the carnivalesque character is also directly linked to the foreboding sphere. And while light colored dots connect the two kissing men, they also provide a connection to the dots within the masked figure and linking the minotaur and the sphere. All of the objects and figures are indeed a neighborhood, a community, even if they are not in full agreement. The title of the piece similarly reflects the two dominant aspects of the artwork.

The first part of the title, *Paradise Terrace*, implies that same-sex eroticism is a wonderful thing, perhaps that it is paradise itself, the greatest thing on earth. It also obliquely and ironically counters exoticizing views of the Caribbean that construct the region as a paradise for outsiders' pleasure and consumption. Interestingly, the title describes not the interior of paradise but its terrace. Given that, according to the *Oxford English Dictionary*, a terrace can be either "a raised walk in a garden" or "a level surface formed in front of a house . . . or on the bank of a river," Atkinson's title endorses Tinsley's argument in *Thiefing Sugar* that the metaphors that reflect Caribbean same-sex desire are more likely to be yards or gardens than closets. As the description of the artist's series states, the drawings' narratives are driven by characters' relationships with each other *and with their environment*, which here consists of the square terrace, a rainbow, and a hovering sphere. The figures in this piece are connected by dots and lines; they inhabit the same universe, even though they are extremely different. That the Couple and the legs of the figure are represented through photographic transfer, as opposed to the free-form drawing and painting used in the rest of the piece, implies that they are *real* representations and that there may be more people like them in the neighborhood community. The second part of the title and the right side of the drawing are more ambivalent. The *mouthful of water* can refer both to the blue coming out of the figure's mouth and to the kiss the two men seem to be engaged in. Thus, this portrayal reflects the sometimes accepting and sometimes troubled incorporation of sexual minorities into Caribbean societies via el secreto abierto.

Paradise Terrace is also interesting because it is one of *fifteen* works by Atkinson—a significant portion of his oeuvre—in the collection of the National Art Gallery of Barbados (NAGB),[87] an institution that defines itself as "the place where a nation nourishes its memory and exerts its imagination—where it connects with its past, and invents its future."[88] Indeed, *Paradise Terrace* is featured on the NAGB website. Galleries and museums, especially national ones, often collect because of a combination of perceived intrinsic economic or artistic worth, perceived popularity, or perceived future worth. As such, they are a permanent part of the official culture and cultural heritage of Barbados.[89] As the home page of the NAGB states, "Culture is a product of diversity. It feeds on differences and it grows through exchanges."[90] The gender and sexual diversity that Atkinson's work portrays and the national pride that is implicitly projected onto these works through the NAGB might point to subtle shifts in Caribbean gender codes and a willingness to reconsider dominant masculinity.

Myths of Exponential Homophobia

I cannot write about Caribglobal homosexuality without addressing the popular myth of the region's exceptional homophobia against men who desire men[91] and the accompanying narrative that posits the region as a "backward" area that through accepting LGBT (lesbian, gay, bisexual, and transgender) rights and tourism can join the "modern," "developed" world.[92] The popular representation of "a particularly Antillean victim subject and a particularly Antillean homophobic subject" assumes Caribbean exceptionalism, as well as a profound lack of agency in the region that necessitates local sexual minorities being saved by international activists.[93]

In 2006, *Time* magazine infamously declared that the Caribbean is "the most homophobic place on earth," but this is only one recent example of many similar statements that have been made in the last twenty-five years or so.[94] When addressing the region as a whole, Jamaica is typically singled out as a place where it is nearly impossible to be *gay*. Notwithstanding the fact that generalizing from one country to the entire region ignores "how, as regards homophobia, 'tolerance levels vary, with places such as St. Thomas in the Virgin Islands, Trinidad and Barbados [being] at the higher end of the continuum of tolerance, while Jamaica, St. Vincent and St. Lucia occupy the lower levels,'"[95] there are unfortunately many examples of intimidation, beatings, rape, and murder in Jamaica. And the representations of such violence in dancehall music lends credence to these arguments, in a rhetorical turn not unlike when right-wing U.S. American fundamentalists use images of New York City or San Francisco's gay pride parades to demonstrate why those cities are present-day Sodoms and Gomorrahs.[96] The charge of a "spectacular" Caribbean homophobia extends to those regional territories that are technically part of the European Union; Agard-Jones writes that the Antilles are often portrayed in France as being "gripped both by a conservative-Christianity-gone-wild and a retrograde set of (black) cultural values" in a "discourse [that] draws the lines of radical cultural difference to ostensibly 'explain' the homophobic violence that occurs in a place like Martinique, even when much the same can be found in a place like Provence [France]."[97] The challenge for those of us who study nonheteronormative sexualities in the Caribbean is determining how to acknowledge real—and yes, sometimes violent—homophobia without endorsing the idea that the Caribbean is uniquely and exceptionally homophobic.

It is particularly frustrating that music and religion are often the only local contexts provided to explain this supposedly exemplary Caribbean homophobia. The *Time* article states that Jamaica "has the world's highest murder rate," and its next sentence adds that "rampant violence against gays and lesbians has [caused it to be called] the most homophobic place on earth."[98] But the author makes no connection between the two statements. In a country with the highest murder rate in the Caribbean and, indeed, one of the highest in the world,[99] the large number of murders of men who desire men cannot be surprising. Similarly, in a country where rape and other violence against women is commonplace, the rape of women who desire women cannot be surprising. My point is not to imply that there is no need to address specifically antihomosexual violence but to point out that this is only one kind of horrible violence that exists in Jamaica, the Caribbean, and elsewhere.

Similarly, it is unfortunate that funders and researchers rarely support or pursue an analysis of the link between other types of violence and the rates of antihomosexual violence in the Caribbean. If one of those international organizations that provides money to document homophobic violence or to try to censor homophobic dancehall lyrics[100] would recognize that their kind of activism "prioritizes certain kinds of visibly queer subjects over other Jamaican victims of state and economic violence and denial of citizenship," then they might consider supporting an analysis of how homosexuality is used by Caribbean politicians to distract poor people from poverty, unemployment, lack of quality free education, and general disenfranchisement.[101] Indeed, "the lack of access to resources around which poor young black men can legitimately develop their masculine identity" can lead to "[h]eterosexual conquests and a hatred of homosexuality" becoming strategies to reinforce masculinity and manhood.[102]

It must also be acknowledged that some Caribbean sexual minorities and sexual minority advocates agree with the exponential homophobia myth, whether because it makes *their* territory (one with less violence) look more "developed" or because it can help them obtain international visibility and funding. One Martinican lesbian was adamant about "how very different Martinique was from a place like Jamaica, a place she understood to be a 'real' (and spectacularly unique) site of homophobic violence in the Caribbean . . . . She understood Martinique to *be* France, not a place in need of some sort of ideological development in order to be *equal to* France."[103] Similarly, some Bahamians believe local sexual minority activism is not necessary, since "the Bahamas is nowhere near as violent as Jamaica or Middle Eastern and certain African states."[104] Other Martinican interlocutors "suggest that in the absence of an ongoing and serious engagement with the lives of people on the ground in the Antilles, these forms of advocacy serve to do little more than benefit the personal political and professional trajectories of the mostly diaspora-based advocates."[105] Indeed, the region's reputation regarding *gay rights* is promoted by the strange bedfellows of local sexual minority activists, international *gay* or *LGBT* rights advocates, and U.S. American fundamentalist Christians who have targeted the Caribbean and Africa to promote agendas that are, right now, less popular in much of the United States. As Robinson writes, a "new sexual order positions the Global South either as backwardly homophobic in relationship to the sexually developed North or as a primitive frontier where the dominion of Christianity can be preserved."[106] This statement has been echoed in the last twenty years by a number of scholars writing about the Caribbean, Latin America, South Asia, the Arab world, and elsewhere.[107]

I have been italicizing *gay* and *LGBT* in this discussion because it is important to recognize that being *gay, lesbian, bisexual,* or *transgender* in France, Canada, or the Netherlands, for example, is not necessarily the same as being a sexual minority in Cuba, Haiti, or Trinidad, for example. In fact, "the rhetoric of the 'homophobic Caribbean'" repeated by the global North "is frequently rooted in a neo-colonial paternalism which misses the often untranslatable way in which sexualities operate in non-Western contexts."[108] As mentioned earlier in this chapter, the concept of el secreto abierto is a more popular way of dealing with same-sex desire in the Caribbean than is the strategy of "coming out" of the "closet," which is more popular in the global North. Three examples of this difference include the much-documented fact that often "macho" men and/or those who are insertive in male homosex may not be considered homosexual in the Spanish Caribbean;[109] the fact that some Haitians accept same-sex desire and non-hegemonic genders in themselves or others because they attribute them to an affinity with Voudoun goddess Erzulie Danto; and the persistence of the mati tradition in the Dutch Caribbean.[110] It is important to attend to these differences because they are not merely linguistic; they refer to particular ways of knowing, and they also "produce circuitries of sociality."[111] The well-known report on the status of sexual minorities in Jamaica points out that the "use of Europe as a standard of reasonable conduct [in relation to sexual minorities] is extremely problematic having [sic] regard to strong nationalist sentiments that prevail in the Caribbean concerning this issue."[112] In fact, there is a long Caribglobal tradition of viewing same-sex desire as something foreign to Caribbean identity, and there is a more recent tradition of viewing attempts to win *gay* or *LGBT* rights as neocolonial, even in territories where the citizens are also part of the European Union. Indeed, in its official documents and promotional materials, the Netherlands implies that the "values and norms to which they adhere are universal," even as the country imposes mortality-related laws on resistant Caribbean territories. Accusations of neocolonialism would seem less accurate if international gay rights organizations based in the global North were more inclusive of southern voices. In this vein, activist Colin Robinson asks, "Why is it the Global North does GLBT equality through domestic politics, but the Global South has to do it through 'human rights' and 'international law' and foreign pressure. That's plain colonial thinking."[113] Unfortunately, this thinking persists in attitudes towards Caribbean sexual minority advocacy.

Ironically, if Caribbean nations and territories tend to view advocacy of *gay rights* as pushing the nation back to a colonial state, many activists in the global North—and some in the global South—view such advocacy as necessary to bring the Caribbean into modernity. Too often, scholars "see an unproblematic unidirectionality in the field of sexual globalization, a triumphant progress and transfer of sexual forms and identities from the West to the Rest."[114] Thus the successful integration of homosexuals, and therefore advancement into modernity, is typically judged by "venues and vehicles for public affirmation and recognition of gay and lesbian identities" and by the presence of "LGBTQ social movements, political activism, and public demonstrations, such as gay pride marches," as well as the decriminalization of homosex, the censorship of homophobic music, and the removal of blocks to gay-specific tourism.[115] If the terms in question are set by the global North, then "coming out" and public, explicit, audible visibility will be prioritized, and Caribbean subjects who engage el secreto abierto—who in fact make up the majority of Caribbean same-sex desiring subjects—will always be considered backward failures.

What is too often missing in discussions about same-sex desire in the Caribbean are the variety of ways in which sexual minorities live and love and work for change, including taking seriously different traditions such as el secreto abierto. Indeed, global North advocacy on behalf of the Caribbean, Africa, and other global South locations regularly occurs without consulting people in those places and is, quite frankly, racist, imperialist, and short sighted, assuming a pervasive, permanent, and unusual lack of agency among sexual minorities in the global South.[116] Agard-Jones explains that the current situation "increasingly inscribes a narrative whereby metropolitan queers are mobilized to 'save' local (Antillean) queers from local (Antillean) people."[117] As Horn writes, "while scholars are quick to acknowledge that queer desires and lives are lived differently in other societies, hardly any effort has been put into understanding how such differences might also lead to different forms of resistance, activism, and visions of sexual justice outside the parameters and paradigms through which we have come to measure these in the global north."[118] While extraregional media and organizations tend to be very occupied with detailing the horrors of Caribbean homophobia, they are rarely concerned with changing Caribbean attitudes towards sexual minorities, and even more rarely do they work with people within the region towards change. And yet, Trinidadian activist Colin Robinson reveals that on his first visit to Jamaica in 2000, instead of an absence of community or people wholly paralyzed by fear, he found "men, women, and transgenders carving out spaces for community and love and celebration amidst oppression in breathtakingly creative ways."[119] Indeed, there are a number of Caribbean-based sexual minority advocacy organizations that are pursuing innovative and pathbreaking strategies, such as CAISO (Coalition for Advancing the Inclusion of Sexual Orientation in Trinidad and Tobago), Suriname Men United, SASOD (Society Against Sexual Orientation Discrimination in Guyana), SEROvie (Haiti), and GrenCHAP (Grenada Caribbean HIV/AIDS Partnership). I will analyze some of these organizations that focus specifically on women in the next chapter. Below I will examine resistance through documentary film, which presents actual Caribbean sexual minorities.

Documentaries of Caribbean Same-Sex "Reality"

If Caribbean exemplary homophobia is a myth, then what is reality? The "real" is something that constantly eludes scholars, whether we are analyzing the crafted "real" of the creative imagination in the arts or whether we are analyzing the crafted "real" of self-presentation provided in situations observed by social scientists. This tension also exists in the examination of documentaries, which purport to provide "real" lives and situations but which can be as crafted and manipulated as any other form. As Michael Renov writes in his introduction to *Theorizing Documentary*, all forms of nonfiction include "any number of 'fictive' elements, moments at which a presumably objective representation of the world encounters the necessity of creative intervention" including "character . . . use of poetic language, narration, or musical accompaniment . . . camera angles," et cetera.[120] Furthermore, the "truth" of "reality" is more than a little swayed both by who is in power and, in terms of documentary, by "whose point of view the viewer agrees" with.[121] Nevertheless, documentary continues to be thought of as being more real, true, or authentic than fiction and visual art. My concern here is with film's *representation* of reality, rather than with the comparison of film to a supposedly pristine reality that I do not have access to either. Interestingly, documentaries generally provide depictions of Caribbean men who desire men that are quite different from those found in other art forms. While Caribbean literature tends to portray men who desire men as ultimately being punished by society for their gender transgressions and visual art tends to provide graphic examples of el secreto abierto, documentary film tends to portray men who desire men as confident, self-aware agents, if not as activists.

Orgullo en Puerto Rico/Pride in Puerto Rico foregrounds visibility and activism by focusing entirely on the eighth annual Gay, Lesbian, Bisexual, Transsexual and Transgender Pride Parade in Condado and on openly (and mostly self-identified) gay and lesbian activists. The parade itself, whose participants include men with painted faces and people with rainbow flags (including Puerto Rican flags with rainbow stripes), will be familiar to anyone who has seen LGBT pride celebrations in North America or Europe. In just seventeen minutes, *Orgullo/Pride* manages to interview two accepting religious leaders, the first openly homosexual candidate for office in Puerto Rico, lesbian parents, heterosexual parents of gay men, and several sexual minority activists and advocates. The clear message is that while many sexual minorities in Puerto Rico want more rights and acceptance and less harassment, the island is hardly a place of extreme homophobia and, in fact, is home to a vibrant and diverse LGBT community (notwithstanding that the film presents few images of trans or dark-skinned Puerto Ricans).

Songs of Freedom takes its title from one of über-Jamaican Bob Marley's famous anthems. Directed by Phillip Pike in 2002, this documentary features interviews with Jamaicans of different classes who practice same-sex desire, including both men and women and one public activist, Larry Chang, who is also the only Asian-Caribbean person included in any of the documentaries. The film portrays a range of experiences, from those of "Bobby,"[122] whose parents threw him out when they found out about his sexuality, to Chang, whose middle-class sister showed uncomfortable "tolerance," to "Miriam," who describes herself as being from the "ghetto" and who herself was surprised when her entire family accepted her sexuality. "Edward" plans to marry a woman and have children because of pressure from his father "to be a man and to have responsibility," while "Louise" is in a "marvelous" relationship with a woman, and "Clarence" is very involved in his church, where the leadership is aware of and accepts his sexuality.

Violence is reported in the film through reports of suicide attempts, beatings, and even murder, and fear is present through most interviewees' decision to have their faces distorted or to be interviewed off-screen. Nevertheless, the overarching message of the film is that most sexual minorities in Jamaica are "able to live a good life, a happy life," as "Henry" puts it. No one is quoted as wanting to emigrate from Jamaica to another country, and the Jamaica of the documentary is one that has gay nightclubs, drag shows and competitions, and (fractured) communities; it is also a country with pervasive class distinctions, corruption, and violence that are not restricted to sexual minorities. Filmed in the belly of the supposedly extremely Caribbean homophobic beast, *Songs of Freedom* refuses to reinforce or reproduce stereotypes. As the description on the film's DVD case states, this "first documentary about gay life in Jamaica" has portrayed "whole persons, full of beauty, complexity and contradictions."

Unlike *Orgullo/Pride* and *Songs of Freedom*, *Of Men and Gods* (2002) interviews no self-proclaimed activists, yet it is similar to these films in that it shows several individuals who live gender-nonconforming and/or same-sex-desiring lives openly, despite varying levels of acceptance from those around them. Focused on Haiti, *Of Men and Gods* differs from the other two films in that its subjects are almost exclusively gender transgressive, a focus the film never explicitly addresses. While this is certainly laudable given the typical lack of such representation, the result is a film that is not less skewed than others but skewed in a different way. Still, the pride and grace with which Innocente, Blondine, Fritzner,[123] and the other subjects live and seek love and eroticism is both striking and moving.

Collectively, these three documentaries contradict mainstream portrayals of the Caribbean as being uniquely and exponentially homophobic and of Caribbean sexual minorities as being permanently and profoundly lacking in agency (unless it is to apply for refugee status in the global North). Clearly, there is a wide range of self-concept, community, erotics, and activism among Caribbean men who desire men and other sexual minorities in the region. These attitudes and activities counter the global North and international gay hegemonic "imagination of Caribbean spaces as sexually backward in superlative and irredeemable ways, and of Caribbean queers as lacking agency and autonomy."[124]

Conclusion: "Is the Answer That Makes the Row"

The title of this section is an aphorism from Trinidad that implies that a row, an argument, requires two people, and if the second person keeps quiet, then there will be no row. This notion takes responsibility away from the instigator in a kind of blame-the-victim mentality that appears often in relationship to same-sex desire in the Caribbean; within this logic, it is not heterosexism, homophobia, or strict gender codes that create problems but the "obvious" people who are "flaunting" their same-sex desire either by demonstrating visible gender variance, by being seen in a same-sex embrace, or by otherwise confirming same-sex attraction.

Criticisms of Caribbean homophobia too often point to a "primitive" or "barbaric" mentality rather than offer serious cultural and historical analyses of systemic heteropatriarchy and sexism. Such criticisms clearly state that Caribbean homophobia is exponentially worse than homophobia in the global North.[125] But as the preceding analysis has shown, Caribbean cultures are often actually tolerant of sexual minorities—if those individuals adhere to traditional gender codes and to the parameters mandated by el secreto abierto. Within—and sometimes beyond—these boundaries, many people are able to live lives in the region that include same-sex desire and love. The ability to comfortably and safely live such a life depends, not surprisingly, on the individual's gender expression, class, and geographic location, among other factors.

Of course, there are also sexual minorities who are discriminated against, harassed, beaten, or even killed for their "predilection." How can we change the discourse about Caribbean sexualities to reduce the number and lessen the severity of the "rows" over it? One way is to change the terms of the discussion. Because gender and sexuality are so connected in the popular imagination, homophobia is intimately connected to transphobia and sexism, and specifically to the intolerance of nondominant masculinities. As Aviston Downes notes, "for any representation of masculinity to become hegemonic, the co-optation or complicity of lesser masculinities is necessary."[126] Interestingly, scholar de Moya has identified what he calls "an exuberant array" of more than two hundred Dominican masculinities, though only a small number of these are approved by society.[127] And, as Tinsley notes, not only have Caribbean realities "generated a spectrum of Creolized names beyond effeminate to designate culturally specific formations of male femininity," Caribbean communities often include "male women . . . as 'natural' parts of the Caribbean cultural landscape [who] occupy recognized places in their communities."[128] If we can begin to accept different types of masculinity and maleness as natural and valid, then gender-nonconforming and same-sex-desiring men will not be seen as "answering back" through their living and loving, and "rows" over gender or sexuality are less likely to erupt. While this may seem to be an academic suggestion, everyone can participate in such change by paying attention to how they and others praise or condemn men's and boys' behavior. Though I would not expect an elimination of hierarchies of Caribbean masculinity (which unfortunately will have less masculine types at the bottom), I do believe we can and should work towards a weakening of the existing hegemony, in part through a lessening of stigma attached to non-hegemonic masculinities.

In addition, international activists should allow direct political action to be led by those located in the region. The title of this subsection can also be understood in another way. If Caribbean people, both heterosexual and nonheterosexual, would only do as international gay activists ask and decriminalize sodomy, censor homophobic lyrics, embrace gay tourism, and have a pride march once a year, then there would be no "row," no threats of reduced aid, no boycotts, and no accusations of backwardness. While we can give the benefit of the doubt to non-Caribbean and Caribbean diaspora activists located in the global North and assume that their work stems from "good intentions and sincere desires" to reduce Caribbean homophobia and its effects, we must also recognize that "both sincerity and good intention were at the heart of most colonizing missions."[129]

In addition to recognizing local traditions of discretion exemplified in el secreto abierto, scholars must take seriously Caribbean activist strategies, even when these do not resemble traditional political activism or the dominant strategies used in the global North. As Tinsley explains, "The tactically obscured has been crucial to Caribbean and North American slave societies, in which dances, ceremonies, sexual encounters, abortions, and slave revolts all took place under the cover of night."[130] While this chapter has explained the open secret of men who desire men, the next chapter will examine the dangers and benefits of the obscurity of Caribbean women who desire women.

"This Is You"

"Invisibility," Community, and Women
Who Desire Women

The issue of revelation discussed in the previous chapter as being dominant in the experiences of Caribbean men who desire other men does exist
for Caribbean women, but it is not the dominant trope for them. Similarly,
the issue of supposed invisibility can be applicable to Caribbean men who
desire men, but it is not the dominant trope for their experiences or representation. If Caribbean men who desire other men are punished less for
their desire than for the gender nonconformity that is considered its visual manifestation, then Caribbean women who desire other women are
erased—made invisible—when their desire and gender expression can be
absorbed by prevailing norms. When they can neither be erased nor absorbed, they are punished for daring *not* to desire men. This chapter deconstructs the supposed invisibility of Caribbean women who desire women,
and explores how their portrayal in the region's literature mirrors strategies pursued by Caribbean organizations created by and serving this same
population. The main objective of this chapter is threefold: first, to deconstruct the myth of the invisible Caribbean lesbian found throughout the
region and its diaspora; second, to demonstrate, through key literary texts
by Dionne Brand (set in Trinidad), by Shani Mootoo (set in Toronto), by
R. Gay (set in Haiti), and by Marilyn Bobes (set in Cuba), *how* invisibility
functions, specifically that it is less a passive absence than it is an active,
enforced disappearing; and third, to reveal how Caribbean women involved
in Grupo OREMI (Cuba) and the Women's Caucus (Trinidad and Tobago)

use activism to battle their isolation and their invisibility, at least to each other, and how these groups, along with the multigender and ally organizations Hombres por la Diversidad (Cuba), the Coalition Advocating for Inclusion of Sexual Orientation (Trinidad and Tobago), and Overlegorgaan Caribische Nederlanders (the Netherlands) in the Caribbean and its diaspora, engage political approaches that reject more separatist strategies popular in the global North. Throughout, it will be clear that, in addition to supporting each other, these women desire to be full and largely unremarkable members of their communities.

However, before the argument unfolds, we must consider terminology. Throughout this chapter, the descriptive and less culturally weighted term *women who desire women* will appear more often than *lesbian*, although sometimes the latter word will be used. Some, but not all Caribbean women who have erotic, romantic, and/or sexual relationships with women identify with the term *lesbian*, as can be seen in several quotations used later in this chapter. As within many communities of people of color in the United States, some people in the Caribbean explicitly identify the term *lesbian* with white North American and European women, while others use local nonderogatory or reclaimed terms such as *zami, mati, buenas amigas, entendida, kambrada*, and various euphemisms such as "so," "funny," or "goes with women," and still others refuse to label their sexuality at all. Furthermore, the diversity of individual sexualities means that women who are married to or have sex with men *and* have sex with other women, women who have sex with other women but profess not to fall in love with them, and women who only engage in particular sex acts with women may not label themselves lesbians or as anything other than heterosexual. Here, when the term *lesbian* is used, it is used consciously and to refer to people who have identified themselves with that word.[1] It is important to note that this issue is not "just" one of word choice. The lived experiences of nonheteronormative sexualities are often different in different places. And, in fact, it is because terms represent lived experiences in particular cultural, geographical, chronological, and social spaces that they make sense to us at all. To use a term in an inappropriate context is to erase the specificity of that context and the agency of the individual, and to superimpose assumptions on them about what it means to inhabit their identity.[2]

Trinidadian Dionne Brand, winner of Canada's prestigious Governor General's Award (1997 and 2006), among many other honors, has published ten collections of poetry, three novels, one short story collection, and two books of original essays. Her prolific publishing record and the breadth of topics, including race, sexuality, immigration, and memory, that Brand's oeuvre addresses make her one of the most important living Caribbean women writers and one of an even smaller group of notable Caribbean writers who identify as lesbian. Brand's poem "Hard against the Soul," which was first published in 1990 in her important collection *No Language Is Neutral*, remains radical today because it holds up a mirror to the Caribbean and names women who desire women as part of its reflection, an approach that is repeatedly seen in Caribbean literature and activism. Because this poem insists not only on the existence of Caribbean female same-sex desire but also on the *Caribbeanness* of that desire, it is an appropriate text with which to begin this chapter.

Each of the six stanzas of "Hard against the Soul" begins with the phrase "this is you girl." The girl addressed in the poem signifies both a female who is not yet a woman and the emphatic "girl" one woman calls another woman in affection or anger. But without a comma to separate them, the girl is also fused to the *you*, and the many Caribbean images of "you girl" found throughout the poem (ocean, sea wall, bush, etc.) are linked to mark her as a kind of Caribbean Everywoman. The poem is full of verbs: the earth is described as "carrying on" and "smoothing" shell and coral; the "sea breeze shaped forest of sand and lanky palm"; the woman and sea "turn"; bodies of water "boil" and "roll"; silence "chatters." The text also includes nouns that can also be verbs (*cut, turn, dip, daub, pulse*), and together these words give the poem a sense of movement and constant transformation that is in turn bestowed on you-girl, so that she and you and we and Trinidad and the Caribbean can be a single stone and/or the entire sea wall; breeze and/or spirit; lover and/or anything at all.[3]

The first three stanzas of this poem/section focus on *place*. You-girl is specific Trinidadian places (Blanchicheuse, Manzanilla, Maracas, etc.); she is the road and the land and the stone that makes up these places, and you-girl is also the ocean that wears these things away and the breeze that caresses them. While these places are indelibly Trinidadian, the fact that "this is you girl, even though you never see it" points to travel and includes the diaspora. Likewise, the lines "La Fillette bay never know / you but you make it wash up from the rocks" indicate that even though the landscape does not know you-girl, she is described as the power behind its movement.[4]

Each of the next three stanzas also mentions place, but in addition they refer to the human experiences of thinking, physical feeling, and erotic desire—that of the speaker specifically and that of humanity generally. In the fourth stanza, you-girl becomes the stone again—"this stone of my youngness . . . turning to burning reason"—but now it is not rock stone, but instead the possibility and burden of the speaker's youth that painfully, "breaking" and "turning," becomes reason, as in knowledge and understanding. In the fifth stanza, you-girl is a poem that does not exist yet which, paradoxically, may be describing itself while it describes the beloved and her "smell of fresh thighs and warm sweat."[5] Though the woman desired here is likened to water, the homoeroticism is clear: you-girl does not just desire another woman, she *is* the desire of one woman for another, for her flesh and smell and sweat.

The final stanza begins "this is you girl, something never waning or forgetting." Only here is the "this" not specific; here "this" and "you-girl" are first "something" and then an unnamed place that enables you-girl to make sense of herself and to take joy in being both alive and awake. This note is sounded in the last, oft-quoted phrase of the poem, which is "to be awake is / more lovely than dreams." The awareness of the poem's conclusion should be read in relationship to memory (you-girl is "never waning or forgetting"), to physical feeling (the night air, sight), and to emotional feeling (this place is connected to her soul and is where she "makes sense").[6] And this delight in *being awake*, in conscious awareness, implicitly applies to all of the Caribbean images described in the poem, from road and land to thighs and sweat.

The full refrain "This is you girl" eschews the tools of simile; you-girl is not *like* these places and sensations but *is* them, is one and the same. Brand holds a mirror up to Trinidad, and the reflection includes female coming-of-age and female same-sex desire. Specific pieces of land and bodies of water are inherently, undeniably Trinidadian and Caribbean, and so is a woman who sexually desires another woman. In what may be the most extensive reading of the collection that includes this poem, Omise'eke Tinsley writes in *Thiefing Sugar* that "*No Language* not only imagines a sexual politics as West Indian as the Caribbean Sea but also charts complex relationships between eroticism, colonialism, militarism, resistance, revolution, poverty, despair, fullness, and hope."[7] This insistence that same-sex desire is indivisible from the Caribbean is also present in the creative and more explicitly political Caribglobal imagination in fiction by and about Caribbean women who desire women and in organizations these women have created in the region and the diaspora. This affirmation of the existence of female same-sex desire in the region flies in the face of the persistent notion that women who desire and love other women do not exist in the Caribbean.

The Trope of Invisibility

When people discuss or write about female same-sex desire in the Caribbean, they most often use descriptions or metaphors of invisibility and silence. While women who desire other women undoubtedly exist in the Caribbean—and though many of them have full romantic, sexual, familial, work, and spiritual lives—sometimes their sexuality is not visible to, legible to, or widely acknowledged by others. This invisibility can be seen in the following quotations from various works of Caribbean literature and scholarship referring to Caribbean women who desire and have sex with other women:

> "the hidden lives of Caribbean lesbians." "Women who have sex with women seemed not to be talked about at all. Lesbians are effectively disappeared." "In Trinidad, as far as lesbianism is concerned . . . it was still something that didn't really exist, except theoretically." "In Suriname being with a woman was accepted, as long as you did not talk about it, did not name yourself." "Keeping the ghost of excluded otherness in its nonplace is the never-ending job of the dominant system, and lesbian desire has been so excluded from the dominant discourse in Cuban culture that its literary expression is scarce." "Woman-Woman relations of a sexual and intimate nature exist in the Caribbean. They are repressed publicly and privately by the dominant social and cultural norms." "Like the female bodies in her poetry, the once prize-winning Faubert became barely visible in Haitian letters." "It was unspoken, hidden and secretive, but at the same time you can't really hide anything there."[8]

This trope of invisibility is found less forcefully and less consistently in creative and nonfiction literature about Caribbean men who desire other men. However, the fact that Caribbean men who are or are perceived to be feminine and/or to desire men are perceived as being more visible than are women who are or are perceived to be masculine and/or to desire other women is not because the men are more "obvious"; it is because men already have greater access to and visibility in public spaces. As anthropologist Ja-fari Allen observes about Cuba, "Men predominate on the streets of Cuban cities and towns. They joke, talk, and play games in the plazas, on street corners, and in parks, while women are mostly seen en route to some ap-pointment indoors."[9] Thus, the generally diminished social status and lesser public visibility of women accrue exponentially onto women who refuse to embody (or to engender) hegemonic, heteropatriarchal femininity. Indeed, critic Myriam Chancy argues that "lesbian identity, more so than gay male identity, has cross-culturally and across time been regarded as an invisible or nonthreatening subject position."[10] Interestingly, notwithstanding docu-mented cases of the murder and rape of Caribbean women perceived to be masculine and/or same-sex desiring,[11] there seems to be a popular per-ception in the English Caribbean that there is little violence against these women.[12] And yet it is well known that most violence against women is ef-fectively "invisible" because it is unlikely to be reported, and if reported too often is not taken seriously, or is simply ignored, especially if it takes place in the home.[13] Discussing the under-representation of violence against women who desire women, activist Maurice Tomlinson commented that "In Jamai-can culture women are generally expected to be quiet about harassment and abuse."[14] This silencing is only augmented for women who are masculine or who engage in what is considered transgressive sexuality. So while the perception that there is very little violence against women who desire other women in the Caribbean is inaccurate, this misperception is not surprising because so little attention is paid to this type of violence. A rare study con-ducted on this topic found, however, that in Cuba "lesbians are generally more socially rejected than gay men" and that "gay men have benefited from state efforts at eliminating homophobia, while the situation of lesbians have [sic] stagnated and, in some measures, slightly deteriorated."[15] Notably, 96 percent of those surveyed believe that "there is a difference between how lesbians and gay men are treated" in Cuba.[16] This difference is also apparent in academia; for instance, one group of scholars has noted that "Themati-cally, studies of queer Latina sexualities and subjectivities . . . are still fewer in comparison to queer Latino sexualities and symbolic practices."[17]

In fact, as detailed in chapter 2, much of the literature on Caribbean men who desire and have sex with other men focuses on their *visibility* and the difficulties many of them have passing and points to this visibility as contributing to the targeting of sexual-minority men for violence. Dudley Ferdinandus, Director of FOKO (Fundashon Orguyo Kòrsou), the local sexual-minority advocacy organization in Curaçao, argues that women who desire women are much more "comfortable" on the island than are men who desire men, in part because it is "very normal to see two women raising up a house[hold] or walking hand in hand," meaning that such touching is not automatically assumed to be erotic.[18] Similarly, Wekker observes that "While the Surinamese state naturalizes and tries to enforce compulsory heterosexuality for men, mainly by ridiculing and animalizing male homosexuals in public debates and speeches, it has mainly ignored female mati, who are not in the habit of naming themselves."[19] Notwithstanding the censure—ranging from "scorning" to "corrective" rape[20]—that women who desire women do receive in the region, it is clear that women and men who engage in same-sex relationships are often treated differently. These differences do not make one group more or less maltreated than the other, but examining these disjunctures is useful for a nuanced understanding of same-sex desire in the region.

Why does this *particular* invisibility and silence around women who desire women persist in Caribbean societies and literature? The invisibility of Caribbean women who desire other women becomes an excuse for broader societies and cultures to ignore them (and for some gay men to ignore or resent them, especially when they presume that lesbians inherently and/ or deliberately participate in "invisibility" by passing, which some do). But we cannot forget the structures and circumstances that allow many of these women to pass, including the heteropatriarchal assumption that all women's sexuality, if it exists at all, is "a nothingness, a lack, an absence," and the commonplace reality of women-headed households in the region.[21] According to sociologist Elizabeth Crespo-Kebler, Puerto Rican lesbians' invisibility is "directly tied to the heterosexual matrix that rules over all women's gender and sex experience . . ." a statement that applies well to the region as a whole.[22] And anthropologist Jafari Allen notes that while invisibility may (seem to) afford women more freedom than men "since women enjoy access to each other's bodies for 'friendly' physical affection without harsh scrutiny," when either the woman's same-sex desire or her gender nonconformity is apparent, "this angst-filled silence is matched in symbolic violence."[23] These social structures and anxieties work from one angle to create the supposed invisibility of Caribbean women who desire women and simultaneously work from another angle to punish them for the existence of that desire.

In the essay "This Body for Itself," Trinidadian poet, activist, and scholar Brand argues that the general absence of any sexuality in black women's writing is a form of "self-preservation." She writes that "In a world where Black women's bodies are so sexualized, avoiding the body as sexual is a strategy. So is writing it in the most conservative terms . . . [and] Leaving pleasure to men, that's a strategy, too."[24] But avoiding sexuality out of a desire to seem "respectable" will not only lead to suppressing and silencing one's own sexuality; it can also lead to the aggressive silencing of anyone else's sexuality that is considered unconventional, transgressive, or abnormal.[25] Audre Lorde famously told readers in *Sister Outsider* that "your silence will not protect you," a truth that Gloria Wekker expounds on when she notes that modesty, sexual secrecy, and "performing asexuality" provide no guarantees against physical, emotional, societal, or epistemic violence.[26]

All of this talk of invisibility belies a "very present absence": the real existence of women who desire other women in Caribglobal communities and cultures.[27] It is instructive to unpack the quotes listed at the beginning of this chapter. Regarding Elwin's reference to "the hidden lives of Caribbean lesbians," it is important to remember that only that which already exists can be hidden.[28] Allen declares that at the time of the Cuban Revolution, while male homosexuality was considered "an artifact of capitalist bourgeois decadence," lesbians were "effectively disappeared"—again, the need to efface these women points to their existence.[29] The speaker in the next quote declares that when she was a child, lesbianism only existed "theoretically," even though as an adult in Trinidad she has had several same-sex relationships. Then one of Gloria Wekker's Surinamese interlocutors describes an acceptance of female same-sex relationships that is predicated on neither naming nor discussing the practice. Bejel argues that the "dominant discourse in Cuban culture" actually works quite hard to exclude lesbian desire—and even then, it leaves a trace, a "ghost" presence. Similarly, in their essay "Sexual Choice as a Human Right [sic] Issue," which addresses tolerance in the English Caribbean, Cave and French clearly state that female homosexuality does exist in the region but is actively repressed. Scholar

Tinsley describes the bodies of women who desire each other in Ida Faubert's poetry, as well as Faubert herself, as being "barely visible," even as Tinsley reveals the importance of both these bodies and the poet in Haitian and Caribbean studies. The final quote, from a Dominican woman who identifies herself only as Daphne, speaks for itself: "It was unspoken, hidden and secretive, *but at the same time* you can't really hide anything" in the Caribbean.[30] Examined closely, all of these quotes sustain Chancy's assertion that in relationship to women's sexuality, any given Caribbean community "knows already what it denies," with the force of that denial reflecting both the strength of that knowledge and the fear that even acknowledging female same-sex desire (much less accepting or "condoning" it) will unravel the national, social, and cultural fabric.[31] And as Cave and French feel compelled to declare, "Woman-woman relations of an intimate and sexual nature exist in the Caribbean. There are established, long-term, consensual sexual relationships between women. Such relationships are not the discovery of the decadent post-War period, nor are they a product of the new feminist movement of the 70s, nor of the social disintegration of the 80s and 90s, nor are they merely examples of the importation of decadent ways from the white North . . . However, the recording of the history of these relationships is fairly recent."[32]

To this litany—only a sampling of similar language that is replicated throughout Caribglobal literature and scholarship—we can add the existence of Caribbean terms and slurs such as *macommère, griti meid, antiman, mati, tortillera, platte borden, zami, kambrada, ma divine,* and *cachapera,* terms that describe real, not mythical, sexual and erotic behavior between women.[33] And to this we can add Gloria Wekker's in-depth descriptions of women's sexuality and mati work in Suriname,[34] Tinsley's collection examining eroticism between women in Caribbean literature, and the work of numerous poets, writers, and critics.[35] Clearly, Caribbean women who desire and have sex with other women *do* exist in the contemporary and *did* exist in the historical Caribbean (and not only its diaspora),[36] as well as in the region's cultural production. Therefore, we cannot assume that invisibility is the same as absence, insignificance, or lack of agency. Nor should we assume that invisibility and silence are always already permanent, having no causes, no beginning, and no end. The truth is that this so-called invisibility is neither complete, nor blameless, nor permanent. In fact, the invisibility of Caribbean women who desire women is actually a *near-invisibility*, a state that supposes—and sometimes promotes—invisibility, even in the presence of actual people or other evidence to the contrary.

The near-invisibility of Caribbean women who desire women is incomplete because, as the close reading of the earlier litany of quotes demonstrates, assertions of invisibility often either imply or are accompanied by tacit acknowledgement of these women's existence. The impossibility of complete invisibility is also proven by the fact that women who desire women (and men who desire men) are not always invisible to each other—and typically not to themselves. Similarly, the near-invisibility of Caribbean women who desire women is not permanent because it is so deeply contextual, depending on place, time, and circumstance, as well as on who is being looked at, who is looking, and how they are able to interpret what they see. The erotic relationship of two long-term women "roommates" may be near-invisible when they have Sunday lunch with each other's families, but it becomes quite visible if a visitor notices that the roommates' apartment has only one bedroom and one bed.

Mati-ism is a long-established, complex cultural practice among Afro-Surinamese working-class women that has same-sex sexuality at its core and which also includes its own specific language, customs, and systems of morality. The unique tradition of mati work, involvement in the mati culture, may at first glance seem an exception to the presumed invisibility of Caribbean women who desire women. In fact, examining Wekker's groundbreaking work reveals that in Suriname the mati tradition is widely known to exist but is rarely explicitly discussed or acknowledged outside of those involved in mati work or with those intimately connected to them. This expectation of discretion outside of mati circles is yet another type of near-invisibility.

The circumstance of being near-invisible is fraught with tension, enforced as it is by prevailing social and cultural norms. This enforced near-invisibility can make it easier for people who contradict heteropatriarchy to be abused. Since Caribbean law and custom have already established that women who desire other women are (or should be) outside of the public sphere and are definitely outside of respectability, it is assumed that abuse of them will receive little, if any, censure or punishment. Near-invisibility can also make it difficult for communities of women who desire other women to be created or even for women who might desire each other to meet. But just as invisibility is not absolute, nor does it always produce abjectness or a complete lack of agency, regardless of how painful, diminishing, and damaging the experience can be. Nor is it true that that which is invisible or near-invisible is insignificant. The very anxiety that produces near-invisibility points to the significance of women's same-sex desire. Agency, eroticism, and love are all possible within the structure of near-invisibility, and this range of experiences is found within Caribglobal literature.

Women Who Desire Women in Caribbean Literature

In his introduction to the reprint edition of Patricia Powell's *A Small Gathering of Bones*, a novel about how three men navigate life, love, and family as HIV/AIDS emerges in Jamaica, author and essayist Thomas Glave argues that the realm of fiction focused on Anglophone Caribbean men who desire men is an "arid landscape of silence and invisibility" compared to the number of publications about their female counterparts.[37] This is, to an extent, true; no openly nonheterosexual Anglophone Caribbean man has achieved the literary or critical success of Dionne Brand and Michelle Cliff, for instance, both of whom are part of the second generation of the "boom" of English Caribbean women's writing that arguably began with the publication of Paule Marshall's novel *Brown Girl, Brownstones* in 1959. The number of short stories featuring English Caribbean men's same-sex desire is slowly increasing, though the number of novels remains extremely small and not all of these authors themselves claim a nonheterosexual identity.

However, it is remarkable that even though the number of self-identified lesbian Caribbean authors has increased in the literary landscape, within novels themselves the number of primary, fully developed Caribbean characters who are women who desire other women has not kept pace. As with men, more same-sex desiring Caribbean women are found in short stories than in full-length texts. Taken together, the authors Glave cites—Brand, Cliff, Makeda Silvera, Nalo Hopkinson, and Powell (some of the most well-known self-identified English Caribbean lesbian or queer women writers)—are more likely to focus their novels on men who desire men, trans people, or heterosexuals than on women who desire women. I support all authors' right to write about whomever they wish, yet it is curious that *collectively* even self-identified nonheterosexual Anglophone Caribbean women shy away from writing novels that focus on women's same-sex desire. Speaking about the absence of women who desire women in her own work, Cliff has said that "part of it is self-censorship. I have to be honest. I think it is. And I think it's having grown up in a society that is enormously homophobic."[38]

The situations in the French, Dutch, and Spanish Caribbean are quite different. The French Caribbean has no major living, openly nonheterosexual writer; anthologies and critics continue to mine the work of the deceased Asotto Saint in part because it is a rare example of such writing.[39] Similarly, in the absence of translations of her work, in particular *Levenslang gedicht* (Lifelong poem, 1987) and *Over de gekte van een vrouw* (On a woman's madness, 1982), editors and critics often rely on Astrid Roemer's 1986 discussion with Audre Lorde or excerpts from work by Gloria Wekker as the only Dutch Caribbean representation in their collections.[40] In Spanish Carib-global literature, there is a great deal more writing that features the lives of nonheterosexuals, including men, women, and people who live in the trans spectrum. In that part of the region, same-sex-desiring men writers and characters outnumber women. As mentioned earlier, in *Gay Cuban Nation* (2001), a detailed analysis of same-sex desire in Cuban literature and political thought, Bejel notes that "lesbian desire" continues to be "scarce" in Cuban culture.[41] In addition, it is important to note that no Spanish Caribbean woman writer approaches the legendary status of Cubans Reinaldo Arenas and José Lezama Lima, both of whom wrote explicitly about male same-sex desire. A closer examination of nonheterosexual writers and characters from throughout the region would likely reveal that the texts produced are the result of a complicated matrix of publishing opportunities, trends in marketing and university syllabi, and personal preference; unfortunately, such analysis exceeds the scope of this chapter.

*   *   *

Contrary to what may be popular belief or expectation, in Caribbean texts that portray women loving and desiring other women, sexuality itself is rarely the focus of the main storyline. Instead, these women are portrayed as being part of a larger Caribbean community that is extremely important to them. One can even say that Caribbean community is a main character of the texts; we often learn enough of its history and attitudes to understand both it and the protagonists better. In this way, the authors emphasize the characters' Caribbeanness along with, and sometimes more than, their sexual orientation. Instead of *the single* focus, sexuality is one priority of many, and it is not always the characters' first priority. Though the word *lesbian* appears in none of the texts examined here, as Gopinath notes in relationship to South Asian texts, "narratives that explicitly name female same-sex desire as 'lesbian' may be less interesting that those moments within the narrative that represent female homoeroticism in the absence of 'lesbians.'"[42] I will briefly discuss three examples: two relatively well known, and one relatively obscure. Analysis of these stories will elucidate the productive potential, as well as the dangers, of near-invisibility.

"Out on Main Street" is a widely anthologized short story by Shani Mootoo set in Toronto, Canada. It addresses the near-invisibility related to different kinds of passing, as well as the spotlight of attention that can result from being unable to pass. The story is an investigation of appearances and authenticity in relationship to ethnicity, gender, and sexuality. The story's location allows an exploration of diverse South Asian experiences and identities; though they are of Indian descent, Janet and Pud (the narrator's nickname) are described as not "real" Indians but rather as "kitchen" Indians and "cultural bastards" because they are Trinidadian.[43] Even so, Pud considers herself "more" Indian than Janet, her girlfriend, because Pud is nominally Hindu while Janet is definitely Presbyterian. Pud is herself soon humiliated, though, by the "real" Indians in a Toronto sweet shop who correct her Hindi—only to find out later that those "real Indians" are actually from Fiji! However, these ethnic and cultural divisions are quickly forgotten when two drunk white men come into the store and behave badly towards the Fijian brothers. In an instant, all of the South Asians come together to support the store owners and mend their pride.

Moments later, the female lovers find solidarity with a group of beautiful South Asian women who have also come to snack at the shop as they all commiserate over the unwanted sexual attention aggressively offered to them by the Fijian brothers. But that solidarity is broken up when two obviously same-sex desiring friends come in. As Pud tells it: "is a dead giveaway dat dey not dressing fuh any man, it have no place in dey life fuh man vibes, and dat in fact dey have a blatant penchant fuh women." The pair's sexuality becomes hypervisible, and at that point, the formerly friendly "Miss

Universe pageant" women ignore Pud and Janet, shunning their implicit homosexuality, one woman looking as though she "was in de presence of a very foul smell."[44]

Although Pud's sexuality goes from being near-invisible to being hyper-visible ("over-exposed" in her own words), her self-presentation is consistent.[45] It is others who have difficulty reconciling the different elements of Pud's life, a complexity we all share but which is more apparent when multiple aspects of the self are marked as "other." Indeed, Pud is genuinely invested in many aspects of herself, including her unconventional gender, and she confidently and happily participates in the South Asian, female, and same-sex desiring communities as their boundaries shift around her. Significantly, Pud comments on the women's appearance (for instance, their "Miss Universe" looks and their "Indian-looking" appearance) but does not presume to name the other women's ethnicities or sexualities; thus, the author refuses to have Pud repeat the stereotyping and exclusion to which she has repeatedly been subjected.[46] Furthermore, by portraying a series of situations in which Pud both is and is not accepted, in which she is and is not able to pass, Mootoo refuses to prioritize sexuality above other aspects of her character's identity.

The second story may literally be the least visible of the texts discussed here because it appeared in a collection of lesbian erotica published by a small press, factors that mean its audience has been rather limited.[47] "Of Ghosts and Shadows" (2003) is set in Haiti and was written by a Haitian-American author, who published it under the pseudonym R. Gay.[48] The story's title gestures towards the near-invisibility of its main characters. Marie Françoise, the narrator, remarks that she and her lover Amelie "are women who don't exist." Although she states that they do not exist, the materiality of their bodies and lives show that this is clearly not true. The text underscores that their lives are simultaneously near-invisible—"less than shadows"—and substantial—"more than ghosts." The following sentences speak more clearly: "We're the wayward relatives neighbors gossip about in hushed, horrified tones. We are the women people ignore because two women loving each other is an American thing—not the sort of behavior god-fearing island folk would engage in."[49] And yet the story insists that, despite their sexuality, these two women are part of and inseparable from their compatriot "island folk." The story moves between their emotional and physical desire for each other and the desires they share with their community: desires for small luxuries, for safety, and for peace. The language of the story explicitly links all of these desires and, like Mootoo's, does not privilege sexuality.

The first part of "Of Ghosts and Shadows" is set in the market, an everyday *communal* space. Walking through the market, the lovers watch each other from afar "because it is too dangerous to do anything but watch" each other. Turning her gaze away from her beloved for a moment, the narrator is filled with a desire to weep because she sees a group of schoolchildren and remarks, "they too want things they cannot have." What the women want but cannot have is, of course, each other, but that want is also linked to their own poverty—to "imagining what it would be like to own" something—a state that Amelie and Marie Françoise share with those around them.[50]

The lovers are also part of the community of Haitian women left behind after their men have disappeared, having been murdered for political reasons or having fled from persecution or poverty into the forest or to another country. The narrator's mother is only able to escape her sorrow in the "stolen moments" of sleep, when she can forget her husband's imprisonment or murder, her son's absence, her poverty, and the impending political violence all around, as well as (presumably) her daughter's sexual transgression. The narrator uses the same metaphor of stealing in reference to the young women: they only enjoy "stolen moments" of intimacy; they must "steal away" to a friend's house or "steal to the bathroom" at the occasional house party to make love.[51] The reasons for maintaining this near-invisibility are demonstrated when one of these parties is violently interrupted, leaving one man in the hospital. But even though many in their larger community would condemn, if not attack, them, the story insists that those involved in same-sex relationships are part of the Haitian community around them and have more in common with other Haitians than differences from them.

These two stories begin with both the lover *and* with a specific physical and cultural place; like Brand's poem, they emphasize an indivisibility and simultaneity of experience. For the protagonists and for both pairs of lovers, sexuality is a difference and an important difference—a difference that, if discovered, could lead to ostracization or violence. But it is not an *absolute* difference. The stories point out that sexuality is only one of many potential causes of violence in Haiti and only one of many potential points of difference and division in the region and its diaspora. It is not, to the women themselves, a difference that separates them from the communities they were born into, the communities they love.

And, significantly, although others in their family and community want these women to be both silent and invisible, the women refuse. "Of Ghosts and Shadows" ends with the two women making passionate love despite the very real danger of being caught. Similarly, "Out on Main Street" ends with Pud refusing either to disavow her sexuality, confirmed by her having obviously nonheterosexual friends, or to disavow the women with whom she had previously shared a different solidarity. Erotic desire, as well as the desire not to betray one's own self, are stronger here than are threats of social or familial rejection.

Just as near-invisibility does not result in a complete lack of agency, neither does the state of near-invisibility nor the structures that enforce it guarantee their goal: the suppression or elimination of Caribbean same-sex desire and pleasure. Indeed, even in the face of threatened damnation, physical harm, and shunning, the characters persist in claiming their same-sex desire and in pursuing erotic pleasure and the satisfaction of that desire. And even though the reader never hears from Maritza directly in Marilyn Bobes' 2008 short story "Someone Has to Cry" (discussed in detail below), other characters reveal that she took pleasure, at least, in her own body. Presenting an unconventional gender, Maritza is described as having been unusually confident for a teenager—"nervy," even—and "happier" than other young women who were more attractive than her.[52] Unfortunately, without any community support for her difference, without even one confidante, and without a loving partner, this pleasure is not enough to sustain her.

The women in "Of Ghosts and Shadows," however, maintain a loving and sexual relationship despite the threats. Most of the time they hide their love from others, but both love and desire push them "to defy *the rules*" of their enforced invisibility because "such stolen moments are the one small thing [they] have in this big, big world."[53] Similarly, Mootoo's narrator, who in her crew cut, jeans, and boots says she "look like a gender dey forget to classify" and knows that she inspires revulsion and threats in many around her, persists in her gender nonconformity.[54] And even though sometimes she practices behaving in a more feminine way, ultimately she embraces her non-normative gender because it *feels* good and "right" to express her "true colors."[55] Mootoo's story is also funny, and while the narrator addresses serious identity issues (for example, "I wish I could find that place where I am Trinidadian"), her language and style encourage the reader to find pleasure in the story and empathize with its main character.

Just as it is important to recognize that agency and desire are possible within a state of near-invisibility, it cannot be forgotten that near-invisibility can also have negative, even disastrous, consequences. "Someone Has to Cry" by Bobes is an example of the latter. On the surface it would seem that protagonist Maritza is, in fact, invisible because she has committed suicide. And yet near-invisibility applies here as well because she is very present in the thoughts and words of the friends and acquaintances who have gathered for her wake. Each person reveals how their interactions with or observations of the dead woman affected their lives.

Clearly, community is important in this story; it is the mechanism through which the narrative is conveyed, in multiple bursts of first-person narration. Maritza, however, is most often described as having been in the community but not of it; as a teenager she had been considered "unlike" the other girls, and one woman at the wake goes so far as to compare the adult Maritza to an "extraterrestrial." Though she continued to socialize with her friends individually and as a group, Maritza withheld her deepest thoughts even from Cary, her closest friend, who can remember only one time Maritza shared something personal with her.[56] Neither Maritza nor anyone else explicitly confirms her desire for women, but most of the characters believe she was "that way" because of her non-normative gender presentation, unusual confidence, and because another woman lived with her for some time and that woman's departure may have been one of the events that led to Maritza's suicide.

Both friends and acquaintances attend the wake, and though not everyone liked Maritza, everyone has memories of her participating in their circle. Though here the community portrayed is one of friends, they were not particularly friendly towards the deceased. Their internal monologues reveal their censure of everything from Maritza's body language to her career choice to her presumed sexuality, all attitudes that represent those held by the larger society regarding expectations of appropriate female appearance and behavior.[57] Unlike the characters in Gay's story, Maritza was not a full member of the community; she had been often present but apart, "unlike" the others. And unlike Mootoo's Pud, she did not seem fully at ease with herself. The story implies that this lack of support, the barriers to her ability to be honest with others about herself, and the breakup all contributed to a state of despair that resulted in her death. The attitudes towards her gender transgressions, the constant need to reject male advances (including from one of her friend's husbands), the rumors about her sexuality, and the absence of anyone in whom she could fully confide: these factors led to violence that though self-inflicted is no less tragic. The other literary texts examined here and the Caribglobal activism discussed below imply that having had a more supportive community might have prevented the isolation and despair Maritza experienced.

Women Who Desire Women in Caribbean Activism

While literature is a fruitful site of analysis of Caribbean same-sex desire, examination of real-life "texts" and contexts clarifies that the literature reflects the lived experiences of some women in the region. The phenomenon of near-invisibility, itself a result of attempts to render invisible sexualities that do not adhere to, and therefore threaten, heteropatriarchal mores and structures, is not unique to the Caribbean. What is striking, however, is the response of Caribbean sexual minorities to this phenomenon. "To understand" Caribbean sexual minorities, we must "understand the problematics of visibility and the strategies of semivisibility" used within the region.[58] Organizations that specifically serve Caribbean women who desire other women are more rare than organizations in the region that serve sexual minority men or people of multiple genders. Considering structural and official hostility towards women and sexual minorities in the Caribbean, this additional level of near-invisibility is not surprising. Nevertheless, a few such organizations do exist and largely focus on creating safe and supportive social spaces, the kind of spaces that can provide relief from communities that are often hostile or indifferent to same-sex desire. Activism is itself a form of visibility and a way to counter isolation, as is seen in the cases of Grupo OREMI in Cuba, the Women's Caucus in Trinidad, and OCaN in the Netherlands.[59]

Because the Cuban government strongly discourages independent organizing, Grupo OREMI was created under the auspices of CENESEX (Centro Nacional de Educación Sexual), the country's national center for sex education. Founded in 2005, OREMI's original mission was to combat "social isolation" and the "anonymity that makes [lesbians] feel set aside" from the larger society. According to one of the founders, another integral priority was to combat "cultural [read racial] marginalization," since most of the organizers identified as black.[60] At the same time, the organizers took pains to explain that they "[did] not wish to separate themselves from Cuban society."[61] As in the short stories examined earlier, the women of Grupo OREMI wanted to claim cultural and erotic identities simultaneously.

In her study, sociologist Tanya L. Saunders, who studied the organization extensively, writes that "Grupo OREMI created a safe and dependable space for antiracist social critique, lesbian empowerment, and socialization." This took place mainly through social and cultural events; the first gathering was publicized only through word of mouth, yet hundreds of women attended—so many that some had to be turned away.[62] Nonheterosexual women of African descent in Havana were so starved for this type of space that many publicly kissed, and some even had sex, in or near the CENESEX venue. This behavior led to significant public complaint, and as a result, Grupo OREMI was allowed to exist in its original form for only a few months. The organization continues to provide counseling and a limited public presence.[63]

Located in Trinidad, the Women's Caucus has a similar mission to Grupo OREMI. Their Strategic Team defines the Caucus as "a group of women who identify as women who love women (WLW) including lesbians and bisexual[s]" and notes that the group was founded in June 2010 "to examine and identify the needs of WLW in Trinidad and Tobago with a view to creating safe spaces for women to meet and to provide some level of support around specific needs identified by the group."[64] To date, the group has avoided designating any officers or creating any formal organizational structure. It strives to "mirror [the] racial and cultural diversity" of Trinidad and Tobago, and a recent event attracted more than sixty women. In its first year the programming (more than twenty events) focused on social and cultural events, including "chats" (discussion on topics such as fear, homophobia, and broadening perceptions of what a "real lesbian" is like), a beach day, karaoke, and three ecumenical religious services.

Both groups organized around identity because creating internal community and mutual support was a major priority. As one self-identified Caribbean lesbian told an interviewer for a Canadian anthology, "I don't think it is easy to live an entirely gay life in the Caribbean. Especially if you are not wealthy. Because I think you are really isolated."[65] While parties and chat sessions may not seem political, even to some of the people who attend them, these activities counter near-invisibility by creating a community that is at least visible to itself. They reduce isolation and create dialogue that is valuable on its own, though it may also lead to more formal and public political activism or advocacy. In *Queer Latinidad* (2003), Juana María Rodríguez affirms the importance of informal gatherings, but argues that "on a political level, recounting individual narratives within the private confines of identity-based groups is simply no longer sufficient as a means of effectively transforming the social conditions of our lives if we do not also reclaim a vocal public presence."[66] Yet, given the yearning for community repeatedly expressed in the interviews collected by author Rosamund Elwin,[67] it seems that some people do find community gatherings to be a key source of support, if not also of transformation. Furthermore, even if we acknowledge that such gatherings typically do not themselves result in legislative or other formal political change, they often act as personal and social catalysts for the organizations and work that *do* lead to more traditionally political activism.

In the Netherlands there is an example of activism similar in purpose to that of the Women's Caucus and OREMI but housed in a very different type of institution. While a number of sexual-minority advocacy organizations exist within the Dutch Caribbean, including the Women's Way Foundation (Suriname), FOKO and Pink House (Curaçao), and Suriname Men United, in the diaspora such advocacy has recently been undertaken by an organization with a broader mission. Overlegorgaan Caribische Nederlanders, otherwise known as the OCaN Foundation or OCaN, is "the Dutch Consultative Body relating to the integration of Dutch Caribbean citizens in The Netherlands [and] the official interlocutor of the Dutch government on matters relating to integration for Antilleans and Arubans in the Netherlands."[68] It does not officially represent the Netherlands Antilles but is one of "seven individual organisations that conduct talks with the Dutch government on policies concerning ethnic minorities. The government and the collective of organisations have the right to put topics on the agenda. Every organisation promotes the interests of the ethnic minority they represent."[69] As these statements show, OCaN is an NGO that has significant prominence and access to power in the Netherlands. As such, it is notable that OCaN organized the first official Caribbean Dutch presence in the annual

Amsterdam Pride parade, as well as several other events geared towards embracing sexual diversity.

A focus on inclusion and regional identity is clear in OCaN's "Dushi and Proud" activities, including both a 2011 discussion about sexuality in the Caribbean Amsterdam community and the first official Caribbean Dutch boat to participate in Amsterdam Pride that same year. The title is significant; *dushi* means "good" or "sweet" in Papiamento (also spelled *Papiamentu*), a creole spoken in and recognized by the governments of Bonaire, Aruba, and Curaçao, with official status on the latter two islands. The English word *pride* is regularly used by ProGay Amsterdam, the official organizer of Amsterdam Gay Pride (also written in English), and by other LGBT events and organizations in the Netherlands. Thus "Dushi and Proud" uses a uniquely Caribbean language (derived mostly from African, Portuguese, and Spanish influences, with only minor contributions from Dutch, English, and native Caribbean languages) and English to represent a Caribbean diaspora community located in the capital of the Kingdom of the Netherlands. These linguistic choices signify both OCaN's otherness within the Netherlands and its existence within a Caribglobal imaginary community.[70] The phrase proclaims pride both in a specific Caribbean culture and/or heritage, and in nonheterosexual identities or behaviors; like the other Caribbean organizations examined here, OCaN's sexuality-related advocacy insists that sexuality and community should not be conceived of separately; it considers "sexual diversity *in* the Dutch Caribbean community," rather than sexual diversity as separate from that community.[71]

While I want to emphasize the political relevance of groups that organize parties, conversations, limes, and similar activities, I also want to acknowledge that politics is not the only realm in which such activities are important. These groups and their gatherings also represent an ethics of care that prioritizes emotional and moral support over more traditional political activity. Allen writes that everyday, informal, and even unconscious community-building creates "new space, which may become a political organization or a heretical theoretical paradigm, but also may be a new name that defies, reappropriates or refuses old labels, or a complex of acts beyond what is interpolated within prevailing ideologies."[72] Nonheterosexuals within the Caribbean are often criticized by others for not having a movement, for not fighting hard enough or publicly enough for rights privileged by those in Europe and North America. What this actually means is that Caribbean people are being criticized for not having a movement that mimics a Euro-American civil or human rights, identity-based framework and for not replicating tactics used in the United States, Canada, England, France, or the Nertherlands.

This focus on community is counter to the missions of mainstream gay and lesbian organizations in the global North, which tend to focus more on policy work. With over one million members, the Human Rights Campaign (HRC) is a paradigmatic example. HRC describes itself as "America's largest civil rights organization working to achieve lesbian, gay, bisexual and transgender equality," asserting in its mission statement that it "strives to end discrimination against LGBT citizens and realize a nation that achieves fundamental fairness and equality for all" through advocacy strategies in realms such as law, policy (for example, lobbying), public education, outreach, and political elections.[73] Visibility, support, and community are neither words nor concepts that appear in HRC's mission statement. Contrastingly, Saunders argues that Grupo OREMI's politically "inclusive" stance was meant not to focus on the government but rather as "a direct challenge to international discourses that reduce lesbian (and homosexual) marginalization to state repression."[74] HRC and similar large, well-funded institutions in the global North influence international sexuality discourses more than do any of the other organizations mentioned here. But with more local and targeted goals, organizations such as Grupo OREMI and the Women's Caucus can have an important impact in their respective countries, and on individual lives.

Smaller grassroots organizations in the global North that primarily serve immigrants (and their descendants) of color have more in common with Grupo OREMI and The Women's Caucus than with behemoths such as HRC. For instance, the mission statement of Las Buenas Amigas describes the New York-based group as a "Latina Lesbian educational, social/cultural, political, and recreational organization; devoted to the ideal of creating a visible presence in our society, and a unique, safe space in which to address, discuss, inform, act on, and empower ourselves on the issues that affect our community the most (such as homophobia and any and all other forms of oppression)."[75] The mention of visibility, safe spaces, discussion, empowerment, and community mirrors the goals of the Caribbean organizations discussed earlier. However, the mission of multigender and predominantly male sexual-minority advocacy organizations (which in the

Caribbean often are one and the same)[76] tend to differ both from sexual minority advocacy organizations created by and for Caribbean women and multigender/predominantly male organizations in the global North. While the women's organizations focus on community building and support, the predominantly male organizations focus on belonging and coalition strategies.[77] A brief look at the names and mission statements of a few Caribbean and U.S. American sexual-minority advocacy organizations reveals different political priorities.

Mission Statement of Hombres por la Diversidad (HxD):
Nuestra meta es: Promover iniciativas educativas y la implementación de políticas para el reconocimiento y respeto de la libre orientación sexual e identidad de género como derechos humanos.[78] [Our goal is: To promote educational initiatives and policy implementation supporting the recognition and respect for sexual orientation and gender identity freedom as human rights.]

Mission statement for the Coalition Advocating for Inclusion of Sexual Orientation (CAISO):
CAISO aims to educate public decisionmakers about modern understandings of sexual orientation and gender identity, and to help the public embrace the full humanity of Trinidad and Tobago citizens of diverse sexual orientations and gender identities.[79]

Even the names of organizations such as HxD and CAISO demonstrate this focus on coalition strategies, a common strategy in the region which is also seen in the names of organizations such as Suriname Men United, United and Strong (St. Kitts), the Society Against Sexual Orientation Discrimination (SASOD-Guyana), and others. It is also apparent in the case of Puerto Rico's "first gay and lesbian organization," named Comunidad de Orgullo Gay/Gay Pride Community. Both CAISO's and HxD's names clearly point to the organizations' openness to heterosexuals (and to those who choose not to name or identify their sexuality) and imply that involvement does not, ipso facto, mean that one is not heterosexual. Furthermore, neither mission statement refers to a *specific* sexual orientation. While any cursory examination of these groups' activities and affiliations reveals a focus on sexual minorities, their choice of language in their primary documents is one of inclusion, not exclusion. Similarly, while OCaN does not focus exclusively on sexuality, its name and mission clearly reference both the Caribbean and the Netherlands, both the region and the diaspora.[80] The focus on inclusion is reinforced by the fact that CAISO, HxD, and OCaN all prioritize education, which invites those who do not know much about sexuality or gender identity to both learn about related issues and to participate in the organization's activities.

Both CAISO and HxD also make explicit reference to the nation, while OCaN clearly references the Dutch Caribbean subregion. CAISO's mission statement explicitly refers to citizenship and to Trinidad and Tobago, and to promoting a fuller inclusion of sexual minorities into the country's society and culture. In fact, CAISO's acronym invokes national culture, since it references *kaiso*, a colloquial term for calypso music, one of the oldest unique cultural forms in Trinidad and Tobago. While most of HxD's objectives only implicitly focus on Cuba, its fifth objective is, in part, "Investigar y documentar la historia de la diversidad sexual en Cuba" [To investigate and document the history of sexual diversity in Cuba]. In a region where political and religious leaders as well as popular cultural icons have claimed that homosexuality is not indigenous but is imported from the United States or Europe, such a local focus represents an important claim to the contrary.[81]

In fact, *nation* is the primary identity around which Caribbean people have historically organized.[82] This is certainly true for independent states, in which lay citizens and politicians alike proclaim the importance of the nation, proclamations that have recently included dismissing as neocolonial attempts to, for instance, decriminalize sodomy.[83] But nationalism is also a force in the nonindependent Caribbean territories, whether it is a significant contingent advocating for independence, as in Puerto Rico, or whether there is a strong identification with the colonizing country, as in Guadeloupe, or whether the people have largely agreed to an in-between status, as in Aruba, which is a "separate autonomous" entity within the Kingdom of the Netherlands.

It is also significant that Grupo OREMI and the Women's Caucus, as well as the literary texts focus on building and being part of communities and not nation-states. After all, the state is one of the primary entities that codifies heteronormativy and heteropatriarchy. And even though OCaN has a direct relationship with the state of the Netherlands, its activism around sexuality focuses on ethnic and sociocultural community and integration, not integration into the state. And even though CAISO and HxD both invoke the nation, they are not advocating for the existing, restrictive, punitive, and even predatory nation-state. Instead, these organizations are working for a *transformed* nation that is more inclusive of and responsive to all members of its communities.

Interestingly, although there has been a good deal of scholarship that questions the ability and/or willingness of Caribbean nations to conceive of nonheterosexuals as citizens and as legitimate members of the nation, there has been very little written about the desire of sexual minorities to be seen as part of the Caribbean nation.[84] Of course, this kind of progressive homonationalism works to dismantle the nation's attempts to exclude nonheterosexual activities and identities:[85] Allen writes that the Cuban state "has worked hard to curtail any organized identitarian movement in Cuba, which they see as a threat to their socialist and nationalist projects." Similarly, in her groundbreaking work, Jacqui Alexander writes that "Erotic autonomy signals danger to the heterosexual family and to the nation. And because loyalty to the nation as citizen is perennially colonized within reproduction and heterosexuality, erotic autonomy brings with it the potential of undoing the nation entirely, a possible charge of irresponsible citizenship, or no responsibility at all."[86] But via Grupo OREMI, OCaN, CAISO, HxD, SASOD, and other Caribbean organizations, the "threatening" homosexuals simultaneously proclaim their difference *and* their commitment to the vision of a better nation. In these circumstances the organizations implicitly propose a radically different nation, one that retains its pride and culture—but which no longer demonizes, scapegoats, or disappears indigenous same-sex sexuality or those *citizens* who engage in it. It is ironic that so many in the global North consider Caribbean sexual minority activism to be "backwards" when, in fact, Caribbean activists are often proposing nuanced, locally specific, and potentially transformative strategies.

In contrast, mainstream gay and lesbian organizations in the United States focus on single-issue identity politics and specifically on the rights of lesbian, gay, bisexual, and transgender (LGBT) people. According to Negron-Muntaner, "An important ideological difference between Puerto Rico and the US is that in the US . . . one of the foremost political ideologies produced by the gay and lesbian movement is the notion of an identity politics unrelated to class, race and other social determinants."[87] The two largest and most visible organizations advocating for sexual minorities in the United States are the National Gay and Lesbian Task Force (NGLTF), founded in

1973, and the aforementioned Human Rights Campaign (HRC), which was founded in 1980. The first sentence of NGLTF's mission statement focuses on the LGBT community; in fact, the acronym *LGBT* appears three times in four sentences, while the word *nation* appears only once and then is not invoked as an entity that LGBT people are an inherent part of but rather as a benefactor capable of generating (or withholding) respect and generating (or denying) opportunity. The LGBT community is prioritized above all other affiliations and communities. In fact, the sentiments of diversity and respect for everyone, which are prominent in the HxD and CAISO mission statements, appear only in the last sentence of NGLTF's statement.

HRC's rhetoric is more consistently inclusive; its declared goals include "inspiring and engaging all Americans," "increasing public support among all Americans," and "educating Americans." Although the "support" to be increased is presumably support of LGBT concerns, HRC's mission also supports "fundamental fairness and equality for all." Like NGLTF, HRC names the sexual minorities, but HRC's mission explicitly assumes that LGBT people—alternately "LGBT citizens," "LGBT Americans," and "LGBT individuals"—are already part of the nation. But again, the organization's clear priority is helping individuals who identify as (or perhaps are identified by others as) LGBT, in contrast to the preference for coalition and multi-issue work of CAISO, SASOD, and other Caribbean organizations.

Both NGLTF and HRC draw on U.S. identity politics, an organizing strategy in which individuals coalesce around a particular (and necessarily bounded) identity. There is a long—and to a large degree productive—North American history of organizing around identity; even though it is now rather out of favor among U.S. American intellectuals, it is still very frequently used by activists. Gloria Wekker points out that nations in the global North often encourage people in the global South to use the former's sexuality identity markers. She writes that the Dutch state "instructs: if you say, and fashion yourself after the dominant mode of being a lesbian, then that is something we recognize," specifically in the case of applying for political asylum as a lesbian, while the state does not recognize, for instance, identification as a mati or a manroyal.[88] The necessity of such "instruction" emphasizes that a tradition of identity politics does not exist in the Caribbean. Independence and the Caribbean women's movement are the two main political and social justice movements to have taken place in the region during the twentieth century. The first movement was arguably so successful that no subsequent identity can compete with the national one. Even as racial balkanization and heteropatriarchy continue to exist, a strong sense of nationalism tends to pervade all sides of any Caribbean debate.

I point out the differences in these organizations and their mission statements not to criticize any of the institutions, since I assume each accurately represents their purpose.[89] Rather, I wish to reinforce that each organization is responding to the perceived needs of its constituency and all are products of the history, politics, and organizing traditions of their respective countries. The more local and interpersonal approaches should not be seen as "backwards" tactics that will eventually evolve into the "better," more "progressive" or more "political" tactics of larger (and better funded) mainstream organizations. Through OREMI and the Women's Caucus, Caribbean women who desire women can claim social space, create community, and provide support for each other *as Caribbean women*. Similarly, OCaN, HxD and CAISO represent attempts to advocate for sexual minorities not as a separate interest group but as an integral part of the nation.[90] As Allen writes, "exercises of individual agency toward developing *who we are* in changing worlds, despite who we are told we are or *ought* to be—is thus *political* because it challenges the status quo allocation of social and material capital, moving the individual toward improving her or his own felt/lived experience."[91] The very existence of organizations such as OREMI and the Women's Caucus, as well as HxD, CAISO, OCaN, and other regional and diaspora sexual minority advocacy organizations, combats invisibility and contradicts "a developmental, progress narrative of 'gay' identity formation that posits the diaspora as a space of sexual freedom over and against the (home) nation as a space of sexual oppression."[92] By foregrounding being part of a larger national and cultural community, they declare that sexuality is *not* their only focus but must be considered in addition to—and perhaps even looked at through the lens of—those larger communities.

The question of what identity is becomes transformed, Rodríguez points out, as the question of what identity is *for*: "Under what circumstances is it constructed and whose interests does it serve?"[93] OREMI and The Women's Caucus use identity to create space and community *for themselves*, apart from explicit legislative concerns or the agendas of explicitly political organizations. On the other hand, HxD, CAISO, and OCaN encourage people to gather under a goal—the ending of discrimination and the inclusion of sexual minorities as legitimate citizens, respectively—rather than under an identity, thus allowing people to self-identify in a myriad of ways while still coming together for political purposes.

Conclusion: Looking for—and Seeing—the Invisible

Just as we should beware of comparing oranges to apples in terms of advocacy organizations from very different contexts, so must we also beware of reinforcing the myth of lesbian invisibility and an attendant absence of the possibility of agency or pleasure. The difference between invisibility and near-invisibility is much broader than a thin line; the myths of invisibility are perpetuated not only by those who do not see women who desire other women but also by people who disavow or are silent about the women they do see. Dismantling the concept of "invisible" Caribbean women who desire other women requires, in part, attending to who and what is looked for, and to who and what is and is not seen. For instance, trying to identify Caribbean female same-sex desire by looking for overt displays of romantic or erotic affection between women will not yield a lot of results in many Caribbean communities where such displays are rare in public. And even where it is commonplace to see women holding hands, embracing, or laying their heads in each other's laps, these behaviors do not necessarily indicate a sexual, romantic, or erotic relationship. Among the mati of Suriname, even erotic displays of affection between women do not necessarily correspond to sexual identities as they are commonly understood in the global North.

Nor is looking for masculine women a good tactic for finding Caribbean women who desire other women. While those who are gender non-normative are often the most visible sexual transgressors, the norms of gender expression vary greatly across cultures. "Masculinity" and "femininity" function differently in different racial and class communities and in the urban and rural areas of different territories.[94] For instance, a woman smoking a pipe and sitting with her legs spread wide would not necessarily be considered masculine in some parts of the Caribbean. Of course, the concept of "masculine women" does exist in the region; in Jamaica there is even a name for these women—*man royals*. One of Elwin's interviewees remembers such a woman: "She had a husband, he was there, but he was not really there. She wore pants and she ran the bar. There was a sense of strength about her. In North America, people would say she was a closet dyke, but in Jamaica that's a tough woman. A strong woman."[95] And then, man royals do not always desire other women, and not all women who desire other women display masculinity.

The one element shared by all of the fictional texts discussed here is the presence of characters who are made up of many elements. These characters are a mofongo, a pepper pot, a djon-djon, a cook-up—culinary references to the portrayal of characters in such a way that refuses to divide up their identities: nationality here, race here, sexuality there, gender there. Instead, two, three, and sometimes more of these aspects are simultaneously addressed and can often not be picked apart. Because these texts have multiple intertwined themes and portray characters whose complexity is not limited to their sexuality, they might look less "lesbian" and more heteronormative to some. Their sexuality might be seen as invisible when one also has to look at race, nationality, ethnicity, or other aspects of identity. But just because Caribbean female same-sex desire is difficult for some to see does not mean it does not exist.

So how does one see Caribbean women who desire women? The *nearness* of near-invisibility is meant to imply physical proximity as well as a metaphorical not-quiteness. Caribbean women who desire and have sex with other women are in more places, in more bodies, and in more situations than one might think.[96] For those who continue to believe that these women do not exist, the very real participants in organizations such as Grupo OREMI and the Women's Caucus, as well as the Women's Way Foundation (Dutch Antilles), Women for Women (Jamaica), Las Buenas Amigas and SOCA/Sisters of Caribbean Ancestry (both in New York City), and any number of Caribbean multigender organizations, prove them wrong. A growing body of literature—poetry, fiction, and nonfiction; anthropological, sociological, and historical; as well as documentaries such as *T con T* and *Sisters without Misters* also reveal these complex lives. But in order to be convinced that Caribbean women who desire women are not invisible, one has to be willing to see them. Sometimes this entails moving beyond looking *at* to seeing, and moving beyond seeing to acknowledging.

Another type of forced invisibility takes advantage of the fact that Caribbean women who desire women (like Caribbean men who desire men) are less likely to explicitly reveal their sexuality, allowing or encouraging others to choose not to "see" their romantic relationships. As Grenadian

Debbie Douglas noted in an interview, "There is a lack of acknowledgement of the importance of the relationship. So for instance I don't think anybody [would] really say, 'You lesbians, you should be killed.' But people who do know I am in a relationship certainly don't respect that relationship—in terms of feeling that I am free to be picked up, that all I need is a good fuck or that I don't know my mind."[97] As this chapter has shown, the near-invisibility of Caribbean women who desire women is directly linked to systemic sexism and heteropatriarchy and those structures' expectations of women.

Looking, seeing, searching, and *re*searching are not benign activities. We know that the gaze has power. Who and what we look for impacts what we see, but so does *how* we look. We must make sure our gaze on Caribbean women who desire other women and on Caribbean sexual minority advocacy does not reinforce heteropatriarchal or colonial dynamics. And we must be sure that we do not suffer from a myopia that will prevent us from seeing desire between women, whether or not it fits easily into definitions of lesbianism or queerness. Because while near-invisibility does not eliminate agency, it does not promote it either; too often it promotes isolation, fear, and self-loathing. As Silvera notes, denial is a main barrier to visibility, so acknowledging the past existence and the current presence of Caribbean women who desire women in the region is key to eliminating the myth of invisibility. As we look at Caribbean women and their lives and desires, we must be willing to see and respect a range of experiences, or very real lives and bodies will continue to suffer the consequences.

4

"Force-Ripe"

Caribbean Women's Sexual Agency

"Force-ripe" is a colloquial English Caribbean phrase that refers to fruit picked before it is ripe and then forced to ripen early. It is also commonly used to sneer at girls who dress or behave as mature women, usually in a manner perceived as sexual. The likening of women to fruit—ripe or spoiled—is also found in other parts of the Caribbean. For instance, Judith Ortiz Cofer remembers that when she, as a teenager, resisted a white boy's kiss, he said, "in a resentful tone: 'I thought you Latin girls were supposed to mature early'—my first instance of being thought of as a fruit or vegetable—I was supposed to ripen, not just grow into womanhood like other girls."[1] "Force-ripe" is thus an appropriate phrase to use when discussing portrayals of Caribbean women's sexual agency and the sometimes hostile reactions to that work.

While the activism and creative production of Caribbean women who desire women largely insist (contrary to many others' beliefs) that these women are part of their respective Caribbean communities, heterosexual Caribbean women tend to use different strategies in their portrayals of sexual agency. Heterosexual Caribbean women, like all women and men, are subject to strict gender codes. Yet women who have a conventional sexuality and gender presentation can take for granted their inclusion (however problematic) in their community and nation. Caribbean literature that focuses on heterosexual women's sexual agency—including *Lucy* by Jamaica Kincaid (Antigua), *Heremakhonon* by Maryse Condé (Guadeloupe), and *The House of Six Doors* by Patricia Selbert (Curaçao)—often portrays women who reject a range of Caribbean cultural expectations, including traditional gender mores. In popular music, however, the rejection of gender expectations functions within quintessential Caribbean musical forms. Caribbean "Queens" Jocelyne Béroard of zouk, Drupatee Ramgoonai of chutney, Ivy Queen of reggaeton, Alison Hinds of soca, and Rihanna of Top 40 pop music—women at the forefront of their respective musical genres—largely portray women's sexual agency not as a battle or even a question but as a fact. And because such "facts" are presented within a familiar—and danceable—form, their transgressive nature has not diminished the Queens' popularity among Caribbean women and men.

Agency figures in all of the sexual transgressions discussed in *Island Bodies*. But the concept takes on heightened significance for heterosexual Caribbean women because their gender identity and sexual orientation are not inherently transgressive within Caribglobal societies. I use *sexual agency* here to describe the activity of women voicing, advocating for, and/or pursuing control of their own sexuality or erotic pleasure on their own terms. The inclusion of pleasure is key to sexual agency because women's sexuality is traditionally mandated to be in service of men, procreation, and the nation. Agency can take many forms, including engaging in extramarital or nonmonogamous sex, initiating sex, determining whether or not to have sex and under what circumstances, deciding what kind of sex to have, or displaying desire. As will be seen in the music and novels examined here, sometimes the goal of agency is to defy the expectations of family or culture and to discover and claim one's own sense of self or identity. And while women's sexual pleasure is itself not necessarily culturally proscribed, the *public expression* of female desire is prohibited by heteropatriarchy in the Caribbean and elsewhere. Thus, women are expected to express desire only with the man with whom they have a monogamous (and preferably marital) relationship. Women who publicly reveal or express their sexual desires— to parents or other family or community members—risk being labeled a *whore, puta, putain, jamette, slut, Marilisse,* or *force-ripe.*

I agree with critic Donette Francis (whose concept of antiromance will be returned to in this chapter's conclusion) that "agency is not a fixed destination to which one arrives with the originating act forever completed, but rather it is a continuous series of maneuvers to be enacted and reenacted."[2] The literature and music examined in this chapter also support this view, portraying women who are in the process of becoming and who live complicated and often contradictory lives, rather than women who have resolved all of their internal and communal conflicts. This chapter focuses primarily on *Caribbean* gender norms and expectations rather than on stereotypes from the global North. It describes the Caribglobal *cult of true oomanhood*, a set of restrictive gender codes for women and girls found throughout the region and its diaspora. I then describe cultural traditions found in specific ethnic groups or nationalities as examples of Caribbean cultural forms that differ substantially from European Victorian morals but that typically still support heteropatriarchy. The novels by Condé, Kincaid, and Selbert, along with music by Queens Béroard, Drupatee, Ivy Queen, Hinds, and Rihanna are examined. A brief analysis of the song "Faluma" addresses the transgression of same-sex desire among Caribbean women. In these literary and aural texts, sexual agency can help a woman consolidate and/or evolve her own identity and can help create community with other women, especially those who are maligned because of class, race, or color and those willing to publicly exhibit sexual agency and/or desire.

The "Cult of True Oomanhood"

"The cult of true womanhood" refers to the definitions and expectations of ideal European women in the nineteenth century, specifically "four cardinal virtues—piety, purity, submissiveness, and domesticity."[3] The word *cult* belies the madness and unattainability of the ideal.[4] I use the phrase "cult of true oomanhood"—since *ooman* is how *woman* is commonly pronounced in slang in Jamaica and elsewhere in the Anglophone Caribbean—to refer to the Caribglobal manifestation of gender expectations found across ethnicities and cultures throughout the region and its diaspora. The ideal Caribbean woman, with her histories of slavery, indentureship, colonialism, and pervasive poverty, differs from the woman idealized in the original cult in more than geography. In the Caribbean context, piety is a plus but not a requirement and is not restricted to Christianity. Sexual purity in the Caribbean includes serial monogamy and cohabitation, as well as marriage. Domesticity endures as an ideal, though women working and socializing outside of the home are neither unusual nor scandalous. Similarly, Caribbean women are expected and preferred to be submissive to their male partners and to male authority—when the man shares their race and class. Both cults have been endorsed by men and women and also have been resisted by many in many different ways, including the portrayals and advocacy of Caribbean women's sexual agency seen in the literature and music examined here. The cult of true oomanhood is not the only structure that governs Caribglobal femininity, and I will shortly discuss matikor, kwe-kwe, and carnival, three Caribbean traditions not derived from European cultures that impact specific gender expectations. Nevertheless, the roles and behavior most often attributed to "proper" women in Caribbean laws and media and by Caribbean political, religious, and cultural leaders typically correspond to the tenets of the cult of true oomanhood.

As is discussed in chapter 2, which explains the unofficial-official gender codes for Caribbean men, for Caribbean women "the work of socialization is collective."[5] In Caribglobal cultures, women are generally "marginalized, scorned, and disrespected as loose women within local cultural logic if they appear explicitly sexual and engaged in multiple sexual relationships, without this being attached to procreation and economic needs of the family."[6] Single women, or women whose sexuality is independent of men, have been "defined as lasciviously deviant—'good women' were constructed as sexual for procreative purposes and as sexual servants to men."[7] Women's sexuality also figures prominently in Caribbean nationalism, which similarly prescribes "female sexual containment through compulsory heterosexuality, marriage and motherhood."[8] And as "disciplining the body is at the heart of bourgeois nationalist projects," women's sexuality in the Caribbean is often connected to class and respect.[9] And Kamala Kempadoo explains that for "middle-class colored and black women" in the era of Caribbean independence, "marriage and legitimacy became an obsession as they sought respectability for their families. They vociferously denounced what they saw as the promiscuity and immorality of the lower classes and pronounced proper family life increasingly based on western patterns of faithful marriage, legitimate children and nuclear family households."[10] As will be seen in the literature examined in this chapter, public revelation or acknowledgement of erotic desire can be considered transgressive and can place women outside of middle-class norms. For instance, in Martinique "any woman who *does* freely express her desire for a man in public contexts risks being accused of loose, promiscuous behavior by both men and women."[11]

In Indo-Caribbean communities, the cult of true oomanhood often appeals to an ideal Indian heritage, specifically "the perception of Indian women as passive, docile, and subservient to men" that has existed both within and outside of Indo-Caribbean communities.[12] Indo-Caribbean families are also traditionally "organized around the notion of respect, which is deeply embedded in Indian thought," though, as in other cultures, expectations of respect and modesty have primarily been aimed at women. As Thomas Eriksen writes, "great value is placed on purity in women, and the sacred character of matrimony is emphasized" in Indo-Caribbean communities.[13] Peter Manuel's research also found that while Indo-Caribbean men's behavior is rarely curtailed, "it is women who are expected to maintain ideals of family honour and modesty."[14]

When scholars discuss gender roles in the Spanish Caribbean, they typically focus on men and machismo. However, not only does machismo have implications for women, scholars have also increasingly described marianismo as the female correlate of machismo determining women's gender roles. The structure of machismo typically includes "support of the traditional female role of sexual submissiveness, virginity until marriage, and female responsibility for child rearing and nonfinancial household maintenance."[15] In other words, a macho man must be surrounded by a particular type of woman. On the other hand, marianismo specifically focuses on expectations of women. The term is "derived from the name María, or Mary, the mother of Jesus Christ." It includes the tenets of "virginity, chastity, honor and shame, the ability to suffer and willingness to serve" and usually includes tolerance of male infidelity or promiscuity.[16] Marianismo is closely related to another ideal professed throughout the Caribbean, the identification of the "street" or public life with men, and the home or private life with women. For instance, in de Moya's interviews with Dominican men, the interviewees described their "ideal partner" as a "dama en la calle, cuero en la cama y chopa en la casa" (a lady in the streets, a nymphet in bed and a servant at home)."[17]

Rosemary Brana-Shute similarly found in the early 1990s that among women in Suriname being respectable is a key element of women's reputation. As she notes in "Neighbourhood Networks and National Politics among Working-Class Afro-Surinamese Women," being considered "respectable" means that a woman "is recognized as [being] courteous, cooperative, trustworthy and as leading a scandal-free life. The latter is not correlated with being legally married; so long as she is not regarded as promiscuous, the civil status of her intimate relationship[s] is not an issue."[18] And Puerto Rican Ortiz Cofer recalls that when she was a girl, she "was kept under strict surveillance, since virtue and modesty were, by cultural equation, the same as family honor."[19]

Even though they are specifically prescribed for Caribbean women, as with its Victorian precedent, the requirements of the cult of true ooman-hood are largely unattainable and contradict the lived realities of Caribbean women. For example, studies from the first decade of the twenty-first century estimate that 31–59 percent of all Caribbean children live in female-headed households; that number is close to 50 percent in Jamaica and Barbados.[20] Derby notes that typical family structures in the Dominican Republic include "concubinage, serial unions, female-headed households, [and] de facto polygyny," and Kamala Kempadoo notes that "informal polygyny" is "the social norm and is firmly embedded in Caribbean societies."[21] And despite a cultural focus on monogamy and procreation, Kempadoo's study of adolescent girls in the region found that most had sex first for money and second for pleasure.[22] Nevertheless, heterosexual, monogamous, conjugal families remain the Caribglobal ideal, and women's sexual agency "signals danger to respectability" and thus threatens conventional notions of the Caribbean family and nation.[23]

Other Structures Governing Caribbean Gender

Although the cult of true oomanhood dominates scholarly and popular understandings of Caribbean women's appropriate roles and behavior, as Surinamese researcher Gloria Wekker writes, "we should remain careful with assuming that the geologies of sexual subjectivity in a female African diasporic context are the same as those constructed in Western contexts."[24] Nationally and ethnically specific phenomena exist that provide other expectations of Caribbean women's roles and behavior, sometimes more liberal and sometimes restrictive in different ways from the cult of true oomanhood. Significant examples of these traditions are matikor, kwe-kwe, and carnival.

Matikor is an exclusively female ceremony held before a Hindu wedding and encompassing dance, song, stories, and advice.[25] It was brought to the Caribbean by indentured Indians in the nineteenth century and is still performed today in Suriname, Trinidad, and Guyana. Musicologist Peter Manuel provides a detailed description of a matikor ceremony:

With the [male] drummers standing at a discreet distance and looking away, the women sing lewd songs and perform whimsically erotic
dances, perhaps using an aubergine (eggplant) to imitate a phallus
or inserting a pillow in their blouse to look pregnant. Similar singing and dancing by women may also occur on the festive 'cooking
night' preceding the wedding day, and immediately after the wedding
itself. Women also sing ribald songs behind closed doors after the tur-
meric anointment of the bride, along with similarly erotic songs (for
instance, *chatni sohar*) in private *chatthi* and *barhi* childbirth celebrations in which they would accompany themselves on dholak (drum)
or by tapping two coins on a brass plate.[26]

Bergman's more recent research confirms Manuel's description, adding that
the purpose of the ceremony is both to encourage the new couple's fertility
and "to educate the bride about the sexual act."[27] Although the latter goal
does represent "women's assertion of their independent sexuality and resistance to control," the former goal—a successful marriage via procreation—
implies that we cannot assume matikor does not also provide a way for
women to perpetuate heteropatriarchy through modeling ideal sexuality.[28]
Indeed, at least one scholar notes that matikor "presented no lasting threat"
to gendered hegemonies because it "remained under the supervision of the
male social managers."[29] More research must be done on the specific mores
promoted in matikor and on any emphases on female and/or male pleasure
in order to have a better understanding of the role this ceremony plays in
Hindu Caribbean women's culture.

Kwe-Kwe (also spelled *queh-queh*) is a premarriage ceremony performed
in Guyana before the union "of a couple at least one of whom is an Afro-
Guyanese."[30] Though it is "an in-group, non-public activity" and a largely
working-class phenomenon like matikor, kwe-kwe differs in several respects
from the Hindu tradition; both men and women participate in kwe-kwe, and
many Guyanese dismiss the former as "vulgar" or "indecent."[31] The primary
components of all-night kwe-kwe ceremonies are the hiding and discovery
of the bride, the "ritual 'buying' of the bride," and a ring song and dance
with sexually instructive and explicit lyrics.[32] Typically, the groom and his
friends and family will travel for a kwe-kwe to the bride's home, where she
will be either hiding or in disguise—portraying, according to Edwards, "a
sexually-approved role—that of the reluctant bride"[33] The "buying" of the

bride (found in many other traditions) consists of guests pinning money to the bride's clothing. Finally, those present will participate for hours in a ring-dance, accompanied by one to three live musicians who play a basic rhythm for call-and-response songs that suggest appropriate behavior for the couple's future life. Examples of such songs include "Wash Yu Bembe," (referring to female genitalia) "Maloni Board Am" [Mount her], and "Show Me Yu Science."

In kwe-kwe we see the same ambivalence towards sexual transgression found in matikor. Rohlehr argues that this tradition "suggests that under the heavy overlay of puritanical prudery that has been part of Caribbean male and female socialization lay, and perhaps still may lie, an openness of acceptance [of bodies and eroticism] deeper than the ethic of decency about respectability that controlled both sexuality itself and discourse about it."[34] Nevertheless, though some songs promote women's knowledge of and pleasure in sex, as a whole, kwe-kwe reinforces heteropatriarchy through advocating that men should be workers outside of the home and that women should be homemakers, child-bearers, and child-rearers.[35]

While a majority of Caribbean territories have some kind of annual carnival, as is discussed in chapter 1, many of these were created in the twentieth century to resemble Trinidadian carnival and to attract tourists. The largest, most imitated, and one of the oldest festivals in the region, Trinidadian carnival has a long history of sexually suggestive characters and sexually explicit behavior. In addition to the trans characters discussed in this book's first chapter, nineteenth-century Trinidadian carnival included women dressed as men and near-naked men. Of course, one of the most persistent sexual explicitness of Trinidadian carnival, still obvious today, is found in the double entendre lyrics of the music associated with the festival, and in wining, the dance that most often accompanies this music.[36] Over the last 150 years, legal and cultural restrictions have successively excluded carnival participation by colonial white women, Afro-Trinidadians, and Indo-Trinidadians. Though carnival became dominated by Afro-Trinidadians in the twentieth century, in the twenty-first century the event has become increasingly diverse, and the presence of both misogynist and empowering lyrics is part of that diversity.

Although the Caribbean traditions of matikor, kwe-kwe, and carnival are not always less heteropatriarchal or restrictive than the cult of true oomanhood, each acknowledges women as active participants in their own sexuality, which allows for at least the possibility of women's agency and pleasure in particular contexts. These cultural practices also reveal persistent Caribbean traditions not rooted in Christian or Victorian European morality. And as the rest of this chapter details, these traditions resonate in both Caribglobal literature and culture. Nevertheless, women's sexual agency largely remains transgressive outside of ritual spaces. Thus, as will be seen in the literature and music discussed below, those seeking to constrain Caribbean women's sexuality may appeal to broad notions of true oomanhood as well as other, more specific cultural expectations.

Women's Sexual Agency in Caribbean Literature

Since the term "force-ripe" addresses the "inappropriate" transition between girlhood and womanhood, the bildungsroman is an appropriate genre through which to explore Caribbean women's transgressive sexual agency. The bildungsroman is literally a novel of "education" and, more informally, a coming-of-age story. Judith Halberstam notes that "If adolescence for boys represents a rite of passage (much celebrated in Western literature in the form of the bildungsroman), and an ascension to some version (however attenuated) of social power, for girls, adolescence is a lesson in restraint, punishment, and repression."[37] This is also true in the Caribbean, where the bildungsroman has become a popular, even paradigmatic form that men authors such as George Lamming (Barbados), Joseph Zobel (Martinique), René Marqués (Puerto Rico), and V. S. Naipaul (Trinidad and Tobago) have used to connect individuals' coming of age to national independence and development, in particular through formal education, often outside of the colony, as preparation for leadership. In fiction by Caribbean women, however, the bildungsroman form highlights different experiences. Significant attention is often given to sexual maturation and sexual activity, with the former representing transition into adulthood and *womanhood*, and the latter often signifying rebellion against traditional conservative Caribbean upbringings and expectations.

   Lucy and *Heremakhonon* are coming-of-age novels by two of the most revered living Caribbean women writers, Jamaica Kincaid and Maryse Condé, respectively. Both books are considered classics. The third novel examined here, *The House of Six Doors* by Patricia Selbert, is a valuable but virtually unknown book from the Dutch Caribbean diaspora. All three novels are explicit about the authors' opinions of the gendered moral expectations of their novels' middle-class or aspiring middle-class Caribbean communities. The morals explicitly imparted to Caribbean girls are decidedly conservative, proscribing sex before marriage and extramarital sex. And, yet, implicitly they receive messages that are more mixed, especially those conveyed through the behavior of Caribbean men. All of these works portray characters who consider sex an important, even primary, component of their rebellion against Caribbean morality and specifically against their families. In Caribbean literature, the young women who embrace sexual agency do so precisely because their behavior departs from traditional gender expectations. Often this agency is not limited to sexuality but also contributes to the consolidation of an adult identity and is linked to power or agency in other areas, such as independence from one's family or the ability to choose one's profession. The young women in these novels often discover, however, that sex alone cannot liberate them from a restrictive society and that they have a greater affinity for their Caribbean culture than they had realized.

Lucy

Many of Jamaica Kincaid's texts engage the cult of true oomanhood through their portrayals of mothers' obsession with sexual purity, which of course corresponds with and inspires an obsession with sexual "impurity." Her 1990 novel *Lucy* explores these issues in detail through a young Caribbean woman's first year in the United States as an au pair for a well-off family in New York City. The novel is set in the late twentieth century and focuses on Lucy's project of self-development through distancing herself from the cult of true oomanhood, her Caribbean homeland, her mother, and from all they represent.

The title character describes her family's and society's hopes and expectations of her as follows: "I had been a girl of whom certain things were expected, none of them too bad: a career as a nurse, for example; a sense of duty to my parents; obedience to the law and worship of convention." A major aspect of that "convention" is not to engage in premarital sexual activity. Lucy declares that her "whole upbringing had been devoted to preventing [her] from becoming a slut" and that she had thought erotic and sexual pleasure were "unavailable" to her until she actually experienced them. In fact, the career path and moral standards Lucy is expected to follow are in large part determined by her gender. She bitterly describes how she "came to hate" her mother: while Lucy is expected to be a nurse, her parents—"with great seriousness"—plan for her brothers to "go to university in England and study to become a doctor or lawyer or someone who would occupy an important and influential position in society." According to Lucy, there are "no accompanying scenarios" expected or even conceived of for her.[38] While Lucy's brothers are expected to economically and socially achieve more than she does, *less* is expected of them in the area of sexual morality. Lucy explains, "Where I came from, it was well known that some women and *all men in general* could not be trusted in certain areas. My father had perhaps thirty children; he did not know for sure."[39] Men's sexual *irresponsibility* is expected and encouraged to the point where Lucy's father does not even keep track of his dozens of offspring, nor feel any remorse or shame for this fact.

Lucy's first section, "Poor Visitor," focuses on the protagonist's arrival in a large city in the United States and on how strange much of the place and the things in it are to her, including the white American family she works for and their home. This oddness, the difference from her life in the Caribbean, pleases Lucy—an emotional reaction that also relates to her sex life. Once she arrives in the United States, Lucy begins to *systematically* distance herself from her mother, her society, her island, and their morals and ideals. Her most marked departure from her upbringing is in the realm of sexual morals, closely connected to her resentment of her mother, who imparted those morals. Lucy voices three main complaints of her unnamed mother: that her mother's love "was designed solely to make [her] into an echo of" the mother, that Lucy's "whole upbringing had been devoted to preventing [her] from becoming a slut," and that there was a vast difference in the upbringing of her and her brothers.[40] Having sex allows Lucy to address all three of these complaints; it distances her from her apparently chaste mother, links her to the "slut" figure her mother abhors, and reduces the distance between the conservative morals projected onto Lucy and the license allowed for her brothers' (and father's) sexual behavior and life possibilities.

Sexual agency is explicitly linked to a rejection of Lucy's family and community's morality. When discussing "the first time [she] did everything you can do with a boy," Lucy comments that she "did not care about being a virgin and had long been looking forward to the day when [she] could rid [her]self of that status."[41] This statement implies, in fact, that she followed the mandate of remaining a virgin involuntarily and only for lack of opportunity. That no longer being a virgin was as important to Lucy as her remaining a virgin is to her mother clarifies Lucy's interest in using sexual agency to rebel against those morals, and that her rebellion did not begin when she left the Caribbean. On the contrary, her rejection of the cult of true oomanhood seems to have begun from the time she was indoctrinated into it, and only came to full fruition in her self-imposed exile.

In the United States, Lucy is eager to increase the number and variety of her sexual experiences and later to have her mother know about them as well via her letters to the Caribbean. She has sex with men whenever the opportunity and her desire coincide. After a few weeks in the United States, she thinks, "almost everything I did now was something I had never done before, and so the new was no longer thrilling to me unless it reminded me of the past."[42] Sex reminds her of the past because it rejects her mother's lessons, lectures, and moral code, and Lucy becomes aware of her body, both "as a source of resistance and of sexual pleasure," notes Mahlis.[43] In fact, the physical pleasure of sex frequently surprises Lucy because she remarks that "I had not known that such pleasure could exist and, what was more, *be available to me*."[44] This link between not being able to conceive of the heights of sexual pleasure and not knowing she could have access to such pleasure mirrors the link between both aspects of Lucy's sexual agency; her pleasure in her sexual life and her pleasure at the departure that life represents from her Caribbean mother and upbringing.

In an effort to liberate herself by breaking the intense bonds with her family, culture, and society, some time later Lucy sends a letter that even she finds shockingly cold. She writes to her mother:

> I said she had acted like a saint, but that since I was living in this real world I had really wanted just a mother. I reminded her that my whole upbringing had been devoted to preventing me from becoming a slut; I then gave a brief description of my personal life, offering each detail as evidence that my upbringing had been a failure and that, in fact, life as a slut was quite enjoyable, thank you very much.[45]

With this letter and its details, she seeks to seal her rebellion by revealing her sexuality, thereby betraying her mother and her culture and repaying some of the pain Lucy continues to feel at the mother's preferential treatment of her sons. This letter is, nevertheless, a somewhat ambiguous message, since she sends it with a great deal of money. The mother writes back, "No matter what you do, you will always be my daughter," attempting to reinforce the control she has over Lucy and forcing the daughter to choose between reconciliation and a further, even more extreme break. Lucy chooses the latter, refusing to communicate at all with her mother and eventually moving and providing an incorrect address so that her mother cannot effectively communicate with her.

At the end of the novel, Lucy's life represents progress to her; through sexual agency and travel she has successfully avoided walking the paths chosen for her and she has the self-confidence to declare, "I knew that I never wanted to live in that place [the Caribbean] again, but if for some reason I was forced to live there again, I would never accept the harsh judgments made against me by people whose only power to do so was that they had known me from the moment I was born."[46] Lucy thus declares herself free of her home society's moral strictures *and* from its moral authority over her choices, should she ever return there. And yet declaring oneself to be free and *being* free are different conditions, and even after cutting off her mother Lucy finds that much in her new life reminds her of her old one, of the people and places from which she comes. The novel ends not with a neat conclusion but with her moving beyond sexuality to explore yet more new experiences, including living on her own rather than as an au pair.

Heremakhonon

In contrast to Kincaid's protagonist, who professes complete control over her sexuality, Maryse Condé's Veronica in *Heremakhonon*[47] is frequently confused by her own choices and conflicted about what motivates them, a state reflected in the novel's stream-of-consciousness style. Nevertheless, it becomes clear that in this novel too, a young woman uses sexual agency to try to differentiate herself from the gendered expectations of her Caribbean community. Even though Veronica is postadolescent at the start of the novel, she is still trying to find herself, still literally in bildung, in "formation." While Lucy waits until she is outside of the Caribbean to reveal her sexual activity, Veronica is discovered *in flagrante delicto* with her mulatto lover, Jean-Marie, in Guadeloupe. She is shunned by the larger Caribbean society for having extramarital sex, and she is shunned by her family both for the sex and because her lover is not black. This series of events becomes a cycle of Veronica's sexual behavior causing social rejection in a novel that includes explicitly sexual language "rare in Afro-Caribbean women's writing" at the time it was published.[48]

Despite her protests and having already become a social outcast, her family exiles Veronica from the Caribbean. Soon after the affair is revealed she "left by plane . . . Jean-Marie got married shortly afterwards . . . I passed my baccalaureate with distinction in Paris, but the one did not rule out the other [the affair]. They felt I ought not to go back." Veronica's educational achievements do not cancel out her sexual indiscretions, which have permanently marked her as a "whore" and a race-traitor, a "Marilisse."[49]

Veronica lives for a time in Paris and has an affair with a white Frenchman there. Later, in the unnamed African country Veronica goes to as a university lecturer, she begins her third and final affair of the novel. This time her partner is an African government minister—handsome, wealthy, very powerful, and very dark-skinned. In these traits Veronica and the reader discover that what she truly seeks in all of her sexual partners is vicarious personal freedom.[50] She reflects that "I now realize why he fascinates me. He hasn't been branded" by a history of slavery.[51] Ibrahima Sory's history and power make him completely free in Veronica's eyes, free to pursue his own desires, including her, as he wishes. The other African men she meets are beholden to their families or to the bourgeoning political revolution.

Veronica's revelation about her relationship with Ibrahima also explains her other sexual and romantic choices. In every circumstance, Veronica chooses the man whom she perceives to be the most free. Regarding her first affair, she protests that her attraction to him "Wasn't his color, I swear. That's what they all said because, naturally, they could not think of anything else. No, it was his freedom." This is a freedom that Guadeloupian society has granted him because of his skin color, gender, and wealth. Similarly, she notes that the Frenchman Jean-Michel has "the quality I prize most in others, probably because I lack it so terribly. He's at ease with himself."[52] The women around her—in particular her frail mother and domesticated sisters—are paragons of the cult of true oomanhood, but this is not a path that interests Veronica. She is compelled to seek out another path, and because it contradicts gender expectations, she must do so without familial or communal support. To overcome her own sense of inferiority as a dark-skinned female, she seeks out men who have a secure sense of self and appear to be free of the type of cultural mores that have made Veronica's life difficult. The fact that each of these men has more social status and power than Veronica does serves metaphorically (with Jean-Marie and Jean-Michel) and in actuality (with Ibrahima) to elevate her own social status. Others' consistent condemnation of Veronica for her choice of sexual partners only reinforces her feelings of confinement and makes her think that sex with these men itself can constitute freedom.

After being criticized again for sleeping with Ibrahima, Veronica laments, "Why is it that no matter what I do they throw stones at me? They try to destroy me?" And then, "I want to know why, without fail, my conduct is to blame. With Jean-Marie—I was called Marilisse. With Jean-Michel, too—especially Jean-Michel . . . What are they going to invent now to stop me from making love in peace?"[53] But the fact that she has been sleeping with a corrupt, decadent official is not "invented." Veronica continues to be socially rejected because she continues to choose men whom her community deems unsuitable. And she continues to be socially maligned because her communities—correctly—perceive her sexual choices as rejections of them and of existing gender codes. This quote also hints at cultural double standards seen in *Lucy*; in both the Caribbean and African countries where *Heremakhonon* is set, Veronica is punished and ostracized for her sexual agency while her male partners suffer little or no social approbation. Society would let Veronica "make love in peace" if she would do so with a black man to whom she is married.

Though Veronica physically enjoys her affairs, they do not provide freedom from her own insecurities. Perhaps the novel's greatest irony is the very fact that she seeks "freedom" from her culture, since differentiation through transgressive sex demonstrates an enduring preoccupation with the society and mores she flouts. She wants to be free *like* men, instead of being free *from* the system that places men over women. Furthermore, because sexual agency is the only type of agency she uses, she effectively acts as though her freedom can only be found between and through the arms (and legs) of a man. While her willingness to flout gender expectations demonstrates agency, in the end it is not enough to fulfill her. She eventually recognizes this: "In fact, I'm not escaping from anything. Through Ibrahima Sory I'm trying to get back to them [her family] on an idealized level . . . To sum up, I'm not trying to escape them. But to justify myself," to distance herself from the gender expectations of her family and community.[54] The already tense political situation in the African country deteriorates, and two of her friends are caught up in the government's—in Ibrahima's—crackdown. After a time, Veronica realizes that even though she is not in her birth country, she has become part of a community and is no longer able to pursue her own pleasure and search for self without regard for others' wellbeing or for how her lover is implicated in the increasing oppression and violence. She has come to care for the people she meets in this unnamed country, and with that care comes a sense of obligation, if not responsibility. These feelings are what in the end cause her to leave Africa after her friend Saliou, a student dissident, is killed by the government. Just before departing, Veronica refuses a drink, saying "I want to leave with my head clear. Fully conscious of what I'm doing. It's nothing rash. It's not a spur-of-the-moment decision. I've understood. *Understood.* I must leave if I want to maintain a semblance of respect. Because there is a level below which one must not go." This scene demonstrates a growing maturity. Before, when the world around her was too painful or depressing, she would feel the need for either "a double scotch or a man." But here she refuses both and does not abandon herself to physical pleasure. Earlier she had scoffed that "If I understand correctly making love in this country comes down to making a political choice." But by the end of the novel she has realized that all sexual choices are also political choices. She thinks to herself, "I'm leaving because it would be too easy to stay. If I stayed, nothing would change between us. I'd continue to shuttle back and forth between Heremakhonon [their love nest] and the town." At the end of the novel, she concludes, "I looked for myself in the wrong place. In the arms of an assassin."[55] In utilizing sexual agency to end her affair with Ibrahima, Veronica realizes that sex is neither the only nor the best site for her own self-development. Although her journey of self-discovery is far from over, she is unlikely to repeat the cycle of identifying her own freedom with that of the man she is sleeping with.

The House of Six Doors

In *The House of Six Doors*, a little-known novel by Curaçaoan Patricia Selbert, we see another example of how the relative sexual "freedom" of diaspora can be negative as well as positive and how the cult of true oomanhood can drive a wedge between mothers and daughters. In 1972, sisters Serena and Hendrika move away from Curaçao and the stability of their grandmother to the United States with their mother, Gabriela, a little money and no preparation for their new life in a new country, a different language, and a racial system that classifies their light skin as white or Latin, depending on what language they are speaking. The mother's "plan" is that she will work as a nurse while her daughters become movie stars. Although they are old enough to see the problems with her plan, the sisters stay quiet, having witnessed the mother's severe mood swings and multiple suicide attempts when she was contradicted or when events did not go her way. Each daughter claims sexual agency in ways that have significant but very different ramifications for their bildung, their formation into mature adults.

Not surprisingly, the family's situation deteriorates rapidly. Gabriela's California nursing license is not valid in Florida and, at any rate, has expired. They buy a second-hand car and drive to California, living off of canned corn and beans, Coca-Cola, and cigarettes. When they reach Hollywood, they have so little money left that they must sleep in their car. After looking in the classifieds, Gabriela thinks that "dancing" will be an easy way to make money until she can renew her nursing license; after all, she can rumba and salsa. Of course, that is not the kind of dancing that night clubs are looking for. The mother initially balks when the manager gruffly explains that he can "use" the sisters but not Gabriela, paying them ten dollars per night clothed or twenty dollars per night topless. The prospect is unappetizing, but they have less than fifty dollars left to their name and not a lot of choices. Hendrika says she will take the job, and from the backseat Serena observes that "Hendrika was begging Mama to let her dance, something she did not want to do. Mama did not want Hendrika to dance, but she wouldn't stop her."[56] After insisting that Hendrika will only dance clothed, Gabriela does not acknowledge the nature of the work and pretends it will help her daughter's acting career, which is itself a fantasy. In this instance it is the mother who indirectly causes the daughter to become "force-ripe."

Hendrika dances for several weeks, until the family can finally afford an apartment and Gabriela has begun to work. During that time, Hendrika returns to the car increasingly smelling of cigarettes and alcohol and becoming more and more distant from her sister. Hendrika looks for other work, but though she is a high school graduate, she only has access to backbreaking labor at less than the minimum wage because she is an undocumented immigrant. Horrified by this downward mobility and by work options she believes are below their class, Gabriela instead makes Hendrika the unpaid and unacknowledged laborer for their small family. She is the driver, cook, maid, and laundress while the mother is at work and Serena is at school. Gabriela pays for Hendrika's acting "lessons" from a shady agent and expects her to become an overnight star while rarely uttering a kind word to either of her daughters. Not surprisingly, Serena discovers that her sister has begun smoking marijuana. In a fit of anger over yet another unfair insult from her mother, Hendrika reveals how she really fed their family: "I earned that money. I danced topless for it because you couldn't earn anything. . . . You are the one who is irresponsible, taking us to a country you know nothing about."[57] The mother accuses Hendrika of lying and is unable or willing to console her, while the younger Serena is bewildered and does not know what to do or say. Thus even after this difficult revelation, Hendrika has to process these events alone, and she withdraws even further from her family.

Soon after this incident, Hendrika is arrested for possession of marijuana and subsequently deported. Hendrika claimed a sexual agency she did not want, and her family was not able to help her cope with or understand her experiences. Back in Curaçao, Hendrika eventually develops a full-blown cocaine addiction, and the text provides little hope for her recovery. Hendrika becomes for Serena—and the reader—a cautionary tale about familial sacrifice. Serena declares: "I wasn't going to pretend to be someone I wasn't—Hendrika had done that and it had destroyed her," though it takes her some time to fully realize that promise to herself.[58]

While Hendrika is exploring drugs, Serena is exploring love and sex, and the two sisters keep each other's secrets from their mother. Serena had already been lying to her mother about school (where she struggles because she barely speaks English); it is an easy decision to hide her bourgeoning sexuality. Unlike her emotionally abusive mother and her emotionally absent sister, Serena's Romanian boyfriend Sandu makes her feel beautiful, cherished, and loved. When Serena becomes pregnant, Sandu is willing to marry her immediately, but Serena cannot bear to disappoint her mother in such a profound way, so she insists on an abortion.

Both Serena's abortion and Hendrika's topless dancing are their own individual choices, but because they are made under duress, they are not positive examples of agency. Though their mother does not know about the choices at the time, she is the overriding determinant for what her daughters do. Even though their mother profoundly fails to protect them, they both use their bodies to protect her. Although Hendrika remains lost, Serena is eventually able to combine sexual and emotional maturity into a strong individual identity. As in the other texts, the revelation of premarital sexual activity to a parent is a transformative sign of agency. Serena is in a relationship with Sandu for four years before she tells her mother, and during that time she tries to have the best of both worlds, appearing to be an obedient traditional daughter while having a lover. It is also significant that she only tells her mother about the relationship after it has ended; in this way Serena owns her independence without using Sandu as a prop for herself or an excuse for her mother. She thinks to herself, "I didn't know exactly when I had become a woman—was it the first time I saw myself in the mirror looking like a woman, or the first time I made love to Sandu, or the moment I got pregnant, or the moment I decided to have an abortion?"[59] Each of these moments involves sexual agency.

Significantly, although each of these novels takes place largely outside of the region, migration alone is not a guarantor of sexual agency. Indeed, sexual agency and activity begin *within* the region for Lucy and Veronica, though travel enables their intellectual and emotional distance from traditional Caribbean morality to be combined with physical distance. But eventually each of the women becomes disenchanted with life abroad, thinking like Hendrika that "Nothing is the way I thought it would be," or like Serena that "Things in America might be better, but they were not the things I loved."[60] Even when they decide to remain in the diaspora, they continue to be emotionally connected to their families and to the Caribbean if not to the cult of true oomanhood. These texts also remind us that the concept of sexual agency does not itself inhere judgment; agency includes the power to make both good and bad decisions. For instance, Veronica has a tendency to choose men who care little for her, and Hendrika and Serena make choices they believe are bad for them but which will please their mother. The complexity of these situations is not unlike the ambivalence towards women's sexual agency found in Caribbean traditions such as matikor, kwe-kwe, and carnival, an ambivalence also found in songs proclaiming Caribbean women's sexual agency in the region's popular music.

Women's Sexual Agency in Caribbean Music

As mentioned at the start of this chapter, both literature and music hold special significance in Caribbean cultures because their creation has historically been a "revolutionary act."[61] Although early laws restricted the type of instruments used and music played by enslaved people, access to music was not outlawed as completely or effectively as literacy was. Thus, robust musical traditions created by Caribbean people of African and Indian descent have existed for centuries. Because of its ever-presence in and importance to both everyday life and special occasions, popular music "is an important cultural vehicle for defining gender in the Caribbean."[62] This section examines female sexual agency in the lyrics and images of Caribbean "Queens" of different popular music genres. Jocelyne Béroard, "Queen of Zouk"; Drupatee Ramgoonai, "Queen of Chutney"; Ivy Queen, "Queen of Reggaeton"; Alison Hinds, "the Soca Queen"; and Rihanna, the reigning "Queen" of Top 40 pop music—all have achieved major success in their respective genres, which they have used, in part, to present aural and visual images of women's agency.[63]

For a relatively small part of the world, the Caribbean has produced a great variety of music. Traditional forms and antecedents of contemporary popular forms include the quadrille, the bélé, and gwo-ka from the French Caribbean; bomba, salsa, son, and merengue from the Spanish Caribbean; and calypso and tambu bamboo from the English Caribbean. Dutch Caribbean musical traditions include tumba and kawina, and while the local music ritmo is in its early stages of development, to date most popular music is imported into this part of the region. The Dutch Caribbean is, however, engaged in this chapter's discussion of the Surinamese song "Faluma," popularized by Barbadian band Square One, led by Alison Hinds.

All of the genres examined here are *popular* forms of music; their popularity speaks to their currency and significance in the region, while their hybrid formats (detailed in their respective sections below) represent the realities of transnationalism and globalization that continue to affect Caribglobal populations. With the exception of Rihanna, all of these Caribbean Queens can be considered the first female megastars of their relatively new genres.[64]

Individually the Queens can all be considered Caribglobal: Béroard has lived in Paris and Jamaica, and though she is from Guadeloupe, she now lives in Martinique. Ivy Queen was born in New York City but came of age in Puerto Rico; Rihanna was born and raised in Barbados but is now based in the United States, and Alison Hinds was born in England, raised largely in Barbados, and became an international star in part through her popularity in Trinidad. The music itself is also Caribglobal, evolving across locations and languages. As Jennifer Thorington Springer points out, "Regional artists are often in conversation with one another and also engage other aspects of diasporic music," so a Caribglobal analytical approach is appropriate.[65] Each of the songs referred to here has been a hit based on the assessments of fans, critics, and the artists themselves. Since the singers are acknowledged Queens, it is not surprising that serious scholarship exists on their most iconic examples of female empowerment. Since most of this criticism focuses on text, I will gloss the relevant criticism, adding my own analysis where it differs. Then I will analyze the video for each song, and where no video exists I will examine online images of the singer to explore where visual performance and representation coincide with the lyrical message, and where they differ.

Analyses of Caribbean music by scholars who are not trained in musicology (such as myself) tend to exclusively examine lyrics as though they are literary texts; a smaller number of works examines the dancing that often accompanies the music and is an integral part of many live Caribglobal performances. I have chosen to examine online videos and other images in addition to lyrics because the former are, like music itself, part of "a globalized, diffuse, and deterritorialized site" available to anyone with an Internet connection, as opposed to live performances, which are primarily targeted towards specific audiences (though these are also increasingly streamed or uploaded online).[66] At the same time, official images and videos can be assumed to be deliberate representations of the singer and the song that are at least as important as lyrics in today's multimedia context.

While Anglophone Afro-Caribbean artists are often compared to African-American performers and Spanish-Caribbean artists to South American performers, more work should examine Caribbean music across languages and genres. Zouk, chutney, reggaeton, and soca share several traits. For instance, all have a tradition of sexual double-entendre lyrics, and, as Béroard points out, "Every music in the Caribbean is about pleasure and desire."[67] Each also has its roots in a Caribbean working-class—and often also in a dark-skinned—community but is now part of "the Caribbean transnational music industry" that goes beyond any single national territory or language to create a "community of sound."[68] Based on the music itself and the findings of other scholars, this chapter takes for granted that all of the musical genres here are dominated by and generally perpetuate heteropatriarchy and both male and female gender norms—as indeed do most popular music genres in the Caribbean and elsewhere.[69] The singers discussed here, however, subvert the dominant gender roles of their Caribbean communities and their musical genres through their songs and mediascapes. As Belinda Edmondson notes, performance itself is a form of agency, "an act meant to do particular kinds of work or make particular kinds of statements."[70] So the question examined in the remainder of this chapter is what kind of work are the performances of these Queens doing?

Jocelyne Béroard, Queen of Zouk

Martinican Jocelyne Béroard has been singing professionally—and has been Queen of her respective genre—for longer than any other woman discussed here. Known as both the Queen and the Diva of Zouk, she has been the only female member of zouk band Kassav' for most of its thirty years and has also released three original solo albums during that time. Kassav' (which takes its name from a French Caribbean dish made with cassava) invented zouk, "a mixture of African music, Caribbean music, American music, Jamaican music, [and] Brazilian music," and has dominated the genre since their 1984 worldwide smash hit (and French gold record) "Zouk-la sé sèl médikaman nou ni" (Zouk is the only medicine we have).[71] That same year, Béroard released the song "Pa bizwen palé" [No need to talk], which was both "shocking" to and a major success in the French Caribbean.[72] Indeed, I choose to examine "Pa bizwen palé" because, even though it is more than twenty years old, it continues to be played on the radio and is one of her most popular songs, alone or with Kassav'. It also continues to be covered by other artists and remains the song by Béroard that most explicitly addresses women's erotic agency. As Brenda Berrian, who has written extensively about Béroard, observes, "when you go to a Kassav' concert and the minute you start hearing the familiar music of 'Pa bizwen palé,' the women jump up and start screaming, looking at the men and shaking their fingers and 'Pa bizwen palé.'"[73]

The song is a classic example of sexual double-entendre. Berrian argues in her book *Awakening Spaces* that "Pa bizwen palé" is a request for two lovers to "talk about the state of our relationship" and thus is largely a reinforcement of traditional French Caribbean women's gender role as a *dous*, a caring, sweet woman who is submissive to men.[74] Berrian is not entirely wrong, but she has also missed a very important reading of the lyrics as a woman's declaration of her erotic desire. Béroard herself acknowledges both that she intended erotic desire as one of the song's meanings and that she deliberately used double entendre in order *not* to be explicit or "shocking." When she wrote the lyrics "vini pran-y" / "come for it,"[75] she intentionally blurred the meaning, knowing that people would interpret the phrase in different ways.[76] Similarly, other lyrics can be understood as expressing a woman's desire to be heard as she describes her feelings, but they can also be understood as expressing a woman's physical desire, her "frisson" / "shivering" and "frissoné" / "trembling" and the insistent demand that her lover "vini pran-y" / "come for it," her body, her (physical) love. In fact, from the first lines of the song—"Close the door. / Tonight I won't let you go. / . . . / Dim the light / . . . No need to talk"[77]—the woman is asserting her agency, her power over the situation. In addition to the erotic desire, there are clear statements of female agency via control. The woman makes demands of her male partner: "close the door," "dim the light," "listen." She is also conscious that she contradicts patriarchal norms when she acknowledges that "it's generally men who have the right" to speak and dictate (sexual) relationships. As in Caribbean literature, the transgression in the song is perhaps more in the declaration of desire than in the desire itself. Berrian is correct in noting that "Béroard, a realist, understands her Caribbean public and knows how far to go with her lyrics."[78]

Although Kassav' was one of the first French Caribbean bands to produce music videos (including an early one for Béroard's hit "Siwo"), no video was created for "Pa bizwen palé." This could be due to any number of factors, from the challenge of visually portraying a double entendre, to time and funds, to priorities.[79] Though numerous homemade videos, unofficial recordings, covers, tributes, and at least one spoof of the song can be found online, in the absence of an official video, Béroard's photographs from official websites provide insight into how her public image corresponds to some of the sentiments in "Pa bizwen palé." The photos on www.jocelyneBéroard. com are organized by decade, from the 1970s to the present. Scholars such as Berrian and Gladys Francis note that Béroard is extremely aware of her public image and has "cultivated, with great care, a very dignified and gracious public image."[80] While her fabrics and hair styles change, Béroard's official image is remarkably consistent, including her wardrobe's color palette (mostly black and yellow). In posed photos and in images from live concerts, Béroard's arms, legs, and cleavage are largely covered. Though the posed photos are mostly headshots that do not show her body, it is clear that she favors pants for live performances and jeans and t-shirts for casual shots. Interestingly, in the images from the 1990s and the 2000s, a glimpse of a more flirtatious, sensual persona has emerged. Béroard's hair is more freely and casually styled, her outfits more flowing, and her gaze in a few posed shots is looking down or to the side, giving them a sexier feel.[81] Perhaps with age she feels less likely to be sexualized in a demeaning way; perhaps with her career and legacy fully secure, Béroard is more willing to allow her image to have a flexibility reminiscent of the famous double-entendre of "Pa bizwen palé." Although they send different meanings, both the song and the images portray women's sexual agency. In "Pa bizwen palé" a woman flouts the cult of true oomanhood by openly expressing sexual desire. In contrast, Béroard—even while singing her most erotically daring song—has refused to participate in the trend of female singers wearing and posing in revealing and provocative clothing.

Drupatee, Queen of Chutney

Drupatee Ramgoonai's lyrics and performances, like those of Jocelyne Béroard, will seem tame to some listeners. But taken in the context of the Indo-Caribbean community of the 1980s when she became popular, Drupatee's songs and performances were scandalous. Usually known only by her first name, Drupatee has been both celebrated and vilified as the earliest—and the first female—star of chutney soca, a genre usually understood as being "a fusion of chutney, an Indo-Trinidadian folk music performed during Hindu weddings, and soca," another form of dance music originating in Trinidad, and largely identified with people of African descent.[82] The reference to Hindu weddings indicates that chutney soca's roots include the matikor tradition. As with soca and other forms of dance or "party" music, "driving, danceable rhythms" and catchy hooks are typically more important than lyrics or vocal ability.[83] Sundar Popo, the "Father" or "King" of chutney, in 1970 sang "Nana and Nani," the genre's first major hit to extend beyond the Indo-Caribbean community. While Popo, along with several Guyanese artists, continued to sing chutney, another genre, called Indian soca, was being developed. In 1987 *this* genre (which would soon be called chutney soca) had its first major hits, "Pepper Pepper" and "Hotter Than a Chulha,"[84] both recorded by Drupatee in 1987. Both songs gesture towards women's sexual agency, with the latter song proving particularly rich for analysis.

"Hotter Than a Chulha" describes "Indian soca" as being a fusion of Afro- and Indo-Caribbean cultures, a cultural evolution and revolution. The chorus is as follows: "Indian soca (ah-ha) / soundin' sweeter (oh-ho) / hotter than a chula! / Riddim from Africa and India (oh! oh!) / blend together is a perfect mixture (oh! oh!) / all we doin' is addin' new flavor (oh! oh!) / so let we get down to the Indian soca (oh! oh!)." But the catchy song's message of cultural mixing also activates in its listeners some deep fears about miscegenation, specifically sexual relationships between Indian women and African men.[85] In the song's verses, Drupatee repeatedly invokes Laventille, an overwhelmingly poor, Afro-Trinidadian community, and the "panman" (a steel-band player or arranger), men who are also nearly all of African descent, to represent one strain of chutney soca. The other strain is represented by Caroni, a rural, largely East Indian area of Trinidad. Drupatee herself is the unspoken representative of that community. Phrases such as "panman come a little closer" and "we gone and interfere with the soca" (*interfere* being a common term for sexual interaction, consensual or not), combined with words and phrases such as "hotter," "racy," and "this style . . . go send you wild," make a sexual reading of the lyrics not unreasonable.[86]

Relationships and sexuality are common topics in traditional chutney; in chutney soca, "the themes remain but their articulation changes both literally, in the sense that English becomes the primary language, and figuratively, as their articulation is influenced by multiple sex/gender systems" of both Indo- and Afro-Caribbean working class cultures.[87] Sundar Popo sang lyrics that were extremely sexually suggestive, using the double-entendre of *nani*, which means maternal grandmother in Hindi but which is also slang for vagina in Trinidad. Despite this, it is Drupatee, "far more than male Indo-Trinidadian calypso or soca-chutney singers," who has been vilified by conservative, middle-class Hindu organizations. "Hotter Than a Chulha" also includes a reference to her critics and the metaphorical "blows" she has taken for singing soca. The frequent and at times virulent criticisms of Drupatee and female chutney-soca fans' dancing and other "lewd," "dutty" (dirty), and "vulgar" behavior has been detailed by A. Mohammed ("Love and Anxiety: Gender Negotiations in Chutney-Soca Lyrics in Trinidad"), Manuel ("Chutney and Indo-Trinidadian Cultural Identity"), Niranjana ("'Left to the Imagination': Indian Nationalisms and Female Sexuality in

Trinidad"), Puri (*The Caribbean Postcolonial*), Pinto ("Why Must All Girls Want to Be Flag Women?"), and others. These scholars connect such attacks to discomfort with miscegenation, specifically to an assumption that women's independence from Indo-Caribbean men means that they are sexually aligned with other men, not that the women are independent. Put another way, women's sexual agency is seen as a loss for Hindu-Caribbean men who (like men of other cultures) "both as individuals and communities, have always seen themselves as the guardians of Hindu women's sexuality."[88] The criticism of chutney soca's women is also connected to their image, in which they are dressed largely not in traditional saris or salwar kameez but in the same tight and revealing "Western" clothing worn by Afro-Caribbean women dancing to soca.

Drupatee has the most minimal online presence of any of the Queens discussed here; though she has an active Facebook account with nearly 4,500 "likes," she has no official website, Twitter account, or YouTube channel. This situation may be due to her recently ended twelve-year hiatus from performing, as well as the fact that chutney soca is still building an audience large enough to provide the market that can support the production of more diverse and robust mediascapes. The images on Drupatee's Facebook page are, however, instructive. In the more than two hundred pictures posted, there is something for everyone. The snapshots span her career and show Drupatee performing in saris, cholis, pants, and evening gowns. The performer's equal-opportunity fashion style shows that the harsh criticism early in her career has not deterred her from portraying her body in any way she chooses.[89] "Hotter Than a Chulha" and Drupatee's images promote women's sexual agency through their insistence that Indo-Caribbean women can flout the cult of true oomanhood and sing and dance provocatively in front of audiences that include a mix of races and genders. At the end of "Hotter Than a Chulha," Drupatee sings that chutney soca is "a brand new stage." The public stage was new to Indo-Caribbean women in the 1980s, since for some hundred years prior, most Indo-Caribbean women's musical performances had been in private gender and race-segregated spaces. But the phrase "new stage" is also metaphorical, excitedly heralding a time when Indo-Caribbean women can publicly embrace and celebrate both their sexuality and their complex culture.

Ivy Queen, Queen of Reggaeton

While the first two syllables of *reggaeton* take their name from Jamaica's best-known musical export, the musical genre of reggaeton actually draws predominantly from Jamaican dancehall, Panamanian reggae en español, and hip-hop.[90] Reggaeton differs from the other musical genres discussed here because it does not have "any single specifiable place of origin . . . no *cuna* (cradle) in the sense of a 'hood' or even national setting from which it sprang."[91] Indeed, because it has been embraced by many Spanish- and English-speaking youth throughout the Americas, scholars have taken to calling reggaeton a "pan-Latino" phenomenon.[92] Although there is no agreement on a physical birthplace for this music, there is agreement that its psychic space of origin is among black, working-class urban youth in the Spanish Caribbean and Central America. Indeed, sex, race, class, and masculinity are referred to far more often in the music itself than is any kind of pan-Latino identity. Its lyrics forego double-entendre for explicit sexual content, and, as with hip hop and dancehall, sex "was—and is—reggaeton's organizing register."[93] The genre's sexual material has been decried as "vulgar" throughout the Americas and in 2012 was unofficially banned in Cuba.[94]

In the early 1990s, Martha Ivelisse Pesante entered the masculinist world of "underground" Puerto Rican music, first as a songwriter, then as a member of The Noise, and in 1997 as a solo artist, with the album *En mi imperio* [In my empire], which won her a People's Favorite Rap Singer award from the magazine *Artista*. Although she is no longer the only woman in Puerto Rico willing to freestyle on stage, Ivy Queen continues to be "the most highly visible female artist in this hyper-masculine genre," the undisputed Queen of Reggaeton, and, because she frequently addresses issues of women's power, "perhaps the only [reggaeton] performer to structure her career with a gender difference in mind."[95] Ivy Queen has referred to herself as a "feminista," and while her image has radically changed from "rude" hip-hop style to "glam," each of her eight original albums has included songs that place women in positions of power and agency, as Hector Ayala has noted. The Queen herself has said that her own mother, who raised seven children alone, inspires her to write and sing mostly "about females that are strong."[96] One of these songs, "Quiero Bailar," spent eight weeks on the *Billboard* Latin charts, reaching No. 29.

In the lyrics of "Quiero Bailar," a woman tells a man that she wants to dance reggaeton with him, and she knows he wants to "sudar" / "sweat,"[97] but that just because she dances with him and may even find him attractive, he cannot assume that she will sleep with him—"Tú me puedes provocar / Eso no quiere decir / Que pa'la cama voy" [You can provoke me / But that doesn't mean / That in your bed I'll be]. Here, sexual agency is about the power of saying no and having control by creating boundaries and declining advances. While this message may seem to endorse the cult of true oomanhood's morality, because Ivy Queen's performances and style are sexually suggestive and her lyrics tend to advocate for women's power in relationships, it is clear that her message is not restricted by traditional gender mores. In probably the most in-depth scholarly analysis of Ivy Queen and this song, Jillian Báez writes that the Queen "challenges the pervasive virgin/whore dichotomy in suggesting that women can express their sexuality and still be respected . . . asserting agency on a very grounded level with everyday interactions such as dancing."[98] The song also challenges class-based stereotypes, namely that the urban, working-class, culturally if not phenotypically black women affiliated with reggaeton are not always sexually available because they dance in a sexually suggestive way.

Given the song's lyrics, one would expect that the video would have a lot of bailando (dancing), but it portrays no dancing to speak of; instead, it features the same head-nodding and posturing (including the artist flipping off the camera and viewer) found in many men's reggaeton and hip-hop videos. And not only is there an absence of dancing in general in the video, there is also a particular absence of perreo, the dance style most affiliated with reggaeton and an aspect commonly derided as vulgar. Perreo, literally "doggy style," consists of a man standing still or only moving his hips while a woman stands in front of him and faces away from him, moving her hips rhythmically on top of his pelvic area. Not only does the dance mimic sexual activity, it also can become the occasion for it; occasionally couples take advantage of dark corners in clubs and actually have sex in this position.[99] Ivy Queen's lyric that "bailo reggaeton pero no soy chica fácil" [I dance reggaeton but that doesn't mean I'm easy] seems to refer to perreo dancing.[100] However, perreo's absence from the "Quiero Bailar" video is less surprising when one realizes that Ivy Queen has not danced this way in *any* of her videos, even when she frequently appeared in them with fellow reggaeton star and then-husband Grand Omar when she was married to him. Thus Ivy

Queen endorses Caribbean women's ability to choose different types of sexual agency, advocating for women's right to dance in any way they choose and still maintain control over their bodies while she herself uses this right to avoid being seen dancing in such a suggestive way, not unlike Béroard's choices about her public image. Though Ivy Queen has changed her public persona from "rude girl" with braids and baggy jeans to hyperfeminine diva in dresses revealing her recently "enhanced" body,[101] her lyrics continue to refute the cult of true oomanhood and do not acquiesce to "a normative Puerto Rican femininity, particularly that of polite femininity."[102]

Rihanna, Queen of Top 40

As of this writing, Rihanna, born Robyn Rihanna Fenty in Barbados and living, it seems, wherever she happens to be performing at the time, is on a lot of Top 10 lists. She has been one of *Time* magazine's One Hundred Most Influential People in the World, No. 4 on *Forbes'* Most Powerful Celebrities, second in followers on Facebook (with more than 54.7 million fans), and one of the Top 10 celebrities on Twitter (with more than 32 million followers).[103] She has had nine No. 1 songs (and nine more in the Top 10 of *Billboard*'s Hot 100) from her six albums. And Rihanna has "sold more digital singles than any other artist—a hundred and twenty million."[104] How do these numbers add up? Rihanna is undoubtedly both "the queen of urban pop, and the consummate artist of the digital age."[105] Yet it seems that more has been written about her very public relationships and sex life than about her music. While Rihanna has referenced The Incident with numerous staged photographs in which she appears with a patch over her eye,[106] as well as various songs and videos (including Chris Brown appearing on one of her songs and her appearing on one of his), I want to invert the typical approach to this artist and analyze her by focusing on a song and its video, with only tangential references to her relationship choices.

As regularly occurs with black Caribbean people in the United States, there Rihanna's Caribbeanness usually gets subsumed under blackness or a more general African-Americanness, especially since the Caribbean beats of her first album *Music of the Sun* have mostly disappeared from subsequent albums.[107] In effect, her popularity in North America and her global fame have largely erased her Caribbean context. But Rihanna herself often asserts her Bajanness, and because she was raised in Barbados until the age of sixteen, we can assume that she is as aware of local gender expectations as are other Caribbean women. Rihanna returns to Barbados often, calls it home and "her favorite place on earth," as well as the place she feels happiest.[108] Furthermore, her Caribbeanness is evident in her noticeable accent whenever she speaks, and in the "S&M" video discussed below, the dress she wears in the press conference scenes has *Barbados* written across the bodice.

In 2011 "S&M" spent thirteen weeks on the *Billboard* Hot 100 chart, peaking at No. 2 (the remix with Britney Spears finally hit No. 1 for one week). In addition to the inherent controversy because of its content and gestures to The Incident, the song's success can be attributed to its driving beat and the rhythmic beckoning of the hook "na na na na na *come on!*" The first words of "S&M" are "Feels so good being bad," and the chorus repeats, "I may be bad but / I'm perfectly good at it." These lines suggest that Rihanna dated Chris Brown because "pain is [her] pleasure" and "affliction . . . leaves [her] wanting more." While the song and video are sexually transgressive to the "respectable" middle-class realities of heteropatriarchy in both the Caribbean and the United States because of their references to sadomasochism, the video presents the sexual references along with a critique of the media's interest in the young star.

The attention to detail in the "S&M" video begs for multiple viewings and close readings. The sexually suggestive scenes—dismissed by at least one writer as "soft core"—alternate between portraying Rihanna as restricted and as being in control. She is restricted under plastic sheeting at the opening "press conference," but the press is gagged and nods at everything she says. In another scene she is sitting with popcorn as though watching a movie, but when it is revealed that the star is surrounded by at least eight security-style cameras, it becomes clear that she *is* the movie, until she gets up and walks into a room in which the press, déshabillé, are tied up and terrified, subject both to Rihanna and her pink whip and to the cameras now trained on them. As in the first scenes, first she is the object, but then she is the powerful subject. The sexual images—including those of being tied up, leading a (white) man on a leash, and romping with a roomful of people, many of whom, because of their appearance, dress, and behavior, would be labeled "freaks" or "perverts"—are completely tongue-in-cheek. The press, however, is targeted for more serious critique. The reporters (some of whom also play the "perverts") are dressed conservatively at the beginning of the video's press conference but with ball gags in their mouths.[109] In the media of the music video, only Rihanna gets to "speak." By the end of the video, the press is in clown makeup, implying that Rihanna is less ridiculous for living her life than the media is for obsessing over it. The video's overall message is that by pillorying her with "abuse," the media is unintentionally giving her "pleasure" by helping her career.

The video's candy-colored palate and the fact that celebrity blogger Perez Hilton is her man/dog on a leash contribute to the video's campiness.[110] And though her obvious pleasure (smiling, laughing, smirking) throughout the video removes any question about her willingness to be in these situations, the paradox of "S&M" is closely related to the paradox of Rihanna's public life. Her constant presence on Facebook and Twitter and her explicit mention of her sex life in those fora contribute to her ever-presence in "traditional" media, all of which contribute to her persona as Queen of Pop. Significantly, the song's chorus includes the phrase "sticks and stones may break my bones" but ends with "chains and whips excite me" instead of "words will never hurt me" because, while they may have hurt Robyn Fenty, at least in terms of her career, they have not hurt pop star Rihanna but have only made her more notorious and quite possibly both more popular and more marketable. Only at the very beginning of the video, when the press physically drags her into a room and places her under plastic, is Rihanna portrayed as both not in control and unhappy (literally kicking and screaming). But once she is under the plastic, she is smiling and coy. The overtones are clear: she may not have chosen how she was thrust into the media's spotlight, but now that she is there, she is going to enjoy—and milk—every minute of it, keeping us all well informed on the sexuality of her star persona and her "real" life.

Alison Hinds, Soca Queen

Rihanna has skyrocketed to international superstardom, and Alison Hinds, the "Soca Queen," hopes to follow in her countrywoman's footsteps by bringing soca to a broader international audience. Although many believe soca derives from a combination of U.S. American soul or R&B music and calypso, a Trinidadian creation, singer Ras Shorty I insists that in the early 1970s he created *sokah* (his original spelling) to be the "new national music" of Trinidad and Tobago. In his vision, sokah would draw on both African and Indian rhythms, representing the full nation and the true soul of calypso.[111] Despite the consistent confusion over its origins, soca is "the most popular form of music in Trinidad and Tobago" today.[112] Like reggaeton, it is generally considered a "black cultural form of party music" preoccupied with "public sexuality, and licentiousness."[113] Although it continues to be a male-dominated genre, many women soca singers have found some success, including Destra, Sanelle Dempster, and Denise Belfon. However, there is only one Soca Queen, and for over a decade that has been Alison Hinds, "the first woman ever to win Road March and Party Monarch titles in Barbados."[114] Hinds recalls that fans and media crowned her Queen long before she went solo, when she was the only female member of Barbadian soca band Square One. Hinds has both a strong voice and a powerful stage presence with which she celebrates her own sexuality and that of her fans (especially the ability to wine). Of course, her choice of material has been an important element of her success, and two songs in particular—"Roll It Gal" and "Faluma"—have helped Hinds reach iconic status in the Carib-global world of soca.

"Roll It Gal," released in 2005 just a year after Hinds left Square One, "topped the regional charts instantly" and continues to be a fan favorite, even being called an anthem to women's empowerment.[115] It manages to encourage and celebrate women's sexuality, independence, health, religion, strength, motherhood, work ethic, pride, and intelligence—all in just under four minutes—to an infectious and eminently danceable beat. The stretching out of *gal* in the verses emphasizes a word that can be used in derision or intimacy. In the song, it is an endearment, but it also implies that if someone "fly up in yu face" and calls a woman "gal" to demean her, the woman can respond with "class" and "pride." This elongation is also repeated in the "Roll" of the chorus, and its juxtaposition with the quick three beats of "roll it gal" creates anticipation and excitement, as well as an excellent opportunity to showcase one's ability to wine at different tempos. Though many soca songs celebrate wining, as Jennifer Thorington Springer points out in her detailed analysis, Hinds in "Roll It Gal" "also expands our understanding of 'respectable' womanhood" by insisting that sexually suggestive dancing in no way lessens a woman's value—sexual or otherwise.[116] And though soca is often derided for its lack of political content, this song manages to be both "party music" and "message music"; as Hinds herself explains, "not only is the message there and the message is strong—but there are still clever hook lines, there's good melody, [and] it's still very danceable."[117]

The video for "Roll It Gal" highlights the embodied freedom the song advocates. It begins with two unabashedly sexy scenes; one consists of quick shots of a woman lying on top of a partially clothed man on a secluded beach, eyes closed, seemingly exhausted after a long night of dancing and/or sex. The other scene portrays longer shots of a wet Alison Hinds walking out of the sea in a short, clingy, dripping-wet white top. The rest of the video alternates between staged scenes featuring single women dancing alone and a seemingly unstaged club scene, in which men and women dance in groups, alone, and in couples. While Hinds owns every scene she is in, her dredlocked hair and curvy figure strictly contrast with the appearance of the female dancers in both scenes, who are almost universally skinny with straightened hair. While the dominant message of the video remains empowerment for all women, the more subtle message is that Hinds is the exception proving the rule that *certain* female bodies remain more valued than others.[118]

Conclusion: The Failure of Upbringing

Though it looks and sounds different in each context, there is sexual agency in all of the books and the music discussed in this chapter, agency that often retains an affinity for Caribbean culture while it contradicts upbringings that largely reinforced the cult of true oomanhood. And as much as art can be a reflection or comment on its culture, it does not exist separate from social and political contexts. According to Daly, "In the post-independence era of the 1970s . . . [Caribbean] women began to articulate gender issues in the public arena."[119] In the 1980s and '90s, these efforts developed into a broader women's movement in the Caribbean region. *Heremakhonon* and *Lucy* were published at this time, and their portrayals of women's sexual agency were criticized by some as being in poor taste. Condé recalls that "The uproar about my novel *Heremakhonon* was largely caused by Veronica, the heroine, expressing her own sexuality. For the first time a woman had the right to enjoy sex and to say it."[120] Caribbean popular music, more accustomed to both implicit and explicit sexuality, was generally more welcoming of women artists and women's agency. The 1980s and 1990s were also when Jocelyne Béroard was earning her first gold records, when Ivy Queen released her first album, when Alison Hinds won national music awards in Barbados, and when Drupatee became both famous and infamous in

Trinidad. During this time, women also became more prominent in education, law, and politics. Although Barbados had a woman minister in 1951, and many Caribbean territories did not have their first female ministers until the twenty-first century, the region saw several women first appointed to ministries or other high offices in the 1980s. In 1977, Lucinda da Costa Gomez-Mattheeuws became the first female prime minister of the Netherlands Antilles, and in 1980, Prime Minister Eugenia Charles of Dominica became the first elected woman leader of the Americas.[121] These officials have been followed in recent years by the historic elections of Portia Simpson-Miller and Kamla Persad-Bissessar, the first female prime ministers of Jamaica and Trinidad and Tobago, respectively. The sharp rise of individual Caribbean women's profiles and achievements has been accompanied in the twenty-first century by a "growing hypermasculinization of the state and increasing ideological hostility towards women," as well as a backlash in academia, politics, and culture that includes claims of "'male marginalization' that seeks to (re)center the focus of gender policy on men, particularly young men and boys."[122]

All of the texts discussed here fit scholar Donette Francis' notion of the antiromance, which she describes as including "three major themes: rewriting the heterosexual love plot through an adult-narrated *bildungsroman*, rethinking alternative ways of belonging to the nation by shifting the focus to the sexual complexities of dwelling at home and abroad, and, finally, resisting canonical historical representation by creating counterarchival sources to replot history."[123] Although Francis focuses on novels in her critical study *Fictions of Feminine Citizenship*, the musical texts and mediascapes discussed here can also be considered antiromances. Each of the novels clearly rewrites the heterosexual "love plot"; love is problematized and made secondary to sex in *Heremakhonon* and *Lucy*. In *The House of Six Doors* although a love affair exists, the protagonist herself prevents a traditional "happy ending" through her own reasoning. The songs "Pa bizwen palé," "Hotter Than a Chulha," "Quiero Bailar," "S&M," and "Roll It" also resist the structure of traditional love plots and those of traditional love songs. The novel's protagonists continue to rethink their belonging as they struggle to embrace the Caribbean nation because its culture has proscribed their own agency. Serena, in *The House of Six Doors*, comes closest to resolution both because she is able to separate her mother from her larger culture and nation and because she has a very different female figure to look to, her grandmother.

The songs also present alternative ways of belonging to Caribglobal national and diasporic communities, largely through their insistence on women's ability to determine the nature of their sexual relationships and through the fact that each singer is fiercely and publicly proud of belonging to her nation and the region. The lyrics and images of Béroard, Drupatee, Ivy Queen, and Hinds present different ways of thinking about Caribbean culture, including music and dancing, in ways that empower women. As Susan Harewood asserts, performances such as these "articulate notions of citizenship and nationhood that challenge masculinist, bourgeois, state definitions of the nation."[124] Music and video are themselves counterarchives, so the Queens' productions inherently provide a different mechanism to read and understand women's sexual agency. All three novels present a first-person bildungsroman as an intimate counterarchive to official documents. Other alternate sources of information and knowledge include the Curaçaoan spiritual traditions mentioned in Selbert's novel, the letters between Lucy and her mother, and Veronica's almost diary-like narration.

The concept of the antiromance helps to unpack structurally how these texts portray and promote women's agency. Yet, as was mentioned at the start of this chapter, agency is an ongoing journey more than it is a destination, and that journey is replete with complexity, ambiguity, and contradiction. One such element is the implied limit of women's sexual agency. While the novels portray sexual exploration beyond conjugal monogamy, that exploration does not extend to same-sex desire. Similarly, each of the Queens of Caribbean music has taken pains to publicly emphasize her heterosexual family life. Even though Rihanna, known for sex-related controversy, has erotic scenes with a female model in her "Te Amo" video (banned in the United States), the song's lyrics proclaim "I'm not that way" and ask the woman to "let [her] go." Heterosexuality and homosexuality (portrayed by authors discussed in the previous chapters, and by musicians such as Cuban hip-hop group Las Krudas, Dominican Rita Indiana Hernandez, and Prosas, a lesbian reggaeton group)[125] remain separate in Caribbean literature and music in a manner that is probably much more stark and less fluid than the lived realities of Caribglobal sexualities.

Unlike the other songs discussed above, which use the language spoken by the majority of their fans, "Faluma" has succeeded despite its lyrics being in Surinamese Sranan Tongo, a language spoken by less than half a million people. When Barbadian soca band Square One was preparing to perform in Suriname, they adapted this traditional Kawina song for stage performances as a gesture to the local audience.[126] It was so popular that Square One then asked permission to record it, and it went on to become "one of the biggest pan-Caribbean hits of 1999," perhaps vying with Kassav's "Zouk" for the biggest pan-Caribbean hit ever.[127] Hinds re-released "Faluma" on her 2007 solo album, and the song continues to receive regular airplay and is a soca classic guaranteed to get people dancing.

For this discussion about women's sexual agency, the bridge is the most interesting part of this song; its lyrics include "a woman a woman . . . a mati a mati / I love her I love her." This is one of the few moments in the song where English appears *and* seems to be linked to the Surinamese creole. Mati-ism is a long-established, complex cultural practice among Afro-Surinamese working-class women that has same-sex sexuality at its core and which also includes its own specific language, customs, and systems of morality. (Gloria Wekker's work on this is essential.) It appears that one of the most popular soca songs ever, sung by the single most popular female soca singer ever, mentions same-sex desire in a positive way. Does such a reference matter if the audience does not understand it? The media, activists, scholars, and music lovers have made much of the dancehall tune "Boom Bye-Bye," which became popular outside of Jamaica partly because of its catchy tune and partly because most global North (and some non-Jamaican Caribbean) listeners did not understand the words, which call for violence against homosexuals. This controversy continues with any number of dancehall stars and their "fyah bun" [fire burn] songs, which argue that homosexuals will burn in hell and some of which imply that they should be burned here on earth as well.[128] While a translation and analysis of the complete song and its original source exceeds the scope of the current project,[129] if activists and scholars are going to argue that negative views of same-sex desire can infiltrate a culture even when they are not understood, then I think we should consider the potential effects of revealing the loving, homoerotic undertones of "Faluma."

*   *   *

Comparing the lyrics and images of Caribbean women performers points to an overall ambivalence about women's gender roles. Of the performers discussed here, only Béroard and Drupatee have an image that eschews explicit sex appeal. While this may well be by choice, it is unlikely to be a choice separated from the demands of the music marketplace. As Guilbault writes about soca, "the hypersexualization of bodies through outfits and performance gestures amplifies prescribed gender roles and performances."[130] Harewood agrees that "popular culture participates so much in the rich, messy, complexity of the social that it is rarely, if ever, wholly emancipatory or wholly disciplined."[131] With all of the possibilities that these texts present, none describes a utopia free of the complexity of Caribbean women's contemporary lives. The worlds of these creative texts include domineering parents, strict cultural expectations, predators, and hurtful gossip—as well as women's erotic and emotional power, control, and pleasure. The agency these Caribglobal texts describe is rarely consistent or complete. As discussed early in this chapter, the cult of true oomanhood and other traditional Caribbean gender roles and expectations are not the reality for the majority of Caribbean people, regardless of their location, language, or race. And just as millions of Caribbean individuals daily contradict received heteropatriarchal norms—norms they may themselves endorse—so too do some writers and musicians contradict aspects of hegemonic gender norms. Furthermore, while the texts often focus on sex, the messages focus as much on a gendered liberation of identity—the ability to choose one's identity and expression of self—as on sexual agency. And yet while the sexual experiences are an important part of growth, the process of individual development is larger than these.

* * *

Should woman be perennial daughter raised as lady, always already defined by her relationship to men? Or, should woman and citizenship signify a certain autonomy—what we might regard as erotic autonomy—and sexual agency?

Jacqui M. Alexander, *Pedagogies of Crossing*, 22

Whenever women speak out, they displease, shock, or disturb.

Maryse Condé, "Order, Disorder, Freedom," 161

These epigraphs by two major Caribbean thinkers speak to each other and to the issue of Caribbean women's sexual agency. Alexander advocates for women's self-definition and control over their bodies and sexualities, while Condé points out the negative reactions that follow women voicing their desires. In the various texts examined here, Caribbean women use sexual agency either to attempt to subvert the patriarchal order or to obtain some personal freedom within it. As is clearly seen in the cases of Drupatee and Condé, who were publicly criticized for their embrace of sexual agency, and in the artists' insistence on their own heterosexuality, there are limits to the types of transgression women can advocate for or perform while still being accepted by a wider Caribglobal public. Whereas for Caribbean men particular kinds of public desire and sex are prohibited—particularly same-sex desire and sometimes interracial relationships—for Caribbean women *any* public display of sexual agency or desire is prohibited. In fact, when it comes to sexual agency, all Caribbean women could be labeled force-ripe, since respectable Caribbean women and girls by definition do not publicly acknowledge, let alone assert, their own erotic desire. Once sexually "ripened" through public discovery or disclosure, it is difficult to return to traditional roles.

Scholar Jocelyne Guibault writes in her analysis of Alison Hinds that her "study is not about pleasure per se but about the *politics of pleasure* that animate soca performances."[132] In contrast, my definition of agency includes both pleasure per se and the politics of pleasure. In aural and literary texts by Caribbean women, sexual agency includes acknowledging desire and choosing pleasure, as well as being aware of one's place in the world and being willing to both desire a different kind of life and to take what steps one can toward that change. Blogger Linda West writes that the notion of "women owning their sexual pleasure veers dangerously close to women wanting to own their bodies," and as with the other transgressive sexualities examined in *Island Bodies*, desire and pleasure can be motivators more powerful than convention, tradition, and the possibility of public censure.[133]

5

One Love?

Caribbean Men and White Women

Caribbean men of color are largely portrayed in the Caribglobal imagination as heteronormative, patriarchal heroes. This is true in historical narratives of Great Men who fought or defeated slavery (for example, Toussaint L'Ouverture and Cuffy), colonialism (Eric Williams, Frantz Fanon, and José Martí), or imperialism (Che Guevera and Maurice Bishop). It is also true in the mostly hypermasculine music traditions discussed in the previous chapter and in Caribbean literary texts, especially those written before around 1975, when significantly more literature by Caribbean women began to be published along with a more diverse range of Caribbean men's literature. This reification of the Caribbean man is a relatively recent phenomenon, since it is directly connected to Caribbean people having some political self-determination and some control over the region's cultural narratives and products. During the hundreds of years after Christopher Columbus became fabulously lost and before the era of flag independence, Europeans dominated the portrayals of Caribbean people—and those depictions were rarely positive. Those portrayals helped create the stereotypes of the "Latin Lover," the "Docile Indian," and the "Black Stud" that persist to this day.

The reification of the Caribbean male hero coexists uneasily with the political and socioeconomic realities these men helped to shape. In relationship to these realities, Raphael Dalleo documents several contemporaneous events as follows: "Cuba's epic failure in 1970 to produce a large enough sugar harvest to break free of international economic hierarchies, the Central Intelligence Agency-funded opponents of Michael Manley's 'We Are

Not for Sale' campaign launching a virtual civil war in Jamaica leading to his electoral defeat in 1980, and finally the overturning of Grenada's revolutionary government by U.S. Marines in 1983 appeared to mark the futility of a truly independent Caribbean."[1] To this we can add the U.S. American troops sent to "stabilize" Haiti in 1994, as well as the failure of several Dutch territories to obtain increased sovereignty until the twenty-first century, and the persistent political dependence of other Caribbean entities, including the French Antilles and Puerto Rico. Dalleo is correct to read these events as the failure of "true" Caribbean independence. But they can also be seen as a spectacular failure of male leadership, if not of Caribbean masculinity, especially as the 1970s and '80s also saw the bourgeoning of Caribbean feminism and the beginning of the perceived "decline" of Caribbean men's dominance. The texts examined here take place just before and just after the time period Dalleo delineates, reflecting the optimism of the independence era and the cynicism and poverty that followed it, and in both cases portraying sex with white women as a way to reinforce Caribbean masculinity.

Interracial relationships between Caribbean men of color and white women appear regularly in Caribbean history, film, and literature. Rhoda Reddock writes that "interethnic relations in these societies are often expressed as a contest among men, where control of political power and the state serves to legitimize claims of citizenship and becomes a symbol of 'manhood.'"[2] This is also true in the diaspora, where a man of color's hombría (manhood) may be questioned due to economics, racism, and/or xenophobia and where white women can themselves be physically dominated while also serving as a metaphorical if temporary conquest of white men. This chapter focuses on the racialized erotic affairs between Caribbean men of color and white women, recognizing that an "absence of interrogating white female sexual desire in the Caribbean renders invisible the workings of white female power."[3] It begins with an introduction to stereotypes of both white women and men of color, and then examines how those stereotypes are imbricated in male sex work with female tourists in two very different feature films, *The Lunatic* (1991, directed by Lol Crème) and *Vers le sud/Heading South* (2005, directed by Lauren Cantet), set in Haiti and Jamaica, respectively. Scholar Donette Francis has written that "such interracial intimacies [between white women and black men] have been central to many twentieth-century, anticolonial narratives of male writers," and three texts portraying interracial relationships—*The Mimic Men* (1967), "How to

Date a Browngirl, Blackgirl, Whitegirl or Halfie" (1995), and *Comment faire l'amour avec un Nègre sans se fatiguer/How to Make Love to a Negro without Getting Tired* (1985/1987/2010)—will be discussed in the following section. Finally, the chapter describes three Caribbean men and their relationships with white women: icons of Caribbean masculinity Porfirio Rubirosa and Bob Marley, as well as the lesser-known Surinamese World War II resistor Waldemar Nods. The title of this chapter, "One Love?" is, of course, taken from one of Marley's songs. The addition of a question mark in the title is significant, since in fact most of the loves in these relationships are multiple, not singular, and there are typically no expectations of monogamy on either side.

The texts addressed in this chapter represent thematic, geographic, and chronological ranges. In addition to applying the Caribglobal approach used throughout *Island Bodies* by including texts from multiple Caribbean locations and languages, here theme and geography are closely connected. The films portraying sex work are set within the Caribbean, while the literary texts are largely set in the diaspora and portray relationships not based primarily on financial exchange. The different locations of these two types of relationships is not random, but is connected to real trends of sexual relationships between Caribbean men of color and white women.

Such interracial relationships were rare in the Caribbean from the fifteenth to the nineteenth centuries, both because of the different social statuses of the parties and because they were extremely stigmatized and often illegal. In fact, historically speaking, sex between white women and men of color was rarely acknowledged in the Caribbean. Because it was a threat to white heteropatriarchy, such interracial sex could result in a range of torture or execution for the man, and for the woman in being labeled a prostitute or rape victim, even when the sex was consensual. For example, in Suriname an unmarried white or light-skinned woman "having 'carnal conversation' with a black man would be tortured severely and banished from the colony, while a married woman would undergo the same fate in addition to being branded. The black man would be killed."[4] Caribbean men's access to white women increased significantly in the twentieth century, with both Caribbean immigration to the global North and with female sex tourism to the Caribbean. The economic and political failures described above led in part to depressed economies and an increased reliance on tourism that contributed to the increase in sex tourism to the region. So the appearance of *The*

Lunatic and *Vers le sud/Heading South* at the end of the twentieth century is not surprising.[5]

In contrast, the literary portrayals of relationships between white women and Caribbean men of color represent the development of the Caribbean diaspora. Naipaul's novel *The Mimic Men* both portrays and was published in the wake of the first major wave of Caribbean im/migrants and the era of Caribbean flag independence. Protagonist Singh first travels to England as a privileged colonial seeking a formal education as well as experiences to help him find himself. He arrives before large Caribbean communities were established in Northern metropoles, and at a time when few Caribbean women went abroad, kept home through traditions that limited both their education and their travel. So not only does Singh, as well as the protagonist of Samuel Selvon's 1957 *The Lonely Londoners*, have access to European women because he is in Europe, they are virtually the only women he has any access to at all. Interestingly, Singh is a migrant who does not intend to stay abroad; he returns to the Caribbean for many years, and even when he ends his life in England, he is not of the place, remaining apart and a foreigner.

Twenty and thirty years later, however, the Caribbean men of Laferrière's *How to Make Love* and Díaz's "How to Date" are clearly immigrants, different from the majority but with no intention to return to the Caribbean and belonging in however tenuous a fashion to their Canadian and U.S. American communities. While racism and discrimination persist, the *presence* of Caribbean people is no longer unusual or widely questioned. Women's immigration has also become commonplace, and while Laferrière and Naipaul's narrators seem largely oblivious to women of color's existence, Díaz's main character and the story's title address the range of romantic partners available to him. Another significant difference between the mid- and late twentieth-century Caribbean immigrants in literature is class; both of the later texts' Caribbean characters receive public assistance, and their economic status seems to add, for white women, a reckless flavor to the men's already "exotic" characteristics.

The literary texts discussed here mirror Frantz Fanon's approach to interracial relationships in "The Man of Color and the White Woman," a chapter within *Black Skin, White Masks* (first published in French in 1952). Fanon argues that black Caribbean men who want to sleep with white women want to both use sex as revenge against white men—the "lust for revenge," he calls it—and to *become* white and thus a legitimate man in the powerful Other's eyes.[6] Fanon writes that black men's desire is "to be acknowledged not as *black* but as *white* . . . who but a white woman can do this for me? By loving me she proves that I am worthy of white love. I am loved like a white man. I am a white man."[7] This argument is an extreme version of the conquest narrative identified in this chapter. The men of color in these texts have no delusions that the presence of white women in their lives or beds will cause them to be treated like white men. In fact, they are very aware of the danger they are in once their affairs become public. There is, however, a sense that they have *temporarily* conquered or superseded white men.

Stereotypes of White Women and Caribbean Men of Color

White women have traditionally been considered both the prize and the property of white men, a belief that placed these women on a pedestal while restricting their agency. White men also projected onto black men a violent desire for white women, and in the seventeenth to nineteenth centuries used this supposed desire "to claim that without the restraining effect of slavery, blacks would 'regress' toward their 'natural bestiality.'"[8] Later, accusations of rape or the desire to rape were used as excuses for lynching black men who sought economic or political power—or simply to keep black people in their place, as in the infamous case of African American Emmett Till. Rape of white women was, in fact, used as a tool of war during some slave revolts and independence wars (for example, in Haiti), as rape of black women was used by white men as a method of terror, control, and economic production during slavery. In the Caribbean, the specter of "white slavery" has been raised in the contemporary cases of three white women who have disappeared in Aruba, while recent U.S. American examples of the specter of the black rapist of white women abound, as in the notorious cases of the Willie Horton ads from 1988 and the youths falsely accused of raping the "Central Park Jogger" (exonerated in 2002, after serving up to eleven years in jail).

Another result of the reification of white women is the concept of blanqueamiento, or whitening, the belief that people of African descent will both culturally and genetically improve themselves through miscegenation. Such beliefs persist to varying degrees in the Caribbean and throughout the African diaspora. In some Caribbean nationalist ideologies, the concept of mestizaje, the mixture of European, African, and indigenous peoples, also

"serves to distance Afro-Latinos from blackness."[9] Thus both blanqueamiento and mestizaje maintain white femininity—and white supremacy—
as ideals. These beliefs are not, however, universal. Just as white people
hold stereotypes of nonwhites, nonwhite people also hold stereotypes of
whites. For instance, as in the texts examined here, white women are commonly thought to be overly emotive and either undersexed or hypersexual,
and often less skilled than women of color in areas including lovemaking,
cleanliness, and cooking. One researcher reports that he was told "numerous times" by black Martinican men that "white women are much more
direct in wanting sex whereas Martinican women look good but are hard
to get."[10] And in author Austin Clarke's Toronto Trilogy, Barbadian Boysie's
infatuation with European Brigitte is linked more to her whiteness than her
personality; he remains with her even after he realizes that his black Caribbean wife is more attractive and more hygienic.[11]

* * *

An examination of the stereotypes of men of color could alone comprise an
entire book, so such a study will not be attempted here. Instead, a summary
of stereotypes of "Latin" Caribbean, Indo-Caribbean, and Afro-Caribbean
men is presented below. Because the texts examined in this chapter mostly
portray relationships between Caribbean men of color and white women
from North America, it will discuss stereotypes generally held by people
of color in the Caribbean, as well as by white people in the global North. It
is also important to note that in North America, the Afro-Caribbean man
is often conflated with the African-American man, the Spanish-Caribbean
man with the "Latin," Latino, or Hispanic man, and the Indo-Caribbean
man with the Indian or more general South Asian man. What follows is an
overview of three stereotypes that include, but are not exclusive to Caribbean men of color: the "Latin Lover," the "Docile Indian," and the "Black
Stud."[12] Some familiarity with the dominant stereotypes associated with
men of color will provide insight into the textual analysis, as well as the
implications of interracial relationships.

The "Latin Lover" Stereotype

Ironically, the Latin Lover stereotype now applied to men from or with heritage from South and Central America and the Spanish Caribbean was first

popularized by Italian actor Rudolph Valentino playing an Arab character in *The Sheikh* (1921).[13] Such is the logic of racism. The Latin Lover character is suave, yet volatile; because of his philandering, he is not trustworthy, and he has "an irrepressible libido." And, like most stereotypes of Latinos and Hispanics, he is fair skinned. After its introduction in the 1920s, the Latin Lover "quickly became a film standard" and continues to be frequently found in a variety of contemporary media—from the ongoing popularity of Porfirio Rubirosa (discussed at the end of this chapter), to the U.S. American appellation "Rico Suave" after the 1990 song of the same name.[14]

Macho may be the single word most associated with men from the Spanish Caribbean and South America by those in and outside of the region. The concept of machismo has several similarities with the Latin Lover stereotype; machismo includes sexuality, but it also encompasses an entire constellation of "appropriate" masculine behavior, including "being authoritarian within the family, aggressive, promiscuous, virile, and protective of women and children."[15] Anthropologist Carlos Decena's informants, men in the Dominican Republic and its diaspora, described machismo in similar ways, as encompassing "hypermasculine styles of self-representation, authoritarianism, possessiveness, aggressiveness, propensity to psychological or physical abuse, and so on."[16] As one example, Lauren Derby describes Dominican dictator Rudolph Trujillo as embodying "a traditional [Dominican] genre of masculinity in which his self-aggrandizement was based on the sheer number of women he could lay claim to—women who highlighted his prowess as lover, father, husband, as well as defender of his female liaisons and extended family."[17] As will be seen in both fictional and real-world examples, some Caribbean men as well as any number of white women are invested in and attracted to this stereotype.

The "Docile Indian" Stereotype

Today, Indo-Caribbeans are a majority of the population in Guyana and Trinidad, are a large population in the Dutch Caribbean, exist in much smaller numbers in the French Caribbean, and have very little representation in the Spanish Caribbean. People from India first arrived in the Caribbean en masse at the end of the nineteenth century as indentured servants meant to perform manual labor on plantations more cheaply and reliably than the black former slaves. Thus, although Orientalism had already

stereotyped East Indians as "indolent or irrational" in Asia, in the English
and Dutch Caribbean these stereotypes were "inverted" and "Indian working men were extolled for their docility, industriousness, and respect for the
sanctity of their contract."[18] Indian (and Chinese) Caribbean masculinities
have also been "constructed as effeminate, desexualized and degenerate."[19]
Such representations coexisted uncomfortably with the sensationalist European preoccupation with numerous wife murders that took place in Indo-
Caribbean communities during indentureship—again, such is the nature
of racism. Nevertheless, stereotypes of Indo-Caribbeans as docile and in-
dustrious were specifically meant to provide an alternative to stereotypes
of the "morally-degenerate, lazy" Afro-Caribbeans.[20] David Dabydeen's
protagonist in his novel *The Intended*, similarly distinguishes himself from
Afro-Caribbeans by stating: "I come from their place, I'm dark-skinned like
them, but I'm different . . . I'm an Indian really, deep down I'm decent and
quietly spoken, hard-working and I respect good manners, books, art, philosophy. I'm like the whites, we both have civilisation."[21] In this sense, Asian
Caribbeans have been imagined within and outside of their communities
as a "model minority" not unlike similar constructions in North America.
In relationship to sexuality, Indo-Caribbean men have not historically been
considered a major threat to white womanhood or white masculinity. Besides, already having a majority black underclass that they feared, the European and white Caribbean psyche could hardly justify importing a "buffer
class" that they also feared. In more recent times, the stereotype of Indian
men as docile means that white women traveling to the Caribbean are unlikely to seek them out for sex. It is precisely the "powerful" and "barbaric"
black men that they want—or the tempestuous Latin Lover. If they want an
"Asiatic" lover, they are likely to proceed directly to Asia itself.

The "Black Stud" Stereotype

In fact, in the global North, dangerous or aggressive masculinity is itself
raced as black—often predatory sexuality by men of whatever color is
accompanied by references to "swarthiness" or "darkness." Both the supposedly docile Indian and the assumedly mestizaje or mulatto "Latin" are
contrasted with the hypersexual and violent, predatory stereotypes of black
men. These stereotypes have existed at least since the combined rise of colonialism and slavery in the sixteenth century, perhaps unwittingly created as

a mirror image of how Europeans treated Africans, indigenous Americans, and Indians and other Asians. Interestingly, while some stereotypes have evolved, the stereotype of the dangerous, hypersexual black man, whether the "buck," the "stud," or the "thug," has remained rather consistent for the last six hundred or so years and is found throughout the Caribbean and the other Americas. Its purview did not take long to be held by non-Europeans as well. In Suriname, Indians are described as considering Afro-Caribbeans as "uncivilized, lazy, and pretentious creatures."[22] And Spanish Caribbeans, historically eager to distance themselves from their own African heritage, have been some of the worst perpetrators of discrimination, ranging from contemporary systematic racism, to the 1912 massacre of more than three thousand Afro-Cubans, to the 1937 massacre of more than twenty thousand Haitians and black Dominicans in the Dominican Republic.[23]

Aline Helg, in "Black Men, Racial Stereotyping, and Violence in the U.S. South and Cuba at the Turn of the Century," provides an insightful examination of the paramount importance of demography, economics, and politics to "racial stereotypes and violence." It is worth quoting part of her argument at length:

> White males seemed to lose control over their female relatives at the same time as they were often losing the ownership of the land. As the [economic] depression of the 1890s made white males' condition more precarious, both the destitute black and the more successful black became more threatening. In this context, the myth of the black rapist justified the repression, segregation, and disenfranchisement of black men, while simultaneously bringing white women under the wing of white men.[24]

Analyses such as Helg's imply that stereotypes of black men do not persist solely out of self-perpetuation. Rather, structures of white supremacy continue to exist, and continue to rely upon cultural tropes and beliefs—as well as on divide and conquer strategies among nonwhites—to sustain existing power dynamics.

During slavery, in the Americas of the eighteenth and nineteenth centuries, the image of the lascivious, threatening black "stud," scheming to rape the delicate white woman, helped sustain oppressive legal, social, and economic systems meant to keep political as well as physical threats at bay. Today these images of sexually "unrestrained" black men and ultradesirable white women persist, as do systematic violence and hysteria directed at black men because of real, fabricated, or perceived lust for white women.[25] This violence stems from a historically constructed fear "within white supremacist, patriarchal culture [which] is first and foremost about sexuality—about heterosexuality, about interracial sex."[26] This fear, in turn, results in the simultaneous eroticization and criminalization of black men. Sexual liaisons and relationships between black men and white women continue to be stigmatized, especially in the global North, and therefore remain inherently transgressive.

Women's Sex Tourism in Caribbean Film

Contrary to the stereotypes previously discussed, white women who enter into sexual and/or romantic relationships with men of color in the Caribbean are in most instances hardly prey; their skin color, nationality, and money give them both sexual access to local men and license to break the moral codes that local Caribbean women are expected to adhere to (as well as the codes tourist women might adhere to in their own countries). There are strict gender expectations of Caribbean men and women that generally prohibit women's promiscuity and public displays of female desire, as well as (the appearance of) female-dominated relationships. In the case of women's sex tourism, the Caribbean men's submission to female sexual direction (though she may direct him to be sexually aggressive or dominant, and acknowledges his expertise in all things local) and their financial dependence on women differ from traditional gender roles, straying from the physically dominant, financially contributing, but perhaps emotionally distant participant in the relationship.[27] However, there is little public approbation of the women, whose money, passports, and skin color protect them, nor of the men, whose immediate and extended families may benefit from such transactions.

In the late twentieth century, divorce rates significantly increased while heterosexual marriage decreased in the global North, meaning that for many the dream of the marital nuclear family became cracked, if not shattered.[28] And from the post-World War II period to the present, white women in Europe and North America increasingly entered the work force.[29] These cultural and economic changes combined to provide more heterosexual women with the disposable income and confidence to vacation without men, either alone, in small groups, or on trips designed for them. Not surprisingly, female sex tourism was part of these trends, especially in the global South, where locals were more likely to be in serious economic need, and where one can experience a relatively luxurious vacation (for instance, an "all-inclusive" resort) for a relatively low price.[30] (The very popular book and film *How Stella Got Her Groove Back* also did their part for this trend among African-American women.) Indeed, even working-class tourists can change their location in "economic, gendered, or raced hierarchies of power" through travel by saving and maximizing the value of their currency.[31] Tourism is about pleasure and adventure, and different travelers seek to find their pleasure in different ways. As a result, "Western European and North American women are increasingly participants in a form of tourism that demands sexual participation from the local population" and which, in the Caribbean, can be traced back to sixteenth-century "exoticizing" discourses.[32] In today's Jamaica and Barbados, for instance, "the darker [the man] is, the more able he is to secure a [tourist] woman's attention."[33]

The names for men who have sex with or befriend female tourists for pay tend to be diminutive and imply humor: the generic *beach boys, sanky panky* (Dominican Republic), *rent-a-dreads* (Jamaica), et cetera. But despite the playfulness of these terms, it is important to recognize that what these men do *is work* that supports them and their families, and which, in some places, is also a significant aspect of the informal economy. Scholars such as Kamala Kempadoo (*Sun, Sex, and Gold* and *Sexing the Caribbean*), Cabezas (*Economies of Desire*), and others have encouraged analyses of sex work that acknowledge the possibility of agency and pleasure in the worker;[34] similarly, the two films examined in this chapter—*The Lunatic* (1991), set in Jamaica, and *Vers le sud/Heading South* (2005), set in Haiti—provide rich examples of how Caribbean men are both objects and subjects in their relationships with tourist women. Both films are based on books of the same titles by Jamaican Anthony C. Winkler and Haitian Dany Laferrière, respectively. Each film provides a countertext to movies set in the region but with few characters from there or which include a few Caribbean characters whose lives are given little to no depth or backstory.

*   *   *

Critics and reviewers of Anthony Winkler's books most often comment on his ear for Jamaican English and his humor. This combination is a testament to his writing, since even non-Jamaican reviewers are able to appreciate his humor and recommend it to readers in the global North. Winkler's most popular novel, and the only one to be made into a feature film, is *The Lunatic*.[35] The film is faithful to its source text in both content and tone. It focuses on Aloysius, the homeless madman of a rural Jamaican village whose only companionship comes from the bushes and trees that shelter him, feed him—and converse with him. Aloysius' difficult but predictable life is irrevocably altered when German tourist Inga Schmidt chooses him to satisfy her huge and varied sexual appetite and eventually to commit robbery for her.

Winkler has been called both Jamaica's Mark Twain and its P. G. Wodehouse.[36] Indeed, his novel *The Lunatic* is a satire that in turn makes the white tourist Inga, the white Caribbean patriarch Busha, and the black middle-class Widow Dawkins look as ridiculous as the madman. The foreign white woman, however, is the brunt of the most jokes. In the film we are introduced to Inga through her camera. After Aloysius has earned some money diving for shells for tourists, he eats and then loosens his belt and lies down under a tree for a siesta, not knowing that soon he will be paid for "servicing white femininity" in a more direct way.[37] The film shows extreme close-ups of Inga fondling tubular plants and globes of fruit—works of nature that blatantly resemble male genitalia—alternated with extreme close-ups of one of her eyes and of her licking her lips. The montage culminates in images of her taking pictures of these wonders. When she happens upon the madman, Inga moves from photographing foliage to taking pictures of Aloysius—first his whole body, but quickly focusing on his genitalia, moving closer until she stands over and straddles him to get a close-up. When he wakes with her face in his crotch, Aloysius jumps up and screams, but it is Inga who shouts "Unhand me, nasty sex maniac!" invoking the aforementioned stereotypes of black men. Of course, it is Inga who is the sex maniac. In short order, she insists on having sex in unusual locations (from a boat to a cemetery) and positions (she often proclaims she has "a new trick" to show Aloysius or Service, a local butcher and another lover she acquires). How often she wants to have sex, how long each session must last, her insistence on new places and positions, and her desire to tie him up all confound and offend Aloysius. Yet he gives in to Inga's every whim, having been starved for human company and for sex and having been saved from near-starvation by her money.

In the sex scenes, Inga is always portrayed holding down Aloysius by his wrists, bobbing up and down wildly, and flailing her blonde hair. She rules over Aloysius and Service in every way; the latter character names her regime "pum-pum rule," after a Jamaican slang term for female genitalia, and later Aloysius facetiously declares that "rule of the pum-pum is worse tyranny than colonialism!" The moniker "pum-pum rule" is accurate because the men only stay with Inga because of the frequent sex they can have with her, albeit on her terms. But pum-pum rule is also symbolic of Inga's foreignness, since in the film Jamaican men believe they are the sexually and socially dominant gender, whether or not this is actually the case. While Aloysius' acquiescence to pum-pum rule is consensual (though sometimes reluctant), Inga is portrayed as a selfish predator. During their first and second liaisons, Inga slaps Aloysius for climaxing before her. She eventually claims to love Aloysius, but her behavior is consistently selfish and manipulative. After her wealthy father cuts off her money, Inga rejects Aloysius' suggestion that they forage and work for their food, and she convinces him that stealing is the only way she can stay in Jamaica. Terrified of losing Inga, Aloysius gives in, and when the robbery goes wrong, he prevents Service from committing murder. All three are arrested; Inga's father smuggles her out of the country before the trial has even ended, while Service is sentenced to hard labor and Aloysius is acquitted. At the close of the film, Aloysius is in the care of the black Jamaican Widow Dawkins who, by teaching him manners and how to read, is converting him into an "acceptable" companion and sexual partner.[38] In the film's last scene, the widow reads Aloysius a letter from Inga, censoring the white woman's many "rude" reminiscences of sex with Aloysius. Inga meets Aloysius when photographing his genitalia, and one gets the sense that she will always view him and Jamaica with an exoticizing, infantilizing gaze.

The bilingual film *Vers le sud/Heading South* is as serious as *The Lunatic* is funny, and the former focuses on sensuality as much as the latter focuses on crassness. The viewer is immediately presented with Haiti's contradictions. The film opens with a woman offering to give her prepubescent daughter to Albert, a hotel worker, because "being beautiful and poor in this country, she doesn't stand a chance." The woman wants to save her daughter from "them," and though the *them* is not named, given the time frame we can presume she is referring to dictator Baby Doc's henchmen or any of the others who wield corrupt power in Haiti. Albert, who declines the woman's offer, is at the airport to meet Brenda, a white American tourist, and most of the rest of the film focuses on this perspective. We soon find out what Brenda and the other white women (all in their forties or fifties) want: young, dark Haitian men who are also beautiful and poor. Immediately after arriving, Brenda changes into her swimsuit and goes to the beach, where she finds Legba, who asks her first, "You're all alone?" and then, "So you came for some fun?" She answers both questions in the affirmative. When he was about fifteen, Legba was Brenda's first extramarital affair, her first Haitian tryst, her first black sexual partner, and the source of her first orgasm. As will be detailed shortly, his name also portends his importance to the women and the narrative, despite his youth and poverty.[39]

The quiet monologues provided by the tourist women contribute to *Heading South*'s often languid tone. Directly addressing the camera as though they are speaking to a journalist or researcher—or as though they are confessing—each woman describes why she returns to Haiti and why she has sex with Haitian men. The women fit the three types described in the 2001 scholarly essay "Female Tourists and Beach Boys: Romance or Sex Tourism?" by Herold, Garcia, and DeMoya. The character Sue, a factory manager in Montreal, is the "romantic returnee" type who has been to the Caribbean before, "had a romantic relationship with a local man," and has returned "to maintain this love relationship." Ellen, played by well-known British actress Charlotte Rampling, is a French professor at Wellesley College who is infatuated with Legba. Ellen proclaims that "There's nothing in Boston for women over 40" and exemplifies the "committed sex tourist," described by researchers as a minority of women who "return with the objective of maximizing their sexual pleasure" with one partner. And Brenda, startled by her experience with Legba, begins the film as a romantic returnee but at its conclusion has become an "adventurer sex tourist" who "prefer[s] to have casual sex with a number of partners."[40] After less than forty-eight hours of mourning Legba's murder, Brenda sails away from Haiti and declares "I want nothing to do with men from the North. I want to visit other islands in the Caribbean. Cuba, Guadeloupe, Barbados, Martinique, Trinidad, the Bahamas—they have such lovely names. I want to know them all." Despite their slightly different attitudes towards sex with Haitian men, each of the women is involved in a transactional relationship in which "sexuality and economics converge in discreet ways," such as when Brenda slips cash into Legba's pants pocket while he is bathing.[41] Though it seems that the

women—and their money—are in control, the men sometimes successfully manipulate them, as when Legba plays Brenda and Ellen against each
other, getting more money and gifts out of both of them. Indeed, Brenda
says that when she met Legba, he was a starving teenager whom she and
her husband first fed, then befriended, and whom she eventually seduced.
But it is unclear whether this story is true or whether it is a situation Legba
fabricates for the benefit of the tourists' conscience and for his own pocket.

Legba's name is actually an indicator of significant power. In Voudoun,
Legba is the lwa or god of the crossroads and of destiny. He has two manifestations, notes Delgado: "as a Rada lwa, he is the guardian of destiny, the
one who holds the keys to that destiny and makes certain that a person's
life follows the preordained plan . . . as a Petro lwa, he is the trickster who
arranges unexpected accidents to cause human lives to deviate from the
Almighty's plan."[42] Not coincidentally, he is often portrayed with an en-
larged penis, as well as with an umbilical cord, to represent his ability to
mediate both between life and death and between the sexes; in the case
of *Heading South*, he also mediates between white and black people. The
white women in the film seem to think Legba is their Petro lwa, a happy accident who revives and enriches their sex lives. But in such circumstances,
research implies that the thousands of men like Legba in the Caribbean
(and in Africa, South America, Asia, and elsewhere in the global South)
are Rada lwa, deliberately guiding the women toward a preordained plan.
As Herold, Garcia, and DeMoya discuss in the section of their essay titled
"The Seduction Process," young men working as so-called beach boys in the
Dominican Republic report that they "approach women in a manner which
is friendly and non-threatening," presumably the opposite of what some of
these women would expect from black men. In the film and in the essay,
"the ones who are more successful are those who . . . present themselves as
well mannered, friendly, attractive men who know their way around and can
provide the woman with a good time."[43] Asked by a less-successful hustler
what his secret is, Legba tells the other man he talks too much; he has to
listen more. At the end of the film, when the investigating policeman tells
Ellen "you knew nothing about Legba," he is right in more ways than one.

Contemporary gender and performance theory have convinced us that
all self-presentation is performance. In the cases of the tourist women and
local Caribbean men, however, this reality role-playing is heightened, as
each party performs a persona different from that of their everyday life. The

woman self-presents as someone who has more freedom than usual and fewer inhibitions and restrictions than at home, including the number and background of her lovers. The men must embody "eroticized racial ideals" so that the women can live their fantasies and get their money's worth.[44] They are relaxed yet fun, sexually aggressive while allowing the women to set the boundaries and maintain control. In the only actual sex scene in the film, Ellen and Legba are flirting until he playfully bites her. She pushes him away roughly, admonishing "I don't like it like that," and he immediately apologizes. This interaction is representative of these relationships; the man may play the aggressor, but the woman largely controls the existence, pace, and tone of the relationship. The men are aware that their fit bodies' "youth, 'race,' cheapness, and controllable masculinity are what make them desirable," and they perform accordingly.[45] If any of these traits falters, the men may lose their lover/client.

White women sex tourists want to have their stereotypes both ways. They want—all in the same person—both the aggressive, oversexed black man who is always ready for sex *and* the jovial, docile black man who will always obey them and always be pleasant, regardless of what may be happening in his life. They also want to have casual sex without its seeming casual, even, or especially, to themselves. Research demonstrates that women who engage in transactional sex while traveling are even less likely than similar men to label themselves sex tourists; many women identify their affairs as "'friendships' or 'romance.'"[46] This tendency is seen in *Heading South*, in which all of the women insist that they love their sexual partners, and in *The Lunatic*, where Inga replies in kind after Aloysius declares his love for her.[47] Finally, the white women want to break the stereotype of themselves as undersexed and sheltered while still being directly protected from any potential harm by a man; ironically, they are probably not aware that in having affairs with island men they are fulfilling a dominant Caribbean stereotype of white women as oversexed.

The performance of eroticized racial stereotypes is also found in the literature examined here, especially in Díaz's short story, where the young man changes his demeanor—and his sexual expectations—based on the race of the girl he is with. In Caribglobal literature and film, white women are able to enter and exit their relationships with Caribbean men of color as easily as the women can board a plane out of the country or a subway out of a Caribbean diaspora neighborhood. They can claim cultural competency in another world, *and* they have been thoroughly sexually satisfied. The Caribbean men can also leave the relationships at any time, but as long as they are being paid, they are less likely to do so unless another lucrative prospect is available. In these circumstances, the Caribbean men rarely become rich but they are able to live better, for as long as the money they are given lasts. At the end of the affairs, the men are either in the same position they were in before they met the women or, as in Legba's case, they are dead. As Laferrière's narrator of *How to Make Love*, discussed in the next section, puts it: while in a relationship with a white woman, "I surrender to the least bit of naïveté, even for a second, and I'm one dead nigger. Literally."[48]

Interracial Relationships in Diaspora Literature

In those locations in the global North where (for the time being) white people continue to hold the majority of economic, political, and cultural power, their stereotypes of men of color largely remain the same as those from previous centuries. And there are a number of similarities between how interracial relationships between Caribbean men of color and white women function in the region and in the diaspora. For instance, the white women's skin color, nationality, and money (if they have it) continue to protect them and give them the power to expect sex largely on their terms from their Caribbean partners. And in both places the Caribbean man is expected to be a kind of cultural tour guide for the white woman. However, the context of interracial relationships between Caribbean men of color and white women is quite different in the diaspora than within the region. In Europe and North America, the men's skin color and foreignness makes them always presumed morally, if not criminally, suspect. Caribbean diaspora literature focuses on the perspective of men of color involved in these relationships in the global North. Even though the men's material realities are similarly impoverished in the Caribbean and in the diaspora, the cultural and political contexts they live in are quite different. In the global North, men of color are a stigmatized and sometimes feared minority. Moreover, immigration often initially results in downward mobility, contributing to economic and emotional stress.[49] In literature there are numerous examples of the use of "black male sexual prowess and sexual conquest of the white female body to prove not only the virility but the viability of black men's sociopolitical power," such as those found in novels by George Lamming,

Austin Clarke, and David Dabydeen.[50] Literature by Dany Laferrière, V. S. Naipaul, and Junot Díaz provides portrayals of diaspora interracial relationships that the men consider metaphorical conquest of whiteness and white men, depicting how the fear of and desire for racial and sexual stereotypes are performed in interracial relationships. In all of the texts, sex with white women results in a sense of conquest—or even revenge—for the black men involved.[51]

Dany Laferrière's novel *How to Make Love to a Negro without Getting Tired* (first published in French 1985) is set in 1980s Montreal and explicitly relates black men's having sex with white women to conquest and revenge. As the title of this "erotico-satiric novel" indicates, its vignettes focus on the main characters' sexual escapades. The implication is that white readers' libidos cannot match those of "Negroes" or niggers, both of which terms are closer translations of the French word *nègre* than the less incendiary *black*.[52] Thus, from the title of the book to its end, Laferrière's first novel plays with explosive racial and sexual stereotypes.

The novel begins with a section titled "Nigger Narcissus," which sets its scene: two black men, the unnamed narrator and his black Canadian roommate Bouba, live in a "meager pigsty" of an apartment in a Montreal slum area.[53] Like the men characters in the two films, neither is employed in any formal capacity. Unlike the other literary and film characters, though, it is clear that Laferrière's narrator and Bouba, who spend their days reading the likes of Freud, Hemingway, and Richard Wright, as well as having sex, sleeping, listening to jazz, and—for Bouba—meditating, have access to "high" culture and may be very well educated. The novel is more a series of vignettes about the men's sexual escapades than a single, continuous narrative. At its end, the narrator meets unexpected success with a scandalous erotic novel and realizes writing might give him a more secure life than hustling the white women he sleeps with.

There are too many references to interracial sex as conquest and revenge in *How to Make Love* to include them all here. In one significant passage, however, the narrator describes a consensual liaison: the "Big Nigger from Harlem's head spun at the prospect of sodomizing the daughter of the slumlord of 125th Street, fucking her for all the repairs her bastard father never made, fornicating for the horrible winter last year when his younger brother died of TB." The narrator later describes his own role in a sexual liaison in a college student's family home: "Everything here has its place—except me . . . I'm here to fuck the daughter of these haughty diplomats who once whacked us with their sticks."[54] For both men, sex is motivated by conquest and revenge. The difference between them is based on ethnicity; the African-American man seeks revenge for the combined evils and emasculations of racism, including lynchings, poverty, and poor housing, while the Afro-Caribbean man seeks redress for the combined evils and emasculations of colonialism and racism.

The many similar liaisons described in How to Make Love are, for the narrator, linked to his basic theory that the "only true sexual relation is between unequals." According to the protagonist, since the white woman "must give white men pleasure," that is since her pleasure must be sublimated to his, she can only achieve pleasure by having sex with a man of color, over whom she is socially dominant.[55] Thus even though this satire's protagonist seeks to temporarily conquer and take revenge on white patriarchy, he continues to endorse a more general patriarchal structure.

The narrator's theory is described with the book's only description of oral sex, an act he had "dreamed" of but "didn't dare" ask to be performed. The narrator explains, "I knew that as long as she hadn't done it [fellatio], she wouldn't be completely mine. That's the key in sexual relations between black and white: as long as the woman hasn't done something judged degrading, you can never be sure."[56] Again, he thinks more about the symbolism and power dynamics of the sex than about how he or she feels, physically or emotionally. This character argues that for a black man to truly conquer a white woman, she must consent to a sexual act traditionally considered degrading. Yet much of what white women do for Laferrière's narrator and Bouba could be considered degrading—including having sex with one man while the other is in the room, financially supporting them, and cooking and cleaning for them while they make it clear they have little affection or respect for the women. In How to Make Love, it seems black men get a sense of conquest both by having sex with white women and by making the women their maids. Like the film protagonists, Laferrière's literary characters survive off of white women's money and gifts, in exchange for sex.

Indeed, while sex and not love is the core of these relationships, class and money are also important factors in all of the texts, though in different ways. The How to Make Love narrator and Bouba are "on the dole" and are heavily subsidized by their sexual partners. Money also introduces another volatile power dynamic into the relationships—one over which the women have control. The white women in *How to Make Love* rarely mention their (often really their parents') money, although they take great pleasure in providing extravagant meals, alcohol, and more frivolous items such as flowers, that the men surely could not afford on their own without going into debt or doing without some other necessity. Perhaps Laferrière's narrator would argue that true sexual fulfillment requires financial as well as social inequality.

Unlike the *How to Make Love* protagonist, the main character of *The Mimic Men* considers most European women he meets to be beneath him in terms of economic and social status, as well as intellectual capacity. Nobel Prize winner V. S. Naipaul is one of the most widely read living Caribbean authors in the world, with his fiction and nonfiction regularly examined by scholars in the fields of postcolonial, diaspora, Caribbean, Indian, and general literary studies. Still, the issue of sex in *The Mimic Men* is not often taken up by critics. This text traces its protagonist Singh's childhood in the Caribbean as the pampered son of a well-off family, and his young adulthood as a student in England, characterized by promiscuity and a search for self, his return to the fictional Isabella with an English wife, and finally his re-immigration to England after his marriage and political career have failed, all via Singh's own nonlinear memoir.

While in relationship to white women, stereotypes of Latino and black men can be embodied to the men's advantage, Indo-Caribbean men must resist traditional stereotypes. In Naipaul's novel, Singh is far from docile; promiscuity and becoming a sexual connoisseur are just part of "the confident, flippant dandy" character he chooses to create for himself after immigrating to England.[57] Unlike Naipaul's *A House for Mr. Biswas*, *The Mimic Men* does not dwell on Indo-Caribbeanness. The text does, however, make clear that Singh is rather particular about the race and nationality of his many sexual partners. Specifically, he will not sleep with the local white English women from the school he attends, arguing that he "could not separate those earnest scholarship girls from their families, from the bitterness and mean ambitions that had been passed on to them."[58] Furthermore, he prefers to sleep with European women who speak a language other than English, especially languages he does not speak. (Singh never mentions Caribbean women or any women of color while in Europe.) These specifications and his frequent, yet brief, affairs together signal a desire to have as much sex as possible with white women as different from him as possible, while avoiding intimate relationships. In his birthplace, the small Caribbean island of Isabella, many people knew Singh's life story, as well as that of his parents, cousins, aunts, and uncles. But in England, no one knows him, his family, or their collective history. Serial one-night stands and creating personae for himself are ways to relish the anonymity that London allows.

Singh's promiscuity, however, also involves conquest. From the time he was a child, he has had a preoccupation with England and Europe, and upon arrival in London, he expresses his desire to seek the heart of that metropole, "the god of the city."[59] The young man feels he can conquer and truly know the city of London and the larger continent of Europe through numerous sexual liaisons with European women. It is his own form of sexual tourism in which he becomes cosmopolitan by having sex with white women of a certain class. During the process of seduction and the act of sex, Singh feels sure of himself, of what is expected of him, and of his place in the world.

But what begins as adventure—he even keeps a sexual diary—subsequently becomes a chore, a set of actions that are "expected" of him by white women.[60] "I was capable of the act required, but frequently it was in the way that I was capable of getting drunk or eating two dinners," he writes. The encounters become easy and commonplace, with "seduction" sometimes consisting simply of an invitation to bed. At this time his behavior becomes more disturbing. He begins to keep undergarments from the women he has sex with and to be harsher with them; he shouts at one young woman whose skin he finds disgustingly rough. Eventually he drops his class and nationality requirements, and his habit of promiscuity with strangers develops into an addiction to prostitutes. He became preoccupied with "what these women offered, which was less and more than pleasure; the quick stimulation of fear, followed by its immediate dissipation. But it was a grotesque business . . . that prolonged sensation of shock."[61] Finally, in an attempt to find himself, to escape the emptiness he once craved, and still trying to know and conquer Europe, Singh decides to travel the European continent, continuing to sleep with innumerable women.

Unlike Díaz's and Laferrière's characters, Naipaul's protagonist does become involved in a serious, emotional relationship. Singh returns to England, still searching, and begins seeing Sandra, a white woman who breaks both of his rules; she attends his university and is a working class, native English speaker. While with her, Singh realizes that "Language is so important," that his previous affairs "had been conducted in a type of pidgin; they were a strain; I could never assess the degree of complication we had arrived at after the sexual simplicities. . . . With Sandra there was no such frustration; the mere fact of communication was a delight; to this extent I had changed." With "social ambitions" to escape her working class background, Singh's money and knowledge of culture are attractive to Sandra; after they return to the Caribbean married, Singh is seen by Caribbean people as "offering comfort and status to a woman who was denied these things in her own country." Singh is aware of her motives, but the easiness of delighting Sandra pleases him, and takes his mind off of his recurrent introspection and depression. He describes these dubious attractions as "the perfect basis for a relationship," although to others it "seemed a textbook example of the ill-advised mixed marriage."[62]

After Sandra leaves him and he returns to England, Singh has a few more sexual encounters, but he does not have the energy or the desire to engage them as he once did. In his youth Singh had sought "the god of the city" in travel and sex; as he gets older, he seeks himself in solitude and writing. After his marriage has dissolved and his career has ended, Singh admits that, while he never felt sexually skilled, the act now exhausts him and fills him with anxiety.[63] This anxiety proves that his promiscuity was never just about sex, which he is later able to acknowledge; "at the time I thought I was simply playing. . . . As though we ever play." Rather, his numerous sex partners symbolized his preoccupation with Europe and with whiteness, his problems with intimacy, and his search for himself. "I had tried to give myself a personality," he writes. "It was something I had tried more than once before, and waited for the response in the eyes of others. But now I no longer knew what I was; ambition became confused, then faded." His sexual affairs "were a blur: of encounters less with individual bodies than with anonymous flesh. Each occasion pressed me deeper down into emptiness."[64] Like the women in the previous chapter, Singh and the other men characters here eventually realize that the act of sex does not alone lead to a mature identity.

*   *   *

Junot Díaz's short story "How to Date a Browngirl, Blackgirl, Whitegirl, or Halfie" also primarily addresses interracial relationships, and although mixed-race and "whitegirls" come last in the title, more time is spent discussing them than on the other young women in the story. First published in the *New Yorker* in 1995 and appearing a year later in his popular collection *Drown*, "How to Date" is narrated in the second person singular by a teenage Caribbean boy whose attempts at dating instruction reveal his insecurities about his own race and class, as well as about his expertise with girls. The story's title implies the romantic skills emblematic both of machismo and of the Latin Lover, a masculinity in which "his self-aggrandizement was based on the sheer number of women he could lay claim to."[65] Díaz's piece uses the perspective of an adolescent boy and focuses more on the how-tos of seduction—and how to deal with failure and rejection—than the other texts discussed here. Offering little direct information about himself, the narrator is instead revealed through what he wants to hide from the young women he would date, and from the way he describes them. For instance, his blackness is found in the desire to "hide the picture of you with an Afro," and his Caribbeanness is revealed in his desire not to disclose that his mother experienced tear gas "the year the United States invaded your island."[66] As a young Dominican, he aspires to be a Latin Lover—which requires emphasis on his "foreignness" and "Spanishness" while hiding or minimizing his blackness.

This story is also as explicitly about consuming whiteness as it is about conquering it. Significantly, the narrator does not ask, but tells the reader and himself, "The white ones are the ones you want the most, aren't they." Later, his directions include the following: "Tell her [the whitegirl] that you love her hair, that you love her skin, her lips, because, in truth, you love them more than you love your own." The whitegirl is wooed and complimented more than the other young women; her race makes her more of a prize, even though she is also assumed to be the most sexually available; the narrator states that "If she's a white girl you know you'll at least get a hand job." These girls' presumed class also adds to the sense of conquest, since here class and privilege are also explicitly linked to race. In this story, the "outsiders" are young women from the suburbs, while "local girls" from the Terrace (a housing project in New Jersey) are black or Latina.[67] In this text, "browngirls," Latinas, are always from the projects, "blackgirls" may be from the projects or the suburbs (the latter differing from their Terrace counterparts because they "grew up with ballet and Girl Scouts" and "have three cars in their driveway"), and "whitegirls" and "halfies" are always from the suburbs.[68] Thus, as in the other literary texts and films, money and class are associated with whiteness and treated like whiteness, as something to take and conquer respectively. The women's wealth is accepted and appreciated, but it also inspires further envy and anger because material and monetary gifts do not change the men's material circumstances and only emphasize their economic and/or class differences.

In "How to Date," Díaz's narrator largely adheres to the stereotype of adolescent men that says they are preoccupied with sex. Still, there are subtleties in this short story that do not exist in Laferrière's novel. The narrator's actions reveal his ambivalence towards stereotypes that implicate him as a young, black, Latino man: he wants to be foreign, "other," or "ghetto" enough to attract the white girl, but he also wants to be acceptable and Anglo enough to be accepted by her parents. If characters in How to Make Love fantasize about revenge against the "Man" and the white father while having sex with white women, Díaz's narrator imagines his sexual partner's mother, "her old lady coming to get her, what she would say if she knew her daughter had just lain under you and blown your name, pronounced with her eighth-grade Spanish, into your ear." The father is still implicated, however; earlier in the story the narrator describes being afraid of the white father, who sounds "like a principal or police chief, the sort of dude with a big [red?] neck, who never has to watch his back."[69] Thus his exploits pursue conquest against the presumed racist parents as well as against white people in general.

Late in Díaz's story, the phrase "But usually it won't work this way" reveals that the sex and seduction scenes described are more often than not fantasy. After following all of his own (and presumably his friends') directions, lines, and machinations, the narrator discloses that the white girl will usually pull away, acting "like somebody you don't know."[70] And truthfully, playing with racial and sexual stereotypes as well as the usual adolescent dramas, the young men and women in "How to Date" do not know each other at all.

Famous Caribbean Men in Interracial Relationships

Porfirio Rubirosa (1924–63), a functionary of Dominican dictator Raphael Trujillo who dated and married several wealthy and famous white women and who was rumored to have dated Marilyn Monroe, was the Latin Lover made flesh, conquering Europe and the United States through sexuality in a much more fabulous fashion than our fictional protagonists. Rubirosa began life as a military officer from a bourgeois family in the Dominican Republic but quickly graduated to a jet-set life consorting with multimillionaires. By the time he died in a car crash in his Ferrari, he had had "a twenty-five year career as the world's most famous lover."[71]

Rubirosa's success as a gigolo of sorts was directly connected to his race and that of his lovers and wives.[72] The "Dominican Don Juan" was known chiefly for two personal attributes: on the one hand his charm and impeccable comportment, and on the other his legendary phallus and sexual skills. Like the women in Vers le sud/Heading South, Rubirosa's public—both in the United States and in Europe, where "hundreds of articles and photographs" of him were printed, and in the Dominican Republic, where he was similarly lauded—wanted Rubirosa both ways, as a suave (Latin) bon vivant and as an insatiable (black) sex machine with a member of unspeakable proportions. Langston Hughes commented on this dichotomy in an essay written after Rubirosa's death that calls attention to the playboy's official and public label as Latin, even though his skin was darker than "Negro" politician Adam Clayton Powell.[73] Indeed, "Negro" men in the public eye during his time could not exhibit the kind of behavior Rubi engaged in. Jamaican Harry Belafonte and African-American Nat "King" Cole, two of Rubi's black contemporaries, both distanced themselves from the stereotypes of black men through their "clean" good looks and flawless deportment. But this was not all; both stars married visibly black women—and though they may have strayed from the marriage bed, they publicly remained respectably married, monogamous, and intraracial.[74]

Rubirosa's Latin label served as "an alternative to blackness" that enabled "the intersection of a cosmopolitan 'white' identity and a racialized Dominican hyper-sexuality" in ways similar to the media's treatment of contemporary Spanish Caribbean female stars such as Ivy Queen and Jennifer Lopez.[75] The dual nature of Rubi's fame can also be found in comments made by his lovers and the press. And as Paravisini-Gebert and Perió point out, when his sexuality is mentioned, the descriptions become graphic, "venturing into the terrain of racial caricature."[76] He has been referred to as a "stud," "grotesquely proportioned," and "full of animal vitality."[77] Former lover Zsa Zsa Gabor called him "charming, exciting, [and] volatile" while defending him after he allegedly hit her.[78] White women's acceptance of poor treatment, abuse, and occasional violence at the hands of Caribbean men of color is also found in social science research and in literature. Kempadoo observed that some white female tourists complained about Jamaican men's "pushy behavior or abusive comments" but acquiesced because they accepted such behavior as emblematic of Jamaican masculinity. Rubirosa did not publicly complain about such characterizations of his body, his sexuality, or his temper; on the contrary, he seemed to enjoy his notoriety.

Racialized sexuality also played a role in Rubi's choice of lovers. He chose women referred to as "the most beautiful woman in the world" (actresses Danielle Darrieux and Zsa Zsa Gabor) and the most wealthy (heiresses Doris Duke and Barbara Hutton). The same sense of conquest that appears in Caribbean diaspora literature about interracial relationships recurs in writings about Rubirosa, which invariably admire his ability to win one beautiful, rich (white) woman after another. Derby argues that in the Dominican Republic, Rubi's affairs and marriages were seen as "signs of progress," putting his small country onto the world stage and into its highest society.

Rubirosa's life is also emblematic of a specifically Dominican trope—el tiguere (the tiger). The tiguere is both "alpha male" and an "underdog who gains power, prestige and social ascendance through a combination of extra-institutional wits, force of will, sartorial style, and *cojones* (balls)."[79] Rising from relatively humble beginnings, Rubi became a tiguere through using his sexuality to gain wealth and international fame. Though he has largely been forgotten in the United States, Porfirio Rubirosa continues to be seen by Dominicans as the "quintessential tiguere," as any Google search will reveal. And some Parisian waiters still call their largest, longest black peppermills *Rubirosas*, a fact that would no doubt please the notorious playboy.

*   *   *

After a night of marathon partying that Rubirosa survived much better than did Sammy Davis Jr., Rubi reportedly told the latter, "Your profession is being an entertainer. . . . Mine is being a playboy."[80] While Rubi's talents were his charm and sexual skills, Jamaican Robert Nesta Marley (1945–81) continues to be known for his musical skills as well as his sexual prowess. Of course, Bob Marley popularized reggae (as well as dredlocks and Rastafarianism) throughout the world. But as the child of an interracial liaison and a partner in a very public relationship with a Jamaican white woman, his life was one in which race and interracial relationships figured very prominently. Marley never knew his father, known as Captain Norval Marley. The "Captain" (according to the documentary *Marley*, "there is no evidence that he rose above the rank of private") was a white British colonial officer who seemed to do little work other than riding around on a horse surveying the rural area where he was posted. By all accounts, the "relationship" between Cedella Marley, who was between sixteen and eighteen at the time, and the Captain, who was in his fifties or sixties, was extremely brief, and one of many that he had with local women.[81] Cedella Marley does not provide any details about their time together, and her silence implies that his status and wealth, and her youth and poverty may have combined to create a less than consensual relationship. Thousands of similar liaisons continued to take place many years after slavery had ended because the economic power structures that had been established during slavery remained the same, especially in rural areas, for decades after slavery was formally abolished.

While in Europe and North America Bob would have been considered black without a thought, in Jamaica he was *brown* and was teased and rejected as a child because of his lighter skin color and heritage. He wished he was darker, at one point darkening his face with shoe polish, and wife Rita Marley has suggested that part of his attraction to her was that she is "completely" black.[82] After Bob moved from the rural St. Ann parish to Kingston, the capital, he met and became infatuated with Alpharita Constantia Anderson. He pursued dark-skinned Rita, who was initially reluctant, in part because they worked together and in part because, "like other [Jamaican] girls," she had dreamed of marrying a black man, not a "brown-skinned" one.[83] The two married at his insistence in 1966, while he was still an unknown musician. Through talent and sheer will—including legendary practice sessions that lasted for six hours or more—Bob Marley and the Wailers (originally including Rita Marley, Jimmy Cliff, and others) became superstars, with Bob the best-known among them.

Though quiet and shy around women off-stage, Marley had a magnetic personality and, of course, good looks and sex appeal. His conversion, through Rita, to polygamous, heteropatriarchal Rastafarianism (a religion that allowed him to publicly proclaim and embrace his own blackness) and his growing fame meant that he had access to any number of women, and often they pursued him. Marley publicly denied being married, in one interview saying he would not marry because "I make my own law," and sometimes describing Rita as his sister. Although they had five children together and she put up with regular physical and verbal abuse, Rita began to see her role more as a caretaker than lover and was fully aware of his other affairs. In contrast, several "baby mothers" claim that they did not know he was married at the beginning of their relationships, even though the narrator observes: "That Bob was not a one-woman man was common knowledge."[84] In total, Bob had eleven recognized children with seven different women—at least one of whom was only sixteen when he began pursuing her.

Cindy Breakspeare[85] was "the woman most often linked with Bob, other than Rita or his mother Cedella."[86] Cindy—young, lithe, pretty, and white—was a privileged Jamaican because of her skin color and heritage, though her family had "fallen on hard times" when she was very young.[87] Thus, despite her working-class jobs as a dancer and shop girl in Kingston, Cindy was—and continues to be—seen as an "uptown girl," a term that connotes both color and class. Their affair, begun years before Marley became a national hero, "scandalized Jamaica's elitist and largely racist uptown society."[88] She herself has claimed that Bob preferred "Babylonian" women, though he has been linked to and had children with women of various colors. Rumors persist that Bob was attracted to Cindy's white beauty and that she was attracted to his money, ignoring his advances until he became famous and wealthy. Although we will never know what contributed to the longevity of Cindy and Bob's relationship, after they became involved she was crowned Miss World 1976 (a campaign financed by Bob), becoming famous in her own right. Cindy, in particular, made no effort to be discreet about their relationship, declaring immediately after being crowned Miss World that she had to "go home to her rasta."[89] And the tabloid press followed, photographing the black king of reggae with his "unkempt" dredlocks, marijuana-endorsing religion, and deep creole, and the white beauty queen with her otherwise "clean" image and more palatable accent, speculating about the possibility of their marriage. One headline about the couple in the popular British *Daily Mirror* paper referred to them as "The Beauty and the Beast."[90]

Cindy was Bob's *public* relationship, especially as perceived by the world outside of Jamaica. If the media had focused on him with Rita, with her head wrapped and her long skirts, as well as her dark skin, they would have to contend with Rastafarianism's notion of black women as queens, rather than with the much more conventional image of the white beauty queen. Bob's polygamous lifestyle and the complicity of the women connected to him allowed him to proselytize for an all-inclusive "one love" in both his music and his personal life.

*   *   *

The dominant narratives of relationships between white women and

Caribbean men of color that are found in film, in print, and in the lives of prominent figures focus on sexuality, conquest, money, and power. A significant exception to this pattern is the marriage of Surinamese man Waldemar Nods and Dutch woman Rika van der Lans, which is consistently portrayed as a love story. The couple met in 1928, had a son in 1929, were married in 1937, and in 1945 died separately at the hands of the Nazis for the crime of hiding Jews. This epic story was largely unknown until Dutch journalist Annejet van der Zijl wrote the best-selling book *Sonny Boy* (2004) and a successful big-budget film with the same title was released in 2011.[91]

Details are, of course, lost in the translations from fact to literary nonfiction and from book to movie. Much of what is lost to the wider public relates to Waldemar's early life.[92] His mother "was part of the light-colored black elite of Paramaribo," a descendant of a planter from Scotland and a local black woman. His "Creole-Indian" father was not born into wealth but through prospecting for gold "became one of the richest men in Suriname," which enabled him to marry into a "good" family. Although the film depicts the father leaving Suriname with a pretty young woman, other accounts say he "disappeared" while "adventuring" in Brazil.[93] Thus Waldemar was the result of a marriage of mixed color and class backgrounds.

In 1927 Waldemar's family sent him to Holland to study and live with his half brother. But the arrangement was uncomfortable for the brother's young family, and he became a boarder in the home of his brother's niece, Rika. Rika had also undergone major transitions before meeting Waldemar, who was some thirty years her junior. Raised Catholic, she had defied her family and community with her "improper" marriage to a Protestant man.[94] Four children later, she discovered that he was having an affair with the maid, and she left him, taking the children. The separation also resulted in a reduction of her class status, from that of a wealthy homeowner with servants to dweller in a small city apartment, where she had to take in a boarder just to be able to afford the rent. Waldemar and Rika were both lonely outcasts from Dutch society, and it is perhaps not surprising that a love affair developed.

The racial difference was only one taboo of their relationship. The large age difference, as well her status as a woman who was legally married (and thus adulterous) but effectively separated (and thus "disgraced" by divorce), added to the scandal.[95] The film portrays Rika as a free spirit who declares "I can do anything I want" when she is challenged, an attitude that may have contributed to the loss of her children and the couple's eventual arrest and death. Her spirit only falters when she discovers she is pregnant with Waldemar's child; she actually goes to an abortionist, and it is unclear in the film whether the procedure does not work or whether she decides in the end not to go through with it. Waldemar is initially depicted as childlike (he was seventeen when they met), but he becomes the more serious of the two after their son is born and as the war encroaches on their lives.

The film's most-used technique is that of the flashback. In several scenes, Waldemar gazes at Rika and the screen shifts to similar images of his mother. This approach implies that race is not as big a boundary as it may seem, while also reinforcing Waldemar's good character as a man who wants to take care of his wife the way he could not take care of his mother. Of course, Rika is not his mother, although she is old enough to be. If the abortion scene represents Rika's doubts about the relationship, Waldemar's doubts are revealed when one of his sisters unexpectedly visits from Suriname. By this time, the couple has been kicked out of the house they shared, and Rika's husband—having discovered when he tried to reconcile with her that his wife is pregnant by a black man—has won sole custody of their four children. The couple lives with their baby in a single room above a bar. When the sister comes to the door, Rika answers and immediately knows who she is, but Waldemar insists on talking to the sister away from Rika and does not even introduce them. The sister is shocked at where he is living and completely disapproves of his relationship, calling Rika "that woman" and saying their mother would "turn in her grave." Her rejection mirrors that of Rika's husband. But the key moment in these scenes is when Rika complains that he treated her like "trash," and asks if he is ashamed of her. Waldemar's silence speaks volumes. Waldemar is portrayed as truly loving Rika, but this scene implicitly asks whether if he had had other options—if there had been less racism in Holland at the time or more women of color—if he would still have fallen in love with Rika.

Despite these moments, both the book and the film *Sonny Boy* portray a story of a love that cannot be defeated by discrimination or by war, a love that is big enough for an extended family of six children, as well as for the Jews they hide in their home. By publicizing the story of perhaps "the only Surinamese resistance fighter in Holland," the narrative also serves as a *national* romance that deemphasizes both Dutch racism and the power of Dutch Nazi sympathizers, who were responsible for thousands of deaths.[96]

Conclusion: "Let's get together and feel alright"

Many will recognize the title of this chapter as the hit song written and performed by Bob Marley. I've chosen it to headline this study because "One love?" can be seen as a recurring question regarding representations of interracial relationships between Caribbean men of color and white women. Though "One Love" can also be seen as an anti-imperialist, anticapitalist song, it is useful here because Marley was himself the child of an interracial union who was abandoned by the white father and because Bob Marley was publicly in at least one significant relationship with a white woman. Ironically, many Afro-Jamaicans and Afro-Caribbeans consider "One Love" to be an anthem for the African Diaspora, while millions of others the world over consider it a universal, multiracial anthem.

Waldemar Nods' marriage has become a romantic metaphor for Dutch (and by extension, European) racial tolerance, even though both died at the hands of the Nazis. Similarly, Marley's and Rubirosa's relationships with women are significant beyond their own personal lives, not only because they were international celebrities but because they were and continue to be icons of Caribbean masculinity. That two quintessential Caribbean men's ideal romantic and sexual partners were white women, and that the men continue to be celebrated in part for their ability to bed beautiful white women, is emblematic of Caribbean men's continued reification of white women and continued investment in the metaphor of interracial sex as conquest.

*   *   *

Given that heterosexual, gender-conforming men are the center of the Caribglobal heteropatriarchy, privileged in regional and diaspora political, economic, sociological, and familial sectors, their inclusion in a book about transgressive Caribbean sexualities might seem odd. Indeed, the very concept of Caribbean sexuality has historically been "dominated by masculine needs and interests."[97] One example of andro-focused sexual mores is the fact that nonmonogamous and extramarital affairs are *not* considered transgressive for Caribbean men, a fact pointed out by scores of writers and scholars.[98] Examining what types of consensual sexualities might be transgressive for the Caribbean heteropatriarch can help illuminate the structures that maintain existing hegemonies. Interracial relationships between Caribbean men of color and white women are one such example, though such relationships are much more stigmatized in the global North than they are in the Caribbean region.[99]

The men characters discussed in this chapter are from or have their origins in the French, English, Spanish, and Dutch Caribbean. They are middle class, working class, and poor. Some are light-skinned and some are dark-skinned; they identify with various nationalities and consider themselves black, Latin or Latino, and Indian. The texts are also disparate; some are satirical and humorous, while others are serious or chilling. The white women are much more homogenous. Except for Breakspeare, they are all North American and European. Most are middle class or wealthy at home; all are wealthy within Caribbean contexts. The greatest variation among the women is age; in the Caribbean, the women, such as those in *Heading South*, are much more likely to be age fifty or older. In the diaspora, it is more common for young white women to be Caribbean men's sexual partners, perhaps because the younger women are more willing than the older women to be openly rebellious and reckless with their reputations, and perhaps because Caribbean men, when they have the luxury of choice, find the younger women more desirable. Notwithstanding Naipaul's one-night encounters with no expectations and Cindy Breakspeare's trading her "ideal" femininity for Bob Marley's money, most of the white women are willing to financially support the men of color they sleep with.

Consensual sex is typically meant to achieve pleasure, but as in the interracial sex discussed here, that pleasure is often not solely physical. Kempadoo explains this dynamic another way: "Sexuality has multiple meanings in [various] contexts, not all of which have to do with a reciprocity of sexual desire or feelings of love."[100] What all of the individuals in these relationships share is a racialized sexual desire; the men and women are inseparable from their respective races, and their race contributes to their attractiveness to each other, often serving as a symbol of transgression. As Patricia Mohammed writes, "The dishonouring of a man and his masculinity through [acting upon] the female body has been and remains literally a blow below the belt for masculinity," and Mohammed links this to rape as a tool of war.[101] Similarly, through interracial relationships, each party implicitly strikes a blow against hegemonic white masculinity.

These relationships are also part of a long historical tradition among

Caribbean people of "the strategic use of sexuality to obtain 'whiteness.'"[102] Not surprisingly, the transgression of heterosexual interracial relationships between Caribbean men of color and white women is fundamentally different than the other sexualities discussed in *Island Bodies* because it is meant to affirm and uphold heteropatriarchy. The only question here is *which* man will reign. The men of color use conquest of the white female body to attack white men's social, cultural, economic, and sexual power, but because they largely keep the relationships hidden and temporary or occasional, ultimately the men continue to live within and the women continue to support white heteropatriarchal power structures. As Mimi Sheller writes, "The detour into tropical luxuriance must remain only that."[103] Such relationships must not result in miscegenation (in other words, children) or public, long-term, live-in relationships in the North. For the most part, these relationships must also be kept hidden from the family, unless the rebellion is meant to be public. These rules of conduct are true even for this chapter's real-life examples, which include longer, more public relationships. Waldemar and Rika Nods were rejected by both of their families and by the society they lived in. Porfirio Rubirosa and Bob Marley, with money and fame on their side, embraced promiscuity, so even women who married Rubirosa or had children by Marley could "recover" their own public reputations once the Latin Lover or the Black Stud moved on to his next conquest.

Because most of these relationships are temporary, as Sheller observes, "the transgression of racial and moral boundaries serves to reinforce the constitution of geographies of difference that define Europe or North America as 'civilised' and the Caribbean as a chain of 'unreal' fantasy islands," as well as the constructions of racial difference that created the stereotypes mentioned at the beginning of this chapter.[104] Except in Rubirosa's case, these interracial relationships do not result in any lasting change in the men's material circumstances. But because their intention is to subvert white male hegemony, these relationships can be seen as tangential, but nevertheless related, to other, more organized attempts to subvert white, northern, male hegemony. Keith Nurse argues that "The 'nation' is often portrayed as the patriarchal father figure. Serving the nation is thus equivalent to serving the hegemonic masculine. . . . The 'other,' the foreigner, is feminized."[105] So, if the nation itself is equivalent to the man, then the sexual conquest is linked to a nationalist conquest, and the foreigner is literally feminized through the female body.

The title of this chapter signifies in several different ways. Interracial sex and desire are the one and only "love," largely excluding women of color or relegating them to fourth-class status, behind white men, white women, and men of color. (Here we are reminded of Fanon's statement, "I know nothing," about the woman of color.[106]) To quote Marley's song, in the films and literature discussed here, everyone does "get together," and they both "feel alright" afterwards, but their pleasures, though intimately linked, are not the same. The white women are able to reestablish their desirability through sex with desirable men and to have an "exotic" experience, while the men of color are able to confirm their masculinity by bedding the white man's "prize," often while also improving their own finances. But the dynamics of interracial relationships found in Caribglobal film, literature, and social science research also point to larger questions about the status of hegemonic Caribbean masculinity. As noted at the beginning of this chapter, the films and literature examined here take place just before and some thirty years after Caribbean flag independence. Despite some significant political changes, white men persist in controlling international economics and military force and have influence over the Caribbean because of the region's huge debt to the global North and dependence on its tourists. Caribbean men's perceptions of themselves as in crisis *as men* is apparent in both popular culture and scholarly circles. And yet, "rumors of the death of a male-dominated social order are greatly exaggerated."[107] The point is not so much to say that women would ipso facto have been better leaders, as to point out that the strategies of these specifically male and heteropatriarchal regimes and ideologies failed, and yet the failure has not been linked to those ideologies. Perhaps this is part of why so many male Caribbean intellectuals and heads of state have married white women—for love and sexual desire, surely, but perhaps also to hedge their bets and attack white patriarchy on all fronts. In raising the idea of a spectacular failure of Caribbean men's leadership, I hope to provoke a rethinking of Caribglobal political and social life similar to the rethinking of sexual possibility presented in this book's conclusion.

Afterword

At the beginning of this study, I proposed imagination as part of a methodology for the study of sexuality in popular culture and literature. The preceding chapters explore portrayals of transgressive sexualities in diverse creative works, including carnival and festival performances, novels and short stories, feature films and documentaries, and music and visual art. This analysis also engages traditional mores, official laws, and formal and informal activism as imaginative acts, insofar as they reveal the perceived limits and possibilities of Caribglobal sexualities. To conclude this work, then, I propose imagination as a methodology for the inclusion of sexual transgression in Caribbean community- and nation-building. For if nations are, in large part, imagined communities, then *how* we imagine our communities is crucial. Three important Caribbean thinkers, Puerto Rican sociologist Manolo Guzmán, Jamaican author Thomas Glave, and Trinidadian activist and poet Colin Robinson, have also invoked the imagination in relationship to transgressive Caribbean sexualities. In his important book *Gay Hegemony/Latino Homosexualities*, Guzmán addresses what I name in chapter 2 el secreto abierto, the situation in which people "know" someone is a homosexual, though the fact is not openly acknowledged. Guzmán argues that those who criticize el secreto abierto do not understand its context; he writes that "The claim that sexual silence in Latino cultures is a symptom of homophobia is an effect of the *failure to imagine* a thoroughly historicized gay homosexuality. Thus, this so-called silence is not only misconstrued but also conceptualized as a problem in need of remedy."[1] Glave, in his oft-reproduced essay originally published in 1999, "Toward a Nobility of the Imagination: Jamaica's Shame," focuses on Jamaican homophobic ignorance and shame that are the opposite of the "noble imagination" he

dreams of. And Robinson, in direct response to Glave's essay, argues that
Glave and many Caribbean and non-Caribbean LGBT activists outside of
the region suffer from a "poverty of imagination" in relationship to "the humanity of both the Caribbean homophobe and of the means to change his/
her heart."[2] Like Guzmán, Robinson worries that too many activists propa-
gate "a disturbingly neocolonial vision of the Caribbean as backwards on
issues of sexuality and humanism alongside a reductionist vision of Caribbean homophobia as irrational, ignorant and inhumane."

Presumably all of these men want, as Glave writes, "the ability to envi-
sion goodness, even greatness, in all things, and most of all in ourselves;
the ability to love ourselves—all of ourselves, irrespective of color, class,
gender, or sexual orientation."[3] Interestingly, however, they direct their dis-
content to different constituencies. Guzmán targets scholars who misun-
derstand Latino cultures, while Glave criticizes Jamaicans who are ignorant of or hateful towards same-sex desiring people. Robinson, in contrast,
addresses Caribbean LGBT activists and allies. The conversation between
these men's work is instructive and absorbing. However, I want to present a
Caribglobal argument that engages but broadens the discussion of sexuality and the imagination beyond the sociolinguistic boundaries of Latino
cultures, the national boundaries of Jamaica, and the boundaries of sexual
minority activism. Throughout the Caribbean region and its diaspora,
trans people, same-sex desiring individuals, and women who display sexual agency are considered transgressive because they contradict prevailing
gender and sexuality norms and therefore threaten Caribglobal heteropatriarchy. And when interracial relationships between Caribbean men and
white women are considered transgressive, it is because they are thought to
threaten white male hegemony or to threaten racial or territorial nationalism. Yet, as the preceding chapters have demonstrated, there is an abundance of evidence both of transgressive Caribbean sexualities and "native
understandings" of these desires throughout Caribbean history and culture,
in every era, and in every part of the region and its diaspora.[4] Among other
realities, the increasing visibility of heterosexual women's sexual agency in
music and of trans people and other sexual minorities through activism and
in the media makes the realities of their lives more difficult to ignore. The
persistent existence of sexual transgression despite all efforts to suppress
it demonstrates the power of the erotic and shows that resistance exists in

some form everywhere and all the time, even at great risk, and even if that resistance is difficult for some to discern.

Ironically, the visibility of advocates of sexual repression "inadvertently speaks of the malleability" rather than the fixity of sexuality.[5] The simultaneous persistence of notions of "right" and "wrong," "proper" and "indecent" sexuality are neither accidental nor spontaneous but are concepts that undergird heteropatriarchal structures which, in turn, help to determine and perpetuate Caribglobal racial, ethnic, and class hegemonies. When people—especially religious, political, and cultural leaders—condemn consensual adult sexualities as threatening "our way of life," they are correct—but the *us* referred to is usually a narrow subset of the population. Traditional gender roles and sexual mores serve not only to perpetuate heteropatriarchal hegemony but also to serve as a major distraction from economic, social, and political concerns that have a more immediate impact on Caribbean lives than do minorities' sexual choices.

Those who advocate both for and against sexual restrictions in the Caribbean tend to focus on citizenship rather than on community. In the legal language of citizenship, women, same sex-desiring persons, and trans people rarely exist except as pariahs. But in Caribglobal communities, all of these people appear and are more often than not tolerated and, to various degrees, accepted. As discussed in chapter 3, many sexual minority activists based within the region demonstrate how people can claim a transgressive sexuality and social, ethnic, or national community membership, not only in their mission, but also in their actions. For example, in the aftermath of the devastating 2010 earthquake in Haiti, many foreign aid organizations distributed food only to women, making problematic and life-threatening assumptions about local family structures. In response, SEROvie, an organization created to provide HIV/AIDS "prevention and support services for sexual minorities," obtained food aid and "we started doing our own distribution to our beneficiaries and members of our community, *not only LGBT members but everyone!*"[6] This kind of activism correctly assumes that those who engage in transgressive sexualities *are already part of* their local and national Caribbean communities.[7] It is important to change laws that punish homosex, cross-dressing, and women's sexual agency. But throughout the Caribbean, though these laws are selectively applied to those who seem to have little social or economic capital, they are only rarely enforced.

More actual (though less visible) harm is done to those targeted by such laws through widespread pressure to conform, social shunning, and discrimination within families, schools, workplaces, and religious institutions that prevent people not only from loving but also from working and living in ways that fulfill their life possibilities and potential as individuals *and* as community members and citizens. Furthermore, the persistence of official and unofficial condemnation of sexual transgression in French and Dutch Caribbean territories that have no legal prohibitions against them proves that legislative action without attention to community attitudes is not only futile but can also feed negative attitudes because of perceived neocolonialism.

If Caribbean people who embody transgressive desire and our allies combine efforts to reveal both the prevalence of these desires *and* the prevalent acceptance of them, while *also* addressing economic and political issues of pressing concern to larger Caribbean communities, then real and lasting change will be achieved—changes in peoples' minds and behavior, and not only in the laws that govern them. Like Robinson, I believe that "imagination is a critical tool" at least as much as any theory, annotated bibliography, or rubric. But instead of demanding a "noble" imagination or decrying a "poverty" or "failure" of imagination, I argue for a recognition of the breadth of imagination that already exists in Caribglobal communities, not only among people who engage in transgressive desire, but also among those who would decry such desire.

Notes

Introduction: From the Foreign-Local to the Caribglobal

1. This author is, of course, aware that not all of the places that identify as or are identified as Caribbean are islands. Nevertheless, other geographic locations such as Guyana and the Caribbean coasts of Central and South America share a similar history of being exoticized.

2. Sheller, *Consuming the Caribbean*, 5.

3. Grewal and Kaplan, "Global Identities," 664, 655, 665.

4. Tinsley, *Thiefing Sugar*, 30; La Fountain-Stokes, *Uñas pintadas de azul*, 7. A "department" is the rough equivalent to a U.S. American state or a Canadian province.

5. Dalleo, *Caribbean Literature and the Public Sphere*, xi.

6. K. Kempadoo, *Sexing the Caribbean*, 5.

7. Boyce Davies, *Black Women, Writing and Identity*, 204.

8. Hall, "Minimal Selves," 115.

9. K. Kempadoo, *Sexing the Caribbean*, 7.

10. Atluri, "Putting the 'Cool,'" 20.

11. See E. Clarke, *My Mother Who Fathered Me*; Safa, *Myth of the Male Breadwinner*; Solien de González, "Consanguineal Household"; Slater, *Caribbean Family*; Barrow, *Family in the Caribbean*; and Wekker, *Politics of Passion: Women's Sexual Culture*.

12. For statistics on Bahamian children born outside of heterosexual marriage, see Alexander, *Pedagogies of Crossing*, 38. For research on the nonuniversality of heterosexuality in the Caribbean, see Ramírez, *What It Means to Be a Man*; Decena, *Tacit Subjects*; and Jafari Allen, *¡Venceremos?*

13. K. Kempadoo, *Sexing the Caribbean*, 2.

14. Ironically, ultraconservative Christian fundamentalist groups from the United States are working more frequently in the Caribbean, South America, and Africa, where they believe the cultural climate is currently more welcoming to heterosexism than are North America and Europe. See, for instance, Colin Robinson, "Work of Three-Year CAISO," and Center for Constitutional Rights, "Ugandan LGBT Activists File Case."

15. Alexander, *Pedagogies of Crossing*, 22–23.

16. K. Kempadoo, *Sexing the Caribbean*, 28.

17. Tinsley, "Black Atlantic, Queer Atlantic," 198.

18. Alexander, *Pedagogies of Crossing*, 22.

19. See, for instance, the website for Haitian organization KOURAJ, http://kouraj.org/; Robinson, "Patricia Gone with Millicent"; Decena, *Tacit Subjects*; and G. Ayala, "Retiring Behavioral Risk."

20. Seigworth and Gregg, introduction to *Affect Theory Reader*, 1.

21. See Dalleo, *Caribbean Literature and Public Sphere*, 4. I agree with Dalleo in that my conception of public sphere is more democratic than "Habermas's monolithic construction of the bourgeois public sphere."

22. Tim Padgett, "The Most Homophobic Place on Earth?" *Time* online, April 12, 2006, http://www.time.com/time/world/article/0,8599,1182991,00.html.

23. For a similar approach in relation to use of accents, see La Fountain-Stokes, *Queer Ricans* 190, n.5.

24. Tinsley, *Thiefing Sugar*, 28.

25. Wekker, *Politics of Passion*, 76.

26. Ferguson, *Aberrations in Black*, 118.

27. J. Allen, *¡Venceremos?* 58–59.

28. K. Kempadoo, *Sexing the Caribbean*, 4.

Chapter 1. The Caribbean Trans Continuum and Backhanded Re/Presentation

1. For discussion of the term *transgender*, see, for instance, Namaste, *Invisible Lives*, introduction. On surgery, see J. Allen, *¡Venceremos?* 192

2. La Font, "Very Straight Sex," 1.

3. Orsi, "Cuba Transgender Wedding."

4. Adding significantly to the small archive of work on Caribbean trans people, Tinsley's analysis in *Thiefing Sugar* (175) provides some history of Caribbean trans genders. She cites nineteenth- and twentieth-century Haitian, Surinamese, and Cuban references to "male women," remarking that Caribbean realities "generated a spectrum of Creolized names beyond effeminate to designate culturally specific formations of male femininity—including Suriname's male mati, Caribbean Spanish travesti, and the French/Kreyòl masisi and macommère" (175).

5. A Jamaican study by Hron et al. notes that "transgendered individuals (especially men to women) maintain a very low public profile due to the overwhelmingly negative attitudes toward them, and are therefore not commonly subject to public scrutiny. While cases of abuse do occur, no personal statements exist to document them" ("Report on Persecution" 2). Similarly, the entry for Puerto Rico in *The International Dictionary of Sexuality* states that "As in other parts of the world, transvestites and transsexuals do exist in Puerto Rican society. However, scientific data on the extent of this population and its practices are unavailable" (Montesinos and Preciado, "Puerto Rico," n. pag.). This quote comes from the only article in the dictionary that discusses trans people in a Caribbean country. The missing voices and analysis of trans lives in such studies points to their vulnerability and marginality, as well as

to the low priority many sexual minority advocates place on their experiences and well-being.

6. These times were marked, for instance, by the DeSouza case discussed later in this chapter, by the founding of J-FLAG (Jamaican Forum for Lesbians, All-Sexuals, and Gays), by the increased policing of nonheterosexual gender and sexuality in the Caribbean, and by the increased addition of a *T* for *transgender* to the acronyms of many gay and lesbian organizations and movements.

7. *Lantana camara* is the scientific name of a flowering shrub (not the cactus cereus) indigenous to some tropical areas; in Trinidad it is sometimes called white sage. The leaves change color as they age, and the plant can spread widely, causing some to consider it a pest. For the reference to Nurse Tyler, see Mootoo, *Cereus Blooms*, 6.

8. Mootoo, *Cereus Blooms*, 4. The original is completely italicized.

9. Throughout this chapter I will use the same pronouns (*him, her, himself, herself*) to refer to characters that the characters use to refer to themselves.

10. Mootoo, *Cereus Blooms*, 15.

11. Ibid., 99–100 (emphasis added).

12. Ibid., 105, 22. Here, as elsewhere in the chapter, page numbers follow the order in which items are quoted in my text.

13. Ibid., 6, 7, 71, 47–48.

14. Ibid., 19–20, 48.

15. Ibid., 110.

16. This behavior is often applied to people who engage in same-sex sexuality and is reminiscent of the concept of the open secret/el secreto abierto.

17. Mootoo, *Cereus Blooms*, 124 (emphasis in original).

18. Ibid., 124, 77–78 (emphasis added).

19. Ibid., 47–48.

20. Cliff, *No Telephone*, 7. Harry/Harriet is a name the character uses to refer to him/herself until choosing *she* and *Harriet*. Thus, in this text I will use *Harriet* when referring to the character after her choice and *Harry/Harriet* when referring to the character before that choice is made.

21. Tinsley, *Thiefing Sugar*, 180.

22. Color and race are the most prominent subjects in the novel; Harriet's father, like Clare and her father, has black ancestors but is considered white in Jamaica because of his very fair skin. Though Harriet and Clare share a similar racial ancestry, Harriet displays no complex about her racial identity; she acknowledges the privileges her father's skin and money provide but identifies with darker and poorer Jamaicans.

23. *Batty* is Jamaican slang for buttocks; *battyman* and *batty bwoy* are slurs for homosexual men.

24. Cliff, *No Telephone*, 128, 89, 21.

25. Ibid., 140.

26. Ibid., 168.

27. Cliff, interview, 601.

28. Tinsley, *Thiefing Sugar*, 180.

29. Ibid.

30. See de Moya, "Power Games," 27.

31. Santos-Febres, *Sirena Selena* (Lytle trans.), 2, 8. Page numbers follow the order in which items are quoted in my text. All references to this novel in this chapter are to Lytle's English translation.

32. Ibid., 3, 47.

33. Ibid., 13, 10–11.

34. Ibid., 1.

35. Ibid., 168, 5, 45, 83.

36. Ibid., 103, 127, 135, 171, 129, 133.

37. Ibid., 172.

38. Ibid., 1, 134, 164, 6.

39. Morrison, *Playing in the Dark*, viii. Thanks to Gabrielle Civil for reminding me of this work.

40. Ibid., ix.

41. Ibid., 81.

42. Just as the absence of biologically female trans characters looms large in Caribbean literature and studies.

43. Cliff, *No Telephone*, 128.

44. Ibid., 137.

45. For instance, *transgender* is to some an outmoded term; *gender queer, aggressive* or *AG, boi,* and *gender fluid* are some of the other terms used now in the United States.

46. Sarduy, *Written on a Body*, 93–94.

47. Even before we learn of Chandin's incest, gender ideals in *Cereus Blooms* have already been fractured by race. Lavinia, Chandin's adoptive sister and a foreign white woman, is universally admired for being physically strong, intellectual, and aggressive. But Sarah, his wife from a poor Indian background, "knew better than to be seen" emulating her friend (and subsequent lover)(55). Chandin himself remarks that he "admired things in Lavinia that he would have been ashamed to have his wife do" (55). These comments acknowledge that the colonial social order mandates different conventional genders for different races.

48. Santos-Febres, *Sirena Selena* (Lytle trans.), quotation 1, 74; quotation 2, 31–33.

49. Ibid., 133.

50. See Manrique, "Mayra's Siren Song," n. pag. Unfortunately, there is an assumption here that all transvestites are male.

51. Santos-Febres, *Sirena Selena* (Lytle trans.), 133, 2, 129, 15, 214.

52. Ibid., 103, 106, 203, 208.

53. There are a few notable exceptions, such as Puerto Rican Cristina Hayworth, who was part of the 1969 Stonewall uprising, and Jowelle de Souza, known as the first Trinidadian transsexual.

54. See my 2005 essay "Dressing Down" in *Sargasso* for a detailed discussion of traditional transvestite characters in Trinidad and Tobago's carnival.

55. Aching, *Masking and Power*, 5.

56. Loíza is commonly known as a center of black life and culture in Puerto Rico.

57. The significance of Santiago Apóstol (Saint James the Apostle) implies that he should be considered a fifth character. See Harris, "Masking the Site," 361, 363.

58. Alegría, "Fiesta of Santiago Apóstol," 125.

59. This debate is principally about African retentions, European origins and/or adaptations, and local creation, considerations that, unfortunately, are typically not applied to locas specifically.

60. Alegría, "Fiesta of Santiago Apóstol," 131.

61. Moreno Vega's 2001 *The Altar of My Soul* provides a good introduction to Espiritismo and the academic literature around it.

62. Aravind Enrique Adyanthaya, in an e-mail message to the author, December 4, 2003.

63. Loretta Collins, in an e-mail message to the author, December 3, 2003.

64. It is possible that the general elision of the loca from popular and academic discussions of the Loíza festival reflects "the desire of Puerto Ricans to 'Whiten' the population of Puerto Rico by ignoring its African legacy" (Moreno Vega, *Altar of My Soul*, 333).

65. Other spirit guides in Espiritismo include the indio (the Indian), the gypsy, and the Arab. Aravind Enrique Adyanthaya, in an e-mail message to the author, December 4, 2003.

66. Sifuentes-Jáuregui, *Transvestism, Masculinity, and Latin American Literature*, 4. According to master mask-maker Raul Ayala, there is also a difference between a traditional loca and "a man trying to look like a homosexual" (author's personal communication with Ayala, July 25, 2003).

67. La Fountain-Stokes, "Trans-locas," 5.

68. Decena, *Tacit Subjects*, 164.

69. This same group argues that *all* characters should be "traditional," that in addition to "drag queens," Halloween-type masks and other contemporary costumes should not be allowed" (Lowell Fiet, in a discussion with the author, July 17, 2003).

70. Meredith, "Barbadian *Tuk* Music," 96.

71. Drayton, qtd. in Meredith, "Barbadian *Tuk* Music," 96.

72. Tuk is the main indigenous, traditional music of Crop Over and of Barbados. See Meredith, "Barbadian *Tuk* Music," 83.

73. Peter Roberts writes that in 1975, Natalie Davis, "commenting on an Irish connection, associates the name Sally . . . to a character with these [same] exaggerated characteristics" (see Roberts, "Distinctive Features," 35). See also Davis, *Society and Culture in Early Modern France, 149.*

74. "The Irish Indies," February 15, 2002, *Race and History: News and Views.* http://www.raceandhistory.com/cgi-bin/forum/webbbs_config.pl/noframes/read/487.

75. I discuss Dame Lorraine at length in my 2005 essay "Dressing Down," 25–29.

76. Aching, *Masking and Power,* 75, 3.

77. King, "Dressing Down," 30.

78. See King, "New Citizens, New Sexualities," 221–23.

79. World Travel and Tourism Council (WTTC), *Travel and Tourism Economic Impact 2013: Barbados* (London: WTTC, 2013), 1, http://www.wttc.org/site_media/uploads/downloads/barbados2013.pdf; WTTC, *Travel and Tourism Economic Impact 2013: Trinidad and Tobago* (London: WTTC, 2013), 1, http://www.wttc.org/site_media/uploads/downloads/trinidad_and_tobago2013.pdf.

80. "Puerto Rico," *Encyclopedia of the Nations,* http://www.nationsencyclopedia.com/economies/Americas/Puerto-Rico.html.

81. Hernández and Ortega-Brena, "'If God Were Black and from Loíza,'" 66; Swords and Mize, "Beyond Tourist Gazes and Performances," 56–57.

82. Hernández and Ortega-Brena, "'If God Were Black and from Loíza,'" 74.

83. Sifuentes-Jáuregui, *Transvestism, Masculinity, and Latin American Literature,* 128.

84. Bejel, *Gay Cuban Nation,* 197.

85. See "Dominican Republic Carnival/Carnaval Dominicano—Carnival Characters and Masked Beings with Descriptions," *The Colonial Zone,* http://www.colonialzone-dr.com/traditions-carnival_characters.html; and Lynne Guitar, "The Origins of Carnival—And the Special Traditions of Dominican *Carnaval,*" 2007, *domibachata.com,* http://www.domibachata.com/carnival/Carnaval%20Origins_w%20ophotos.pdf.

86. Murray, *Opacity,* 147.

87. See, for instance, the work of Wayne Willock in Barbados through Cultural and Historical Exposure for Kids in Schools (Facebook page at https://www.facebook.com/media/set/?set=a.209357999188524.1073741848.146684118789246&type=3) and Pearl Eintou Springer in Trinidad and Tobago, through the Idakeda Group (http://www.idakedagroup.com/).

88. Meredith, "Barbadian *Tuk* Music," 102.

89. See, for instance, Guitar, note 83.

90. Gordon, Sharpley-Whiting, and White, *Fanon: A Critical Reader,* 1.

91. Fanon, *Peau Noire,* 146; Fanon, *Black Skin,* 180.

92. As the journal *MaComère* notes, the term *macommère* "is widely used by women in the Caribbean to mean 'my child's godmother'; 'my best friend and close female confidante'; 'my bridesmaid, or another female wedding member of a wedding party of which I was a bridesmaid'; 'the godmother of the child to whom I am also godmother'; 'the woman who, by virtue of the depth of her friendship, has rights and privileges over my child and is a surrogate mother.'" The journal also notes that the word is used to refer to "'a womanish or gossipy man'; [or] 'a homosexual.'" See Assn. of Caribbean Women Writers and Scholars, "About the Name," http://www.macomerejournal.com/about.html. This definition is supported by other sources as well, such as Crowley ("Naming Customs in St. Lucia," 87).

93. Fanon, *Black Skin*, 180.

94. Tinsley provocatively points out that there is a documented history of female Caribbean merchants' same-sex desire, which means a relationship between a market woman and a macommère might be far from heteronormative (*Thiefing Sugar*, 146).

95. Because of the general acceptance of men's promiscuity and informal polygamy throughout the Caribbean, it is likely that Martinican men of all cultures might be seduced by market women. What is significant in Fanon's text is that *only* one type of woman is portrayed as potential sex partners for macommères.

96. Fuss, "Interior Colonies," 33.

97. For example, Bejel, in his analysis of the documentary *Mariposas en el andamio*, points to the Cuban town of La Güinera, which includes and accepts a large number of male transvestites who desire men (*Gay Cuban Nation*, 197).

98. While some outlets have called De Souza the first Caribbean person to undergo gender confirmation surgery, it is more likely that she is the first Caribbean person within the region to publicly discuss having done so.

99. A variety of information about the De Souza case is available. See, for instance, "Trinidad Transsexual Praised for Suing State," *CourtTV.com*, http://ai.eecs.umich.edu/people/conway/TSsuccesses/Jowelle/Jowelle.html.

100. Monica Roberts, "Jowelle De Souza-Trini Trans Pioneer." *Trans Griot* (blog), May 2, 2011, http://transgriot.blogspot.com/2011/05/jowelle-de-souza-trini-trans-pioneer.html.

101. An AP wire story that ran on the *Guardian* website and other media outlets pointed out that "One other transgender woman married years ago, but Iriepa is the first to do so having benefited from the new policy" that allows gender confirmation surgery to be covered by state health insurance. See Associated Press, "Gay Man Weds," *Guardian* online, August 14, 2011, http://www.guardian.co.uk/world/2011/aug/14/gay-man-weds-transsexual-woman-cuba.

102. Orsi, "Cuba Transgender Wedding Show," *Yahoo News*, August 13, 2011. Estrada is likely referring to the UMAP or Unidades Militares para Ayudar a la

Producción (Military Units to Aid Production) labor camps, where between 1965 and 1968 feminine and homosexual men were imprisoned in order to make them more "appropriately" masculine.

103. Society against Sexual Orientation Discrimination (SASOD), "Submission to the Global Commission on HIV and the Law," *SASOD-Guyana* (blog), March 29, 2011, http://sasod.blogspot.com/2011/03/normal-o-false-false-false-en-us-x-none.html.

104. Society Against Sexual Orientation Discrimination (SASOD), "Marking World Day of Social Justice, Transgender Citizens, Supported by SASOD, Move to the Courts to Challenge Guyana's Law against 'Cross-Dressing,'" *SASOD-Guyana* (blog), February 22, 2010, http://sasod.blogspot.com/2010_02_01_archive.html.

105. Ibid.

106. Ibid.

107. Ibid.

108. Guyana Cross-Dressing Incident of February 7–8, 2010, Quincy McEwan, Seon Clarke, Joseph Fraser, Seyon Persayd, and the Society Against Sexual Orientation Discrimination (SASOD) vs. Attorney General of Guyana, judgment on jurisdiction, Supreme Court 21-M, Sept. 6, 2013. See "Court Ruling: Constitutional Court Rules Cross-Dressing Is Not a Crime If Not for 'Improper Purpose': Rights Groups Plan Appeal on Dubious Decision," *SASOD Guyana*, Sept. 27, 2013, http://www.sasod.org.gy/blog-tags/court-ruling.

109. Rangelova, "Nationalism, States of Exception," 84.

110. In both countries Indo- and Afro-Caribbeans make up the majority of the population. In Guyana, Indians are a majority of 43.5 percent, and people of African heritage constitute 30.2 percent (Government of Guyana, Bureau of Statistics, "Population and Housing Census 2002: Guyana National Report," 28, *Bureau of Statistics Guyana*, www.statisticsguyana.gov.gy). Similarly, in Trinidad and Tobago, Indians are a majority of 34.4 percent, nearly tied with the 34.2 percent who are of African descent (Raphael John-Lall, "2011 Population Census Report: 4,591 More Men in T&T Than Women," *Trinidad and Tobago Guardian Online*, February 20, 2013, https://guardian.co.tt/news/2013-02-20/2011-population-census-report-4591-more-men-tt-women).

111. Tinsley, *Thiefing Sugar* 170–71.

112. Ibid.

113. Mootoo, *Cereus Blooms*, 247. Even the one physical reference provided, to Tyler's "dark lips," could refer both to someone of Indian and someone of African descent.

114. Santos-Febres, *Sirena Selena* (Lytle trans.), 84, 41.

115. Ibid., 139.

Chapter 2. "El Secreto Abierto": Visibility, Confirmation, and Caribbean Men Who Desire Men

1. Throughout this chapter I will use the Spanish phrase "el secreto abierto," although sometimes I will use the English equivalent "open secret." I could have easily used the latter or "le non-dit," the French phrase used to refer to similar situations, but I choose to repeat el secreto abierto for two reasons: to destabilize the hegemony of English, albeit in a token manner, and because el secreto abierto is frequently used in scholarship about same-sex desire in the Spanish Caribbean, much more so than the specific language of open secret or le non-dit. See, for instance, Montero, "Queer Theories of Severo Sarduy"; Bejel, *Gay Cuban Nation*; and Agard-Jones, "Le Jeu de Qui?"

2. Wekker, *Politics of Passion*, 271 n. 12.

3. Suriname Men United, "Gays Stand Up for One Another." *Suriname Men United*, 2010, http://www.surinamemenunited.com/informatie/krantenberichten-homos-english.html.

4. Murray, *Opacity*, 114.

5. Pourette, "La figure du makòmé," n. pag. The original quotation reads: "Leurs pratiques homosexuelles restent dans le secret et le non-dit, et elles n'interfèrent pas avec leur vie sociale et quotidienne." (All translations of Pourette are my own.)

6. J. Allen, *¡Venceremos?* 128 (emphasis in original).

7. Laguerre, interview, 2011.

8. Decena, *Tacit Subjects*, 18.

9. Agard-Jones, "Le Jeu de Qui?" 11; Steinecke, "Caribbean Can Be Chilly."

10. Gopinath, *Impossible Desires*, 12.

11. Lancaster, "Tolerance and Intolerance," 263–64, qtd. in Horn, "Queer Caribbean Homecomings," 380 n. 30.

12. Decena, *Tacit Subjects*, 33.

13. "La virulence des discours prononcés à l'encontre des hommes qui ont des pratiques homosexuelles contraste avec la discrétion des propos relatifs aux femmes lesbiennes" (Pourette, "La figure du makòmé," n. pag.).

14. Quiroga, *Tropics of Desire*, 124, qtd. in Peña, "'Obvious Gays,'" 495 n. 30.

15. "[L]'existence du makòmé n'est pas cachée. Il fait au contraire l'objet d'une représentation sociale remarquable: on en parle, on en rit et on le connaît" (Pourette, "La figure du makòmé," n. pag.). *Makòmé* (spelled various ways) is a term commonly used in the French and English Caribbean as a slur against men who desire men and against feminine men whose heterosexuality is suspect because of their gender expression. For more detail regarding this term, see chap. 1, n. 90.

16. Tambiah, "Creating (Im)moral Citizens," 13.

17. See, for instance, Ho, "Caribbean Transnationalism as a Gendered Process," and Safa, *Myth of the Male Breadwinner*.

18. J. Allen, *¡Venceremos?* 72 (emphasis added).

19. Interestingly, the U.S. Virgin Islands repealed its sodomy law in 1984, almost twenty years before the U.S. Supreme Court ruled such laws unconstitutional (Painter, "Sensibilities of Our Forefathers," n. pag.).

20. Agard-Jones, "Le Jeu de Qui?" 3.

21. Tinsley, *Thiefing Sugar*, 31; Aviankoi, "A Gay Is Not a Lost Son."

22. J. Allen, *¡Venceremos?* 72.

23. Peña, "'Obvious Gays,'" 487.

24. Tambiah, "Creating (Im)moral Citizens," 12.

25. Peña, "'Obvious Gays,'" 487–89; Hron et al., 4–5.

26. Peña, "'Obvious Gays,'" 487.

27. See, for instance, Hron et al., "Report on Persecution of Sexual Minorities in Jamaica," published in 2003 by Jamaica AIDS Support.

28. Tinsley, *Thiefing Sugar*, 179.

29. One scholar notes that a similar process is happening in the European Netherlands, which is increasingly anti-immigrant and where "cultural/ethnic conditions and restrictions [are] being placed on Netherlands citizenship" (R. Allen, "Complexity of National Identity," 121).

30. Garry Benfold, "Dutch Antilles Go to Polls," *get2vote* (blog), January 22, 2010, http://get2vote.wordpress.com.

31. Willemien Groot, "Dutch Island Horrified by Same-Sex Marriages."

32. R. Allen, "Complexity of National Identity," 117.

33. Garry Benfold, "Dutch Antilles Go to Polls," *get2vote* (blog), January 22, 2010, http://get2vote.wordpress.com.

34. R. Allen, "Complexity of National Identity," 120.

35. J. Allen, *¡Venceremos?* 10–11.

36. Bejel, *Gay Cuban Nation*, xxii.

37. K. Kempadoo, *Sexing the Caribbean* 28.

38. Decena, *Tacit Subjects*, 114.

39. I agree that "the construction of femininity is neither more secure nor less policed than the construction of masculinity" (Skeete, "Representations of Homophobic Violence," 3), and I discuss the former construct in chapter 3, though here I focus on the latter construct.

40. Bejel, *Gay Cuban Nation*, 6–7.

41. "À la Guadeloupe, l'homosexuel est désigné par le terme créole péjoratif makòmé. Le makòmé est un homme, qui affiche généralement des comportements et des attributs féminins (dans son langage, sa tenue vestimentaire et ses attitudes corporelles), et qui met en acte des pratiques homosexuelles avec des hommes masculins, parfois contre une compensation financière. Les discours le présentent non

pas comme un homme véritable, mais comme un homme-femme. Il n'existe pas d'équivalent féminin du makòmé" (Pourette, "La figure du makòmé," n. pag.).

This same term, variously spelled as *macommère, macomé, makòmé, macumè, makumeh, macoomè, macomeh*, etc., is also found in the English-speaking Caribbean. See chap. 1, n. 92.

42. Aviankoi, "A Gay Is Not a Lost Son," n. pag.

43. P. Mohammed, "Unmasking Masculinity," 53.

44. de Moya, "Power Games," 79–80.

45. J. Allen, ¡*Venceremos?* 126.

46. See, for instance, J. Allen, ¡*Venceremos?* and La Fountain-Stokes, *Queer Ricans*.

47. " . . . de conserver une apparence hétérosexuelle. Il importe à ces hommes d'adopter un code vestimentaire et corporel, des façons de s'exprimer, de se déplacer et de se présenter à autrui masculins. Il faut aimer le sport, être 'costaud,' avoir une musculature développée. Le tout est de ne pas paraître efféminé. La volonté de 'rester un homme' et de s'affirmer en tant que tel se manifeste également dans les rôles sexuels" (Pourette, "La figure du makòmé," n. pag.).

48. de Moya, "Power Games," 89–90.

49. Decena, *Tacit Subjects,* 15 (emphasis added).

50. Ibid., 102.

51. Murray, *Opacity,* 26.

52. "La mort sociale, c'est-à-dire l'exclusion et le bannissement du groupe social et familial" (Pourette, "La figure du makòmé," n. pag.).

53. J. Allen, ¡*Venceremos?* 54; de Moya, "Power Games," 72–73.

54. "No jugar con muñecas. No hacer oficios de la casa porque eso no era de hombres. No vestirse de mujeres. No ponerse maquillaje. Cosas así. Que debemos andar con hombres. No debíamos juntarnos tanto con las mujeres. Que por la manera de sentarnos: deberíamos sentarnos de una forma. Las mujeres se sientan de otra" (Decena, *Tacit Subjects,* 47–48, translation by Decena).

55. Decena, *Tacit Subjects,* 136.

56. Ibid., 114.

57. Agard-Jones, "Le Jeu de Qui?" 10.

58. Decena, *Tacit Subjects,* 32.

59. The "Don't Ask, Don't Tell" policy of the U.S. American government was a major exception to this trend during its life, between 1993 and 2011.

60. Larry Chang, in discussion with the author, Brooklyn, NY, June 21, 2011.

61. Murray, *Opacity,* 113.

62. Lancaster, "Tolerance and Intolerance," 263–64, qtd. in Horn, "Queer Caribbean Homecomings," 380 n. 30.

63. Decena, *Tacit Subjects,* 147 (emphasis added); Greene, "History of Rainbow Alliance Bahamas," n. pag.

64. See Schulman, *Ties That Bind* (10–14, 102–106), for a detailed description of contemporary shunning.

65. Gosine, "Sexual Desires, Rights, and Regulations," 2.

66. Miller, *Fear of Stones*, 6.

67. Ibid., 9.

68. Ibid., 10 (emphasis added).

69. Arenas, *The Brightest Star*, 51.

70. The UMAP camps existed in Cuba from approximately 1965 to 1967. Fidel Castro has since apologized for creating them and called homophobia in the Cuban Revolution "a great injustice" (Castro qtd. in Andrew Swift, "Castro Accepts Blame for Revolution's Homophobia," *Foreign Policy* blog, August 31, 2010, http://blog.foreignpolicy.com/posts/2010/08/31/castro_accepts_blame_for_revolutions_homophobia).

71. Arenas, *The Brightest Star*, 6 5.

72. See, for instance, fiction by Kei Miller (*The Fear of Stones*) and Thomas Glave (*Whose Song? and Other Stories*).

73. Arenas, *The Brightest Star*, 68.

74. Decena, *Tacit Subjects*, 120.

75. Arenas, *Before Night Falls*, 77.

76. Author's personal communication with Chang, June 21, 2011. Chang's social class and ethnicity have been underexamined in interviews and scholarship as factors related to his activism.

77. Tinsley, *Thiefing Sugar*, 133.

78. Translated by scholars variously as *homosexual*, *male homosexual*, and *faggot*, the word *masisi* is used in multiple ways by those interviewed in *Of Men and Gods*. In addition to the aforementioned definitions, the film's subjects sometimes use *masisi* to refer to feminine men who desire men, as well as to identify men who do not hide their desire for other men.

79. *Of Men and Gods*. The spellings reproduced here reflect those of the film's captions.

80. Larry Chang, *Larry Chang Timeline*, n.d., http://www.larrychang.info/timeline.html.

81. Alvarez, *Interesting Monsters*, 82.

82. Ibid., 91.

83. Ibid., 86.

84. Atluri, "Putting the 'Cool,'" 5.

85. Bleys, *Images of Ambiente*, 11. Bleys' work is quite problematic because of his belief that Caribbean sexual minorities are developmentally behind those in the global North and because of his sloppy and inaccurate terminology (117–18, 161, 118).

86. Ewan Atkinson, commentary on *Fiction* series, 2006, *Ewan Atkinson* (online portfolio), http://www.ewanatkinson.com/ewanatkinson.com/Fiction.html.

87. NAGB is different from the Barbados Museum and Historical Society, which does display art but devotes most of its resources and space to history and non-fine-art culture. The museum was founded in 1933, and its original mission was to "to study and put on permanent record the history of the Island, its leading families and public men, old buildings and other matters of interest to antiquarians in Barbados and overseas" (Barbados Museum and Historical Society, "Our History," *Barbados Museum and Historical Society* online, 2013, http://www.barbmuse.org.bb/our-history/).

88. Alissandra Cummins, "Welcome," *National Art Gallery Committee* (NAGC) website, March 1, 2008, http://www.nagc.bb.

89. *Paradise Terrace* was featured on the NAGB website as of September 2013.

90. Cummins (see chap. 2, n. 88).

91. In the myth, homophobia against women is generally not included or is included as an aside, probably because many of these reports are in publications geared specifically towards gay-identified men.

92. Mimi Sheller argues in *Consuming the Caribbean* that similar developmental narratives negatively comparing the Caribbean to Europe and North America have existed for more than five hundred years.

93. Agard-Jones, "Le Jeu de Qui?" 10.

94. Padgett, "Most Homophobic Place" (see intro., n. 22). Rinaldo Walcott notes that "Since the eruptions around dancehall signaled by Buju Banton's 'Boom Bye Bye' in the 1990s (1993 to be exact), the Anglo-Caribbean has been cast as one of the most homophobic places in the world—with Jamaica as its *epicenter*" (Walcott, "Queer Returns," 4). For instance, see also *Têtu*'s 2007 article "La Douleur des Makoumés," analyzed in detail by Vanessa Agard-Jones in "Le Jeu de Qui?"

95. Skeete, "Representations of Homophobic Violence," 4. Clearly she is referring to the English Caribbean; a similar continuum would place the Dutch islands and Haiti on one end, the Dominican Republic and Guadeloupe in the middle, and Martinique and Puerto Rico on the opposite end.

96. Lewis, *Culture of Gender*, 109. See Hron et al.'s 2003 "Report on Persecution of Sexual Minorities in Jamaica" for examples of violent incidents there.

97. Agard-Jones, "Le Jeu de Qui?" 8.

98. Padgett, "Most Homophobic Place" (see intro, n. 22).

99. The United Nations Office on Drugs and Crime (UNODC) *2011 Global Study on Homicide* cites Jamaica's per-capita murder rate as being larger by far than that of any other Caribbean territory (UNODC, *2011 Global Study*, 93). While noting that such generalizations depend on a variety of factors and on how the calculations are made, one UN study confirms that "the Caribbean suffers from more murder per capita than any other region of the world" (*UNODC Crime Trends 2007*, as qtd. in UNODC and LAC Region of World Bank, *Crime, Violence, and Development*, 3).

100. Larcher and Robinson point out that "the average NMMM [No More Murder Music] protestor was in fact using his own body to call for homophobic music to be censored, artists banned, and concerts cancelled," despite their and other organizer's efforts to present a different or at least more nuanced approach ("Fighting 'Murder Music,'" 6).

101. Larcher and Robinson, "Fighting 'Murder Music,'" 4.

102. K. Kempadoo, *Sexing the* Caribbean, 46.

103. Agard-Jones, "Le Jeu de Qui?" 13.

104. Greene, "History of Rainbow Alliance Bahamas," n. pag.

105. Agard-Jones, "Le Jeu de Qui?" 11.

106. Robinson, "Patricia Gone with Millicent," 1.

107. See Binnie, *Globalization of Sexuality;* Horn, "Queer Caribbean Homecomings"; Murray, *Opacity;* Walcott, "Queer Returns"; Gopinath, *Impossible Desires;* Altman, *Global Sex;* and Guzmán, *Gay Hegemony/Latino Homosexualities.*

108. Atluri, "Putting the 'Cool,'" 2.

109. In *Tacit Subjects,* Decena provides a useful analysis that suggests that macho-active constructs and active/passive, activo/pasivo distinctions might be less useful than traditionally thought, since the anally receptive partner may in fact be very active.

110. Of course, these Caribbean concepts of and attitudes towards same-sex desire also differ from one another. While they cannot and should not be collapsed into each other, these concepts and attitudes are linked in multiple ways. They are linked by a similar shared history of chattel slavery, plantation economics, geography, European colonialism, and (neo)imperialism, as well as the concepts' connection to cultural nationalism.

111. Decena, *Tacit Subjects,* 2.

112. Horn et al., "Report on Persecution," 9.

113. Colin Robinson, September 14, 2011, *Facebook* posting.

114. Wekker, *Politics of Passion,* 226.

115. Horn, "Queer Caribbean Homecomings," 362, 377 n. 4. Kiesnoski credits "the economic allure of gay tourist dollars and euros with pushing West Indians toward increasing tolerance of same-sex couples, making such travel look both financially and socially profitable," qtd. in Tinsley, *Thiefing Sugar,* 137.

116. This is also apparent in recent efforts to eliminate or reduce aid to countries in the global South if they do not decriminalize sodomy.

117. Agard-Jones, "Le Jeu de Qui?" 9–10.

118. Horn, "Queer Caribbean Homecomings," 376.

119. Larcher and Robinson, "Fighting 'Murder Music,'" 8.

120. Renov, introduction, *Theorizing Documentary,* 2.

121. Minh-ha, "Totalizing Quest of Meaning," 90, 96.

122. All names except Chang's are pseudonyms; most interviewees had their faces distorted, and some are not seen at all.

123. It is unclear whether the names are real or pseudonyms, or nicknames.

124. Robinson, "Transforming Patriarchy," PowerPoint, slide 12.

125. See Padgett, "Most Homophobic Place" (see intro., n. 22), and Agard-Jones, "Le Jeu de Qui?"

126. Downes, "Boys of the Empire," 107.

127. de Moya, "Power Games," 81.

128. Tinsley, *Thiefing Sugar*, 175.

129. Agard-Jones, "Le Jeu de Qui?" 9, 10, 15. Agard-Jones goes on to say that "France's *mission civilisatrice* acted as the standard bearer. Returning to this time-worn yet still present dynamic forces us to acknowledge the limits of our political imaginations" (15). Of course, the United States also believes it is exceptional as a progenitor of equality and human rights.

130. Tinsley, *Thiefing Sugar*, 104.

Chapter 3. "This Is You": "Invisibility," Community, and Women Who Desire Women

1. I occasionally use the term *sexual minority* to refer to those who engage in (or who want to engage in) consensual erotic relationships that are not heterosexual. I eschew the term *queer* in this chapter, in part because "*queer* is only one construction of nonheteronormative sexuality among many—and that listening to other languages, and others' historically specific sexual self-understandings, is crucial to broadening the field" (Tinsley, *Thiefing Sugar*, 6).

2. As in chapter 2, the creative and critical sources cited here reflect the Spanish Caribbean's production of the largest Caribbean archive of materials relating to same-sex desire.

3. Brand, "Hard against the Soul," in *No Language Is Neutral*, 6–7.

4. Ibid.

5. Ibid.

6. Ibid.

7. Tinsley, *Thiefing Sugar*, 204

8. Elwin, Introduction, *Tongues on Fire*, 7; J. Allen, *¿Venceremos?* 68; Clarise in Elwin, *Tongues on Fire*, 121; Wekker, *Politics of Passion*, 237; Bejel, *Gay Cuban Nation*, 189; Cave and French, "Sexual Choice," n. pag.; Tinsley, *Thiefing Sugar*, 109; Daphne in Elwin, *Tongues on Fire*, 64. In my essay "Lesbians in English and Spanish Caribbean Literature," I use ten *different* titles and quotations to make the same point.

9. J. Allen, *¿Venceremos?* 21.

10. Chancy, "Subversive Sexualities," 64.

11. See, for instance, Hanson, "Correcting 'Corrective Rape,'" and Tomlinson, "Jamaican Law, Homophobia, and HIV."

12. "There are no physical threats to lesbians here" (Rhonda Sue in Elwin, *Tongues on Fire*, 25). "Though there have been no incidents of lesbians being attacked, men are attacked. Couples get hassled and names called. But the men they get all kinda thing" (Tinkerbell in Elwin, *Tongues on Fire*, 51). Two interviewees in Elwin's work reported that women who engaged in same-sex relationships had it harder than men.

13. See the 2010 issue of the *Caribbean Review of Gender Studies* (vol. 4) and, for global context, *Progress of the World's Women 2011–2012: In Pursuit of Justice*, by the United Nations Entity for Gender Equality and the Empowerment of Women. Also see *Crime, Violence, and Development*, a 2007 joint report by the UNODC and LAC Region of World Bank.

14. Tomlinson qtd. in Branka Juran, "Jamaica Lesbians Suffer from Under-Reported Violence—Rights Activist," Trustlaw, 2012, http://www.trust.org/trustlaw/news/jamaica-lesbians-suffer-from-under-reported-violence-rights-activist.

15. Acosta et al., qtd. in Saunders, "Grupo OREMI," 173, 168.

16. Saunders, "Grupo OREMI," 174 (trans. by Saunders). She uses the term *lesbian* in her analysis and quotes the women of OREMI using the Spanish *lesbianas* and *homosexuales* to describe themselves.

17. Aponte-Parés et al., introduction to "Puerto Rican Queer Sexualities," 24.

18. Author's interview with Dudley Ferdinandus, Curaçao, June 1, 2011.

19. Wekker, *Politics of Passion*, 253.

20. Silvera describes scorning as acts of public censure, including refusal to eat food cooked by the woman. She also refers explicitly to reports of gang rape and more obliquely to "the danger of being physically 'disciplined' for speaking as a woman-identified woman" (Silvera, "Man Royals," 347, 353).

21. Chancy, "Subversive Sexualities," 64.

22. Lewis, *Culture of Gender*, xvi.

23. J. Allen, *¡Venceremos?* 11.

24. Brand, *Bread Out of Stone*, 93.

25. A great deal of work has been done on respectability in the Caribbean; see, for instance, Peter J. Wilson's *Crab Antics*, Belinda Edmondson's *Caribbean Middlebrow*, and Cecilia A. Green's "Between Respectability and Self-Respect."

26. Lorde, *Sister Outsider*, 41; Wekker, "Politics and Passion," interview, 2.

27. Chancy, "Subversive Sexualities," 58.

28. Elwin, *Tongues on Fire*, 7.

29. J. Allen, *¡Venceremos?* 68.

30. Elwin, *Tongues on Fire*, 64 (emphasis added).

31. Chancy, "Subversive Sexualities," 61.

32. Cave and French, "Sexual Choice as Human Right Issue," n. pag.

33. These terms and slurs are used in the Caribbean as follows: *macommère* (French and English Caribbean), *griti meid* (Sranan), *anti-man* (English Caribbean), *mati* (Surinam), *tortillera* (Spanish Caribbean), *platte borden* (Surinam), *zami* (English Caribbean), *kambrada* (Aruba, Bonaire, Curaçao), *ma divine* (Haiti), and *cachapera* (Aruba, Bonaire, Curaçao).

34. In brief, mati work is "a surviving historical practice among Afro-Surinamese working-class women who create families from relationships that are not limited to blood ties, or a choice between heterosexuality and homosexuality" (abstract of Wekker, "Politics and Passion," interview).

35. In addition to the creative writers discussed in detail in this chapter, see, for instance, Dionne Brand, Michelle Cliff, Ana-Maurine Lara, Audre Lorde, Achy Obejas, Ena Lucía Portela Alzola, Astrid Roemer, Ofelia Rodríguez Acosta, Cheryl Boyce Taylor, Luz María Umpierre, and Sonia Rivera-Valdés. In "Black Atlantic, Queer Atlantic: Queer Imaginings of the Middle Passage," Tinsley lists Eliot Bliss, Ida Faubert, Mayotte Capécia, Michèle Lacrosil, and Nadine Maglore as other Caribbean authors who have written women characters who desire other women.

36. In *Thiefing Sugar*, Tinsley cites nineteenth and early-twentieth-century examples of nonfiction descriptions of same-sex desire.

37. Glave, introduction, vii.

38. Cliff (Interview 604), qtd. in Tinsley, *Thiefing Sugar*, 198.

39. See Assotto Saint, *Spells of a Voodoo Doll*.

40. Part of this discussion is reproduced in Wekker, "*Mati*-ism and Black Lesbianism," 375–77.

41. Bejel, *Gay Cuban Nation*, 189.

42. Gopinath, *Impossible Desires*, 108.

43. Mootoo, *Out on Main Street*, 45, 51. This nickname is the only name provided for the text's protagonist.

44. Ibid., 56, 54.

45. Ibid., 57.

46. Ibid., 54.

47. Because of the dearth of translations and the limitations of my own language skills, the experiences omitted in this chapter are, unfortunately, those of women who desire women in the Dutch-speaking Caribbean.

48. Using a pseudonym is itself another form of invisibility. Gay insists that she has chosen this name for her writing dealing with sex and often published as erotica "strictly out of respect for my family. I have no shame about anything I've written" (author's phone interview with R. Gay, June 9, 2011).

Lawrence La Fountain-Stokes refers to Puerto Rican professor Juanita Díaz-Cotto as "a well-known, and highly respected scholar, writer, and activist," who ironically uses the pseudonym Juanita Ramos "when engaged with issues of lesbian visibility," including when she edits works such as the important collection *Compañeras: Latina Lesbians (An Anthology).* (La Fountain-Stokes, *Queer Ricans,* 66).

49. Gay, "Of Ghosts," 111.

50. Ibid., 109–110.

51. Ibid., 113.

52. Bobes, "Someone Has to Cry," 58–59.

53. Gay, "Of Ghosts," 114.

54. The threat is apparent when Pud explains that men on the street "does look at me like if dey is exactly what I need a taste of to cure me good and proper" (Mootoo, *Out on Main Street,* 48).

55. Mootoo, *Out on Main Street,* 254.

56. Bobes, "Someone Has to Cry," 58, 63, 66.

57. For examples of the characters' censuring thoughts, see Bobes, "Someone Has to Cry," 58, 64, and 65.

58. Tinsley, *Thiefing Sugar,* 134.

59. Jafari Allen notes that *oremi* "literally means 'close friend' in Yoruba" (J. Allen, *¡Venceremos?* 149).

60. Contrary to the official national discourse that claims that racism does not exist, blackness continues to be stigmatized in Cuba. See Saunders, "Grupo OREMI"; J. Allen, *¡Venceremos?;* Kutzinski, *Sugar's Secrets,* etc.

61. Saunders, "Grupo OREMI," 168, 182, 170, 169, 182.

62. Ibid., 170, 183.

63. See Saunders, "Grupo OREMI," 184, and Acosta.

64. All information about the Women's Caucus and their Strategic Team is taken from their 2011 "Chat XII: Year in Review" PowerPoint presentation. My sincere thanks to the Caucus for providing me with this document.

65. Elwin, *Tongues on Fire,* 99.

66. J. M. Rodríguez, *Queer Latinidad,* 44.

67. "It's difficult being a lesbian in Trinidad and Tobago. . . . We don't have anywhere to go and socialize" (Tinkerbell in Elwin, *Tongues on Fire,* 55). "On the whole, I do not think lesbians and gays in Trinidad have a sense of community" (Camile in Elwin, *Tongues on Fire,* 108). "As far as I can tell, there is not much of a lesbian community, but I don't move in that circle very much" (Clarise in Elwin, *Tongues on Fire,* 122–23).

68. Glenn O. Helberg (Chairman of Board of OCaN), "VIA. Making a difference between Dutch and Dutch," speech given to Thomas Hammarberg, Council of Europe Commissioner for Human Rights, at meeting between commissioner and Dutch NGOs, the Hague, September 30, 2008, *Overlegorgaan Caribische Nederlanders (OCaN),* http://www.ocan.nl/OCan-Nieuws/via-making-a-difference-between-dutch-and-dutch.html.

69. Inst. for Multicultural Development, *Factbook,* 17.

70. Wekker suggests that, at least among Surinamese in the Netherlands, sexual practices and/or identities may be similarly combined and complex; she writes that the "cultural space to which the mati work belongs is no longer singular within the national space of Suriname, but it should be situated in a historically and culturally inscribed space of postcolonialism" ("*Mati*-ism and Black Lesbianism," 225).

71. Overlegorgaan Caribische Nederlanders (OCaN), "Dushi and Proud: OCaN trots op succesvolle participatie Amersterdam Pride" [Dushi and Proud: OCaN proud of successful participation in Amsterdam Pride], *OCaN* online, August 22, 2011, http://www.ocan.nl/Algemeen/dushi-a-proud-ocan-trots-op-succesvolle-participatie-amsterdam-pride.html (emphasis added).

72. J. Allen, ¡*Venceremos?* 95.

73. National lesbian organizations in the USA have very specific parameters for their work. For instance, the Mauttner Project focuses on cancer work, and the National Center for Lesbian Rights focuses on legal work for gay, bisexual, and transgender people, as well as lesbians.

The full HRC mission statement follows: "The Human Rights Campaign is America's largest civil rights organization working to achieve lesbian, gay, bisexual and transgender equality. By inspiring and engaging all Americans, HRC strives to end discrimination against LGBT citizens and realize a nation that achieves fundamental fairness and equality for all.

"HRC seeks to improve the lives of LGBT Americans by advocating for equal rights and benefits in the workplace, ensuring families are treated equally under the law and increasing public support among all Americans through innovative advocacy, education and outreach programs. HRC works to secure equal rights for LGBT individuals and families at the federal and state levels by lobbying elected officials, mobilizing grassroots supporters, educating Americans, investing strategically to elect fair-minded officials and partnering with other LGBT organizations" (*Human Rights Campaign,* 2011, http://www.hrc.org/about_us/2528.htm).

74. Saunders, "Grupo OREMI," 183.

75. Las Buenas Amigas, "Mission," Las Buenas Amigas, 2011, http://lasbuenasamigas.org/aboutus.html.

Las Buenas Amigas includes but is not limited to women from or descended from the Spanish Caribbean.

76. For instance, in relationship to Puerto Rico, Negron-Muntaner notes that "like all subsequent mixed gender organizations, the COG's [Comunidad Orgulla Gay] commitment to feminism was never enough to retain its lesbian membership or create a feminist agenda" (Negron-Mutaner, "Echoing Stonewall," 93).

77. In order to compare "oranges to oranges," I am not addressing groups whose main purpose is related to HIV/AIDS, both because they have a more or less different

mission from sexual-minority advocacy organizations and because of their often overwhelming reliance on the international HIV/AIDS funding complex, which can then influence their mission and programs. Such organizations, including SEROvie in Haiti and GrenCHAP in Grenada, are doing very important work.

78. Hombres por la Diversidad, "About Me," *Hombres por la Diversidad*, n.d., http://www.blogger.com/profile/17157478655048928316 (unless otherwise noted, all translations from this website are my own).

79. Coalition Advocating for the Inclusion of Sexual Orientation (CAISO), "Groups Label Gays' Exclusion from National Gender Policy '1919' Thinking: Launch New Coalition with 20/20 Vision of Citizenship and Sexual Orientation," *gspottt: t&t's triggersite for sogi passion and advocacy* (blog), June 29, 2009, http://gspottt.wordpress.com/about/lyrics-to-make-a-politician-cringe-caiso-forms/.

80. OCaN has a special committee dedicated to sexuality, among other committees focusing on youth, seniors, women, legal issues, communication, and education (Overlegorgaan Caribische Nederlanders [OCaN], "OUTLINE CONCEPT Activity," *OCaN*, 2011, http://www.ocan.nl/OCan-Nieuws/outline-concept-activiteiten-plan-ocan-2011.html).

81. See, for instance, Negron-Muntaner: "The long time association between homosexuality and 'foreignness' is evident" in various newspaper reports of the 1960s (Negron-Muntaner, "Echoing Stonewall," 82). Likewise, see M. Jacqui Alexander: "The belief in the perils of American imperialism and homosexuality—that 'the whole concept of the acceptability of homosexual behavior between consenting adults is essentially an American phenomenon' . . . means, at least in the state's view, that there is no space for indigenous agency of lesbians and gay men, who presumably become homosexual by virtue of Western influence" (Alexander, *Pedagogies of Crossing*, 49).

82. The very strong—and sometimes violent—racial allegiances that exist particularly in Guyana and Trinidad often coalesce behind a political party but do not exhibit any significant *organized* groups or strategies outside of governmental politics.

83. See the formal and informal (e.g., online) debates about the decriminalization of sodomy in Jamaica and Belize, as well as Agard-Jones' analysis in "Le Jeu de Qui?" of the controversy around same-sex marriage in Guadeloupe.

84. Works that critically examine Caribbean nations' failure to include nonheterosexuals as full citizens include Negron-Muntaner's "Echoing Stonewall," Alexander's *Pedagogies of Crossing*, and Smith's *Sex and the Citizen*.

85. Jasbir Puar's *Terrorist Assemblages: Homonationalism in Queer Times* (2007) defines *homonationalism* as a structure that allows and encourages (white) U.S. queer subjects' status over other racially and sexually marked subjects. Less work has been done in examining the nationalism of racially marked subjects in or outside of the United States.

86. J. Allen, ¡Venceremos? 191; Alexander, Pedagogies of Crossing, 22–23.

87. Negron-Muntaner, "Echoing Stonewall," 81.

88. Wekker, "Politics and Passion," interview, 6.

89. However, certainly many criticisms can be made of their priorities and policies. Whether or not any of the organizations discussed here actively and inclusively pursue their mission statements (and in particular to what extent women who desire women are involved in their organizations or their work) exceeds the scope of this chapter.

90. Although not all Dutch Caribbean territories—and indeed, not all of the other Caribbean territories—are independent nation-states, nationalism continues to be a relevant sentiment for individual entities.

91. J. Allen, ¡Venceremos? 96–7.

92. Gopinath, Impossible Desires, 14.

93. See Queer Latinidad, 6.

94. As Gopinath reports, Kaushalya Bannerji in A Lotus of Another Color notes that her "'fondness for bright colors, long hair, jewelry'—[are] bodily signs that have multiple meanings for her as an Indian Canadian woman but read simply as markers of a transparent femme identity within a white lesbian context" (Gopinath, Impossible Desires, 154).

95. Elwin, Tongues on Fire, 29.

96. While in Haiti, Omise'eke Tinsley was told that if she wanted to find lesbians she should go to Voudoun ceremonies, not bars (Tinsley, "Summer and Seven Paths," 330).

97. Douglas qtd. in Elwin, Tongues on Fire, 127.

Chapter 4. "Force-Ripe": Caribbean Women's Sexual Agency

1. Ortiz Cofer, "Myth of Latin Woman," 112. Another Caribbean term that has a similar connotation is womanish, "used to define young girls who prematurely demonstrate grown-up behavior" or who are "acting out of place" (Thorington Springer, "'Roll It Gal,'" 122 n. 5).

2. Francis, Fictions of Feminine Citizenship, 12.

3. Welter, "Cult of True Womanhood," 152.

4. For instance, in When and Where I Enter: The Impact of Black Women on Race and Sex in America, Paula Giddings writes that "Failing to adhere to any of [the cult's] tenets—which the overwhelming number of Black [and Caribbean] women could hardly live up to—made one less than a moral 'true' woman" (47).

5. Decena, Tacit Subjects, 136.

6. K. Kempadoo, Sexing the Caribbean, 78.

7. Ibid., 19.

8. Tambiah, "Creating (Im)moral Citizens," 3.

9. Harewood, "Transnational Soca Performances," 31.

10. K. Kempadoo, *Sexing the Caribbean*, 23.

11. Murray, *Opacity*, 23.

12. Haniff, "My Grandmother Worked," 25.

13. Eriksen, "Cultural Contexts," 138.

14. Manuel, "Chutney and Indo-Trinidadian Identity," 33.

15. Salyers Bull, "Machismo/Marianismo Attitudes," 3.

16. Ibid., 3.

17. de Moya, "Power Games," 71. The Caribbean street/home gender divide has been refuted by a number of scholars. See for instance Ho, "Caribbean Transnationalism," and Safa, "From Shanty Town to Public Housing."

18. Brana-Shute, "Neighbourhood Networks," 136.

19. Ortiz Cofer, "Myth of Latin Woman," 110.

20. Baksh, "Women's Economic Achievements, Challenges Since Independence." Earlier statistics show that 40 percent of households are women-headed in Curaçao, and in the Bahamas, 58 percent of all live births have been outside of heterosexual marriage (Alexander, *Pedagogies of Crossing*, 38).

21. Derby, "Dictator's Seduction," 1115; K. Kempadoo, *Sexing the Caribbean*, 176.

22. K. Kempadoo, *Sexing the Caribbean*, 49.

23. Alexander, *Pedagogies of Crossing*, 23.

24. Wekker, *Politics of Passion*, 70.

25. Bergman, "*Matikor,* Chutney," 6–7; Baksh-Soodeen, "Power, Gender, and Chutney," 194. Also spelled *mathkor, matticore, matikoor,* and *matikura.*

26. Manuel, "Chutney and Indo-Trinidadian Identity," 22–23.

27. Bergman, "*Matikor,* Chutney," 6.

28. Ibid., 7.

29. Kanhai, "Masala Stone Sings," 226.

30. Edwards, "Kwe-Kwe Tradition in Guyana," 181. Another interesting tradition that involves female agency is the pare-masque ball, a French Guianese tradition during which women get to be more sexually aggressive than usual. See Aline Belfort-Chanol, *Le bal paré-masqué.*

31. Edwards, "Kwe-Kwe Tradition in Guyana," 187.

32. Comments about kwe-kwe are derived in part from my viewing of and participation in a kwe-kwe performance/demonstration by Rose October on June 10, 2012. The event took place in Brooklyn at the "Bachelorette Bash," part of *Half the Sky: Brooklyn Women in Traditional Performance*, an event sponsored by the Brooklyn Arts Council.

33. Edwards, "Kwe-Kwe Tradition in Guyana," 186.

34. Rohlehr, "I Lawa," 342–43.

35. Edwards, "Kwe-Kwe Tradition in Guyana," 186.

36. Wining (sometimes spelled *winding*) consists of standing with legs planted apart, while moving the hips in a circular motion.

37. Halberstam, *Female Masculinity*, 6.

38. Kincaid, *Lucy*, 113, 127, 113, 129, 130.

39. Ibid., 80–81 (emphasis added).

40. Ibid., 36, 127.

41. Ibid., 82, 83.

42. Ibid., 31–32.

43. Mahlis, "Gender and Exile," 165.

44. Kincaid, *Lucy*, 113 (emphasis added).

45. Ibid., 127–28.

46. Ibid., 51.

47. The term *heremakhonon* is typically translated from the Mende as "welcome house" but can also be read as "good times" (Apter, "Crossover Texts/Creole Tongues," 89). The novel was reissued with the French title *En attendant le bonheur* (Waiting for happiness).

48. Andrade, "Nigger of the Narcissist," 218.

49. Not unlike Mexico's La Malinche or the Lemhi Shoshone's Sackagawea (also known as Pocahontas), to be a Marilisse is to have committed a peculiarly female and explicitly sexual betrayal of family, country, and race.

50. Freedom is mentioned very early in the text (Condé, *Heremakhonon*, 8). For instance, the narrator argues that her black middle-class family envied the mulattoes neither their skin color nor their wealth but their *freedom* (17).

51. Condé, *Heremakhonon*, 37.

52. Ibid., 8, 56.

53. Ibid., 70, 71.

54. Ibid., 100. At one point, Veronica notes that "My lovers have always ridiculed my family. In a way, I chose them so that they could do it for me" (102).

55. Ibid., 173, 48, 69, 175, 176.

56. Selbert, *House of Six Doors*, 85.

57. Ibid., 141.

58. Ibid., 290.

59. Ibid., 247.

60. Ibid., 96, 78.

61. Berrian writes that "music in the French Caribbean, like elsewhere in the African diaspora, has long been a revolutionary act" (Berrian, *Awakening Spaces*, 2).

62. Aparicio, "Así Son," 660.

63. In the interest of examining less-studied Caribbean music genres, dancehall is not addressed here. For a detailed analysis of women in dancehall, see Cooper's

Noises in the Blood. For a summary of the cogent critiques of Cooper's work, see Sharpe and Pinto, "Sweetest Taboo."

64. There are precedents in other genres of women (and a few men) who sang songs that countered the cult of true oomanhood. Most notable among these are Celia Cruz, the "Salsa Diva," Calypso Rose, the "Queen of Calypso," and Lady Saw, the "Queen of Dancehall."

65. Thorington Springer, "'Roll It Gal,'" 95.

66. Pulis, *Religion, Diaspora*, 88.

67. Jocelyne Béroard, interview by Gladys Francis, July 15, 2012, unpublished. A transcript of the interview was read over the phone by Francis to the author.

68. Harewood, "Transnational Soca Performances," 26; Gopinath, *Impossible Desires*, 43.

69. See, for instance, A. Mohammed, "Love and Anxiety"; Jiménez, "(W)rapped in Foil"; Berrian, *Awakening Spaces*; Báez, "'En mi imperio'"; Mahabir, "Rise of Calypso Feminism." Caribbean men artists who sometimes either contradict hegemonic masculinity or who endorse women's agency or empowerment include Calle 13, David Rudder, and the band Kassav'.

70. Edmondson, "Public Spectacles," 2.

71. Berrian, interview, and Berrian, *Awakening Spaces*, 8.

72. Berrian, interview.

73. Ibid.

74. Berrian, *Awakening Spaces*, 97.

75. All transcriptions and translations of "Pa bizwen palé" lyrics are from Berrian, *Awakening Spaces*, 93–97.

76. See G. Francis, n. 67.

77. "Fénmen lapòt la-a / Oswe ya man pé ké ladjé-w / . . . / Limen bouji-ya / . . . Pa bizwen pale."

78. Berrian, *Awakening Spaces*, 98.

79. Béroard frequently states how much she enjoys performing in front of—and interacting with—live audiences, especially those comprised of French Caribbean women. See Berrian, "Zouk Diva," 4–5, and G. Francis (chap. 1, n. 67).

80. Berrian, *Awakening Spaces*, 92.

81. Jocelyne Béroard, *Jocelyne Béroard*, n.d., http://www.jocelyneberoard.be/index.php?rub=photos.

82. A. Mohammed, "Love and Anxiety," 3.

83. Bergman, "*Matikor*, Chutney," 14.

84. In the Caribbean, a chulha is a large, flat cook plate, used to cook the bread roti, among other foods.

85. A panic that, as Carole Boyce Davies notes, "is often explained by claims about

the sexual laxity of Indian women in relation to black men, rather than by stereotypes about the latters' excessive sexual appetite" (Boyce Davies, "She Wants," 128).

86. Drupatee Ramgoonai, "Hotter Than a Chulha," *YouTube* video, 6:22, posted by "Clynton Mann," October 21, 2011. http://www.youtube.com/watch?v=Eb17 Nc4s3ZY.

87. A. Mohammed, "Love and Anxiety," abstract.

88. Baksh-Soodeen, "Power, Gender, and Chutney," 196.

89. Drupatee Ramgoonai's *Facebook* page, accessed October 7, 2013.

90. Báez, "'En mi imperio,'" 64.

91. Rivera, Marshall, and Hernández, *Reggaeton*, x.

92. Reggaeton "was perceived as a quintessentially hybrid Afro-diasporic or pan-Latin genre that could easily accommodate" any number of nationalities (Pacini Hernández, "Dominicans in the Mix, 149).

93. Jiménez, "(W)rapped in Foil," 231.

94. See Fairley, "Dancing Back to Front," 474; and Gonzales, "Ivy Queen" 32.

95. Gonzales, "Ivy Queen," 32; Báez, "'En mi imperio,'" 66; Jiménez, "(W)rapped in Foil," 239.

96. H. Ayala, "Habla la reina del rap," 5; Gonzales, "Ivy Queen," 32.

97. Unless otherwise noted, all transcriptions and translations of "Quiero Bailar" are from Báez, "'En mi imperio,'" 241.

98. Báez, "'En mi imperio,'" 71.

99. Fairley, "Dancing Back to Front," 480.

100. This transcription and translation are my own.

101. In 2005, Ivy Queen had plastic surgery to enlarge her breasts and enhance her face; she has been very public about her choice to do so (Jiménez, "(W)rapped in Foil," 240).

102. Báez, "'En mi imperio,'" 70.

103. Stella McCartney, "Rihanna—The World's Most Influential People: 2012," *Time*, April 18, 2012, http://content.time.com/time/specials/packages/article/0,28804, 2111975_2111976_2111948,00.html; Zavk O'Malley Greenburg, "Forbes Celebrity 100," *Forbes*, June 26, 2013. http://www.forbes.com/profile/rihanna/; Dorothy Pomerantz, "Rihanna Tops Our List of Social Networking Stars," *Forbes*, August 9, 2012, http://www.forbes.com/sites/dorothypomerantz/2012/08/09/rihanna-tops-our-list-of-social-networking-superstars/; "Twitter Top 100: Most Followers," *Twitter Counter*, May 3, 2013, twittercounter.com/rihanna.

104. Seabrook, "The Song Machine," n. pag.

105. Ibid.

106. "The Incident" refers to the felony assault on Rihanna by her then-boyfriend Chris Brown (also a singer), which resulted in visible injuries to Rihanna and to

which Brown pled guilty in 2009. A number of journalists, bloggers, and personalities, from Perez Hilton to Oprah Winfrey, now refer to this assault as The Incident.

107. The Caribbean heritage of Marcus Garvey, Malcolm X, Heavy D, Harry Belafonte, and Minister Louis Farrakhan is also often forgotten, unknown, or ignored.

108. Rihanna, interview by Oprah Winfrey, *Oprah's Next Chapter*, August 19, 2012, *YouTube* video, http://www.youtube.com/watch?v=ZJgZpNUqXfM, accessed August 21, 2012. Excerpts from interview currently available on *Oprah.com*, http://www.oprah.com/own-oprahs-next-chapter/Oprahs-Next-Chapter-Rihanna.

109. Rihanna, "S&M," Island Def Jam Music Group, 2010, *YouTube* video, 4:03, posted by "RihannaVEVO," January 31, 2011, http://www.youtube.com/watch?v=KdS6HFQ_Luc.

110. The campy images were also the cause of a lawsuit for copyright infringement from popular photographer David LaChapelle, which was settled out of court for an undisclosed sum (Sean Michaels, "Rihanna and David LaChapelle Settle Lawsuit over S&M Video," *Guardian* (Manchester), October 20, 2011, http://www.guardian.co.uk).

111. A. Mohammed, "Love and Anxiety," 3.

112. Pinto, "Why Must All Girls," 139.

113. Ibid., 141.

114. Thorington Springer, "'Roll It Gal,'" 101.

115. Ibid.; SpliffieTV and Carib Life Central, "Alison Hinds: 'Queen of Soca' part 3," *YouTube* video, 9:31, March 11, 2008. http://www.youtube.com/watch?v=-KdrZbG FupM&feature=relmfu; Meschino, "Alison Hinds," 68; Thorington Springer, "'Roll It Gal,'" 119; SpliffieTV (see second cite in this note).

116. Thorington Springer, "'Roll It Gal,'" 121.

117. Hinds qtd. on SpliffieTV; see n. 115.

118. Hinds, *Roll It Gal*, directed by David Cropper, *YouTube* video, 3:55, posted by "cariblifecentral," July 29, 2007, http://www.youtube.com/watch?v=9-eAeDLoYQc.

119. Daly, *Developing Legal Status*, 1982.

120. Condé, "Order, Disorder," 163.

121. Edmondson, "Public Spectacles," 3.

122. Barriteau, *Political Economy of Gender*; Harewood, "Transnational Soca Performances," 27.

123. D. Francis, *Fictions of Feminine Citizenship*, 6.

124. See "Transnational Soca Performances," 26.

125. "Soca artists reinforce heteronormative relations, and so far have excluded homosexual expression. In other words, not all pleasures are permissible on the soca stage" (Guilbault, "Music, Politics, and Pleasure," 19). See also Robinson, "Transforming Patriarchy," PowerPoint.

126. Kawina is a traditional Afro-Surinamese dance music that relies on drums and call and response.

127. Bilby, "Caribbean Musical Enigma," 239. "Faluma" was a No. 1 hit in multiple Caribbean countries for almost two years and was No. 1 in Guatemala for over a year (Hinds, "Alison Hinds Speaking about 'Faluma.'").

128. Several dancehall artists, such as Beenie Man, Capleton, and Sizzla, have released or signed statements advocating respect for all persons regardless of sexuality—though they also continue to maintain a disdain for nonheterosexuals because of religious or cultural beliefs. See Jeremy Kisner, "Beenie Man Says He Supports Gay Rights," *TheAdvocate.com*, May 19, 2012, http://www.advocate.com/arts-entertainment/ music/2012/05/19/watch-beenie-man-says-he-supports-gay-rights.

129. A close reading of the musical elements of the song can be found in Dentonio Worrell, "In Full Bloom: Square One, Barbados' Contribution to the Advancement of Soca on the World Arena," http://www.sinc.sunysb.edu/Stu/dworrell/In%20 Full%20Bloom.doc.

130. Guilbault, "Music, Politics, and Pleasure," 19–20.

131. Harewood, "Transnational Soca Performances," 44.

132. Guilbault, "Music, Politics, and Pleasure," 17.

133. Linda West, "Rihanna Does Whatever She Wants to with Her Vagina and for Some Reason That's a Problem," *Jezebel* blog, May 17, 2012, http://jezebel. com/5911023/rihanna-does-whatever-she-wants-with-her-vagina-and-for-some-reason-thats-a-problem.

Chapter 5. One Love? Caribbean Men and White Women

1. Dalleo, *Caribbean Literature and Public Sphere*, 14.

2. Reddock, *Interrogating Caribbean Masculinities*, xxi.

3. D. Francis, *Fictions of Feminine Citizenship*, 109.

4. Wekker, *Politics of Passion*, 162.

5. These films can be contrasted with *Island in the Sun* (1957), in which Harry Belafonte plays a man who refuses to enter into a relationship with a local white woman because it would threaten his chance of becoming the first elected official in his colony. He also rejects her suggestion that they immigrate to England because he knows it would result in his downward mobility and subjection to increased racism and discrimination.

6. Fanon, *Black Skin*, 14.

7. Ibid., 63.

8. Helg, "Black Men, Racial Stereotyping," 578.

9. Godreau et al., "Lessons of Slavery," 116.

10. Murray, *Opacity*, 26.

11. A. Clarke, *Storm*, 213.

12. Of course other stereotypes of these groups exist that do not invoke sexuality, including the clown and the "gang-banger" for both black and Latino/Hispanic men and, most recently for South Asian men, the terrorist.

13. Treviño, "Latino Portrayals."

14. Pinto Alicea, "Sex, Lies, and Stereotypes" n. pag.

15. Salyers Bull, "Machismo/Marianismo Attitudes," 3.

16. Decena, *Tacit Subjects*, 181.

17. Derby, "Dictator's Seduction," 1113.

18. Wahab, "Mapping," 291, 295.

19. Nurse, "Masculinities," 9.

20. Wahab, "Mapping," 295.

21. Dabydeen, *Intended*, 177–78.

22. Hoefte, "Passage to Suriname," 24.

23. For more about the Cuban massacre, see Helg, "Black Men, Racial Stereotyping." For more about the Dominican massacre, see Turits, "A World Destroyed," and Roorda, "Genocide Next Door." For a creative portrayal, see Edwidge Danticat's *The Farming of Bones*.

24. Helg, "Black Men, Racial Stereotyping," 589–90.

25. This does not in any way imply that there is a hierarchy of oppression in which black men were or are worse off than black women, who of course have also long been the objects of physical and epistemic violence.

26. Saint-Aubin, "Testeria," 1058.

27. In addition to major heterosexual-male sex tourism throughout the Caribbean, in various cities there is also significant homosexual-male sex tourism. See for instance Decena, *Tacit Subjects*, and J. Allen, *¡Venceremos?*

28. See work such as Binner and Dines, "Marriage, Divorce, and Legal Change: New Evidence from England and Wales," and Stevenson and Wolfers, "Marriage and Divorce: Changes and Their Driving Forces." The latter article notes that divorce rates fell towards the end of the twentieth century but that this correlates with a decline in rates of marriage.

29. See, for instance, Fisk, "American Labor in the 20th Century," and Costa, "From Mill Town to Board Room: The Rise of Women's Paid Labor."

30. As the narrator in the documentary *Rent-a-Rasta* puts it: "Women who are considered too fat, too old, or too ugly to pull young, fit sexual partners in Chicago or Hamburg are also considered to be too fat, too old, or too ugly in Barcelona or Honolulu."

31. *Rent-a-Rasta.*

32. K. Kempadoo, *Sexing the Caribbean*, 138.

33. Ibid., 130.

34. There has been significant debate among scholars as to whether these women's

practices should be termed "sex tourism" or "romance tourism." Because I have found arguments for the latter to be unconvincing and to rely on sexism, here I use the term "sex work." See Cabezas' *Economies of Desire*, Sánchez Taylor's "Dollars Are a Girl's Best Friend?" and K. Kempadoo's *Sun, Sex, and Gold* and *Sexing the Caribbean* for discussions of these terms.

35. *The Lunatic*, directed by Lol Crème.

36. Marlon James, blurb, of *The Lunatic* (novel), by Anthony C. Winkler, *Akashic Books* online, http://www.akashicbooks.com/catalog/the-lunatic/.

37. Alexander, *Pedagogies of Crossing*, 54.

38. Robinson-Walcott, *Out of Order!* 89.

39. Other elements from Haitian culture are dropped in the film that might escape some viewers, most notably the Erzulie songs that begin and end the film, though the meaning of their plaintive tone is not difficult to discern.

40. Herold, Garcia, and DeMoay, "Female Tourists and Beach Boys," 984.

41. K. Kempadoo, *Sexing the Caribbean*, 118.

42. Delgado, "From *Sacred Wild* to City," 110.

43. Herold, Garcia, and DeMoya, "Female Tourists and Beach Boys," 986.

44. Guzmán, *Gay Hegemony/Latino Homosexualities*, 25.

45. Tate, "Heading South," 44.

46. K. Kempadoo, *Sexing the Caribbean*, 129.

47. Similarly, in Austin Clarke's novel *The Meeting Point*, part of *The Toronto Trilogy*, a Barbadian man's comments about relationships with white women: "They love you, not because they love you, but because they sympathize with you, dig?" Clarke, *Meeting Point*, 274–75.

48. Laferrière, *How to Make Love to a Negro*, 26–27.

49. "[M]igration invariably places Caribbean men and women into lower occupations, performing tasks and jobs shunned by local populations due to the labor conditions and poor salary" (K. Kempadoo, *Sexing the Caribbean*, 163).

50. D. Francis, *Fictions of Feminine Citizenship*, 9. See also George Lamming's *In the Castle of My Skin* and *Season of Adventure*.

51. In addition to the texts discussed in this chapter, this dynamic can be observed in other works such as Clarke's trilogy, Selvon's *The Lonely Londoners*, and Dabydeen's *The Intended*.

52. Homel, introduction to *How to Make Love to a Negro*, by Laferrière, 8.

53. Laferrière, *How to Make Love*, 14. This and subsequent references in this chapter are to the 1987 English-language version.

54. Ibid., 19, 76.

55. Ibid., 38.

56. Ibid.

57. Naipaul, *Mimic Men*, 39.

58. Ibid., 22.

59. Ibid., 18.

60. Ibid., 17.

61. Ibid., 25, 27, 28.

62. Ibid., 44, 41, 46.

63. Ibid., 231, 234.

64. Ibid., 26–28.

65. Derby, "Dictator's Seduction," 1113.

66. Díaz, "How to Date," 143, 146.

67. The narrator consistently makes a distinction between "blacks" and "Latinos," even though he himself could fall into both categories.

68. Díaz, "How to Date," 144–47. The story implies that "halfies" have a white and a black parent.

69. Ibid., 144–48.

70. Ibid., 148.

71. Paravisini-Gebert and Woods Peiró, "'Porfirio Rubirosa,'" 2.

72. Rubirosa's significant relationships can be read as a kind of progress narrative, in which his partners are at first rich and later wealthy (excluding his last wife, but including two women who were, at the time, the wealthiest women in the world). His partners also evolved from somewhat dark-skinned to increasingly whiter and blonder.

73. Hughes discussed in Paravisini-Gebert and Woods Peiró, "'Porfirio Rubirosa,'" 3.

74. Cole was romantically linked to a Swedish actress, though he returned to his wife before his death. Belafonte married twice more; first in 1957 to a woman lighter than himself and then in 2008 to a white woman.

75. Paravisini-Gebert and Woods Peiró, "'Porfirio Rubirosa,'" 3–4.

76. Ibid., 10.

77. Derby, "Dictator's Seduction," 1114, 1131.

78. Ibid., 1131. White women's acceptance of occasional partner violence is also found in Austin Clarke's Toronto Trilogy novels: *The Meeting Point* (1967), *Storm of Fortune* (1973) and *The Bigger Light* (1975).

79. Paravisini-Gebert and Woods Peiró, "'Porfirio Rubirosa,'" 6; Derby, "Dictator's Seduction," 1116. The "tiguere" is also a local Dominican racialized/sexualized ideal.

80. Rubirosa qtd. in Grimes, "A Jet-Set Don Juan."

81. See Z. Marley and Macdonald, radio interview, "Bob Marley's Legend"; *Marley* (film), dir. by K. Macdonald; and G. Roberts, "Revealed: The White Ex-Naval Officer," n. pag.

82. G. Roberts, "Revealed," n. pag.

83. *Marley,* dir. by K. Macdonald.

84. Taylor, *Marley and Me,* 121–25.

85. Breakspeare is herself the product of a mixed marriage of sorts; her mother was Canadian and her father Jamaican. It is unclear whether her father is a white Jamaican or "Jamaican white," a designation common in many parts of the Caribbean that is based on extremely fair skin (especially when combined with wealth) and which designates whiteness, even if the person is known to have some African ancestry. I was unable to find any pictures or information about Breakspeare's father other than his nationality, and all written sources refer to Cindy Breakspeare as white and/or an "uptown girl."

86. Dixon, "Lovers and Children," n. pag.

87. Taylor, *Marley and Me,* 130.

88. Steckles, *Bob Marley: A Life,* 147.

89. Taylor, *Marley and Me,* 127.

90. Salewicz, *Bob Marley: The Untold Story,* 323.

91. The title is from the nickname for Waldy, the couple's son, inspired by the song sung by Al Jolson in a 1920s film. Although the book *Sonny Boy* has been translated into six languages, those do not include English, French, or Spanish. Thus the analysis in this chapter is not based on my own reading of the book; rather, it is taken from the film, reviews, articles, and interviews with the author posted on her English/Dutch website.

92. Such details include the fact that Waldemar's grandmother lived under the power of a Jewish slave-owner, an irony several critics have commented on. According to the author's website, van der Zijl initially wrote a long chapter about Waldemar's life in Suriname, but "the manuscript became unbalanced" so she cut it out. That chapter now appears in a small booklet, as well as some "special issues" of the complete book. See Annejet van der Zijl, "Sonny Boy," *Annejet van der Zijl,* http://annejetvanderzijl.com/boeken/sonny-boy/.

93. "Suriname in WWII," *Liberation for Everyone,* 2013, http://www.bevrijdingintercultureel.nl/bi/eng/suriname.html.

94. "SONNY BOY—Annejet van der Zijl," *Boektoppers,* http://www.boekentoppers.nl/pdf/sonny_boy.pdf (translations are my own, using online translation tools).

95. Ibid.

96. "Suriname in WWII" (see chap. 5, n. 93).

97. K. Kempadoo, *Sexing the Caribbean,* 17.

98. See, for instance, Jamaica Kincaid's *Lucy* and K. Kempadoo's "Caribbean Sexuality."

99. Interracial relationships between Indo-Caribbeans and Afro-Caribbeans continue to be transgressive in both communities, and several scholars have explored

these relationships and the concept of "douglarization" (Shepherd, Puri, Mehta, Bakshi, etc.). However, an examination of such liaisons would overwhelmingly focus on Guyana and Trinidad. Exploring relationships between Caribbean men of color and white women allows for a more Caribglobal analysis that includes perspectives from multiple races and linguistic backgrounds.

100. K. Kempadoo, *Sexing the Caribbean*, 43.

101. P. Mohammed, "Unmasking Masculinity," 56.

102. K. Kempadoo, *Sexing the Caribbean*, 34.

103. Sheller, *Consuming the Caribbean*, 118.

104. Ibid., 165–66.

105. Nurse, "Masculinities in Transition," 16.

106. Fanon, *Black Skin*, 180.

107. D. Francis, *Fictions of Feminine Citizenship*, 20.

Afterword

1. Guzmán, *Gay Hegemony/Latino Homosexualities*, 89 (emphasis added).

2. Glave, "Toward a Nobility of the Imagination," 19, in Glave, *Words to Our Now*; Robinson, "Toward a Strategy of Imagination."

3. Glave, "Toward a Nobility of the Imagination," 19, in Glave, *Words to Our Now*.

4. Robinson, "Toward a Strategy of Imagination," 1.

5. Crawford, "'It's a Girl Thing,'" n. pag.

6. Laguerre, interview (emphasis added).

7. The new Caribbean feminist organization CatchAFyah, which includes sexual minorities and their allies, may provide another useful activist model.

Bibliography

Aching, Gerard. *Masking and Power: Carnival and Popular Culture in the Caribbean.* Minneapolis: University of Minnesota Press, 2002.

Acosta, Dalia. "Cuba Lesbians Demand Fair Health Services." *Havana Times,* November 26, 2010. http://www.havanatimes.org/?p=33674.

Acosta, Dalia, Sara Mas, Dixie Edith, and Mariana Ramírez Corría. "¿Qué Pensamos Sobre Homosexualidad? Un Acercamiento a la Visión de la Población Cubana." Paper presented at 16th World Congress of Sexology, World Association for Sexology, Havana, March 2003.

Agard-Jones, Vanessa. "Le Jeu de Qui? [Whose game?]: Sexual Politics at Play in the French Caribbean." *Caribbean Review of Gender Studies* 3 (2009): 1–18. http://sta.uwi.edu/crgs/november2009/journals/Agard-Jones.pdf.

Ahmed, Sara. *The Cultural Politics of Emotion.* New York: Routledge, 2004.

Alegría, Ricardo E. "The Fiesta of Santiago Apóstol (St. James the Apostle) in Loíza, Puerto Rico." *Journal of American Folklore* 69, no. 272 (1956): 123–34. http://www.jstor.org/stable/537272.

Alexander, M. Jacqui. *Pedagogies of Crossing: Meditations on Feminism, Sexual Politics, Memory, and the Sacred.* Durham: Duke University Press, 2005.

Allen, Jafari. ¡*Venceremos? The Erotics of Black Self-Making in Cuba.* Durham: Duke University Press, 2011.

Allen, Rose Mary. "The Complexity of National Identity Construction in Curaçao, Dutch Caribbean." *European Review of Latin American and Caribbean Studies* 89 (2010): 117–25. http://www.cedla.uva.nl/50_publications/pdf/revista/89RevistaEuropea/89-Allen-ISSN-0924-0608.pdf.

———. Plenary Presentation. Annual Caribbean Studies Association Conference. Curaçao, May 29, 2012.

Als, Hilton. *The Women.* New York: Farrar, Straus and Giroux, 1998.

Altman, Dennis. *Global Sex.* Chicago: University of Chicago Press, 2002.

Alvarez, Aldo. *Interesting Monsters.* New York: Graywolf, 2001.

Anderson, Benedict. *Imagined Communities: Reflections on the Origin and Spread of Nationalism.* New York: Verso, 1992.

Andrade, Susan Z. "The Nigger of the Narcissist: History, Sexuality and Intertextuality in Maryse Condé's *Heremakhonon.*" *Callaloo* 16, no. 1 (1993): 213–26.

Aparicio, Frances R. "Así Son: Salsa Music, Female Narratives, and Gender (De) Construction in Puerto Rico." *Poetics Today* 15, no. 4 (1994): 659–84.

Aparicio, Frances R., and Cándida F. Jáquez, eds. *Musical Migrations: Transnationalism and Cultural Hybridity in Latin/o America*. Vol. 1. New York: Palgrave, 2002.

Aponte-Parés, Luis Jossianna Arroyo, Elizabeth Crespo-Kebler, Lawrence La Fountain-Stokes, and Frances Negrón-Muntaner. Introduction to "Puerto Rican Queer Sexualities," special issue, *CENTRO Journal* 19 no. 1 (2007): 4–24.

Appadurai, Arjun. "Grassroots Globalization and the Research Imagination." *Public Culture* 12, no. 1 (2000): 1–19.

Apter, Emily. "Crossover Texts/Creole Tongues: A Conversation with Maryse Condé." *Public Culture* 13, no. 1 (2001): 89–96.

Arenas, Reinaldo. *Before Night Falls: A Memoir*. Translated by Dolores M. Koch. New York: Penguin, 1994. Originally published in Spanish as *Antes que anochezca: autobiografía*, Barcelona: Tusquets Editores, 1992. All citations in *Island Bodies* are to the 1994 edition of the Koch translation.

———. *The Brightest Star*. New York: Grove, 1994. Originally published in Spanish as *Arturo, la estrella más brillante*, Barcelona: Montesinos, 1984. Translated to English by Andrew Hurley and published with *Old Rosa* as *Old Rosa: A Novel in Two Stories*, New York: Grove, 1989. All English-language citations in *Island Bodies* are to the Grove 1994 paperback edition.

———. *Old Rosa: A Novel in Two Stories*. Translated by Ann Tashi Slater. New York: Grove, 1994. Originally published in Spanish as *La vieja Rosa*, Caracas: Cruz del Sur, 1980. First published in English with translation by Slater, together with *The Brightest Star*, trans. Andrew Hurley, as *Old Rosa: A Novel in Two Stories*, New York: Grove, 1989. All English-language citations in *Island Bodies* are to the Grove 1994 paperback edition.

Associated Press. "Gay Man Weds Transsexual Woman in Cuba." *Guardian* (*Manchester*), August 14, 2011. http://www.guardian.co.uk/world/2011/aug/14/gay-man-weds-transsexual-woman-cuba.

Association of Caribbean Women Writers and Scholars. "About the Name." *MaComère*. Association of Caribbean Women Writers and Scholars. n.d. http://www.macomerejournal.com/about.html.

Atkinson, Ewan. *Paradise Terrace and a Mouthful of Water*. Mixed media, 2007. Viewable in the *Fiction* series online at http://www.ewanatkinson.com/Fiction.html.

Atluri, Tara. "Putting the 'Cool' in Coolie: *Disidentification*, Desire and Dissent in the Work of Filmmaker Michelle Mohabeer." *Caribbean Review of Gender Studies* 3 (2009): 1–25. http://sta.uwi.edu/crgs/november2009/taraatluri.asp.

Aviankoi, Erna. "A Gay Is Not a Lost Son." *Sexoh! Suriname Men United*. March 16, 2010. http://www.surinamemenunited.com/informatie/sexho-lost-son.html.

———. "Sexoh! Acceptance Is the Key!" *Suriname Men United*. March 16, 2010. http://www.surinamemenunited.com/informatie/sexho-acceptation.html.

Ayala, George. "Retiring Behavioral Risk, Disease, and Deficit Models: Sexual

Health Frameworks for Latino Gay Men and Other Men Who Enjoy Sex with Men." In *Latina/o Sexualities: Probing Powers, Passions, Practices, and Policies*, edited by Marysol Asencio, 274–78. New Brunswick: Rutgers University Press, 2010.

Ayala, Hector. "Habla la reina del rap." *Dialogo*, March 1998, 4–5.

Báez, Jillian M. "'En mi imperio': Competing Discourses of Agency in Ivy Queen's Reggaetón." *CENTRO Journal* 18, no. 11 (2006): 63–81.

Bakshi, Anita. "Breaking with Tradition: Hybridity, Identity, and Resistance in Indo-Caribbean Women's Writing." In *Bindi: The Multifaceted Lives of Indo-Caribbean Women*, edited by Rosanne Kanhai, 208–24. Kingston: University of the West Indies Press, 2011.

Baksh, Rawwida. "Woman's Economic Achievements, Challenges since Independence." *Sunday Guardian* (Port-of-Spain), August 12, 2012.

Baksh-Soodeen, Rawwida. "Power, Gender, and Chutney." In Kanhai, *Matikor*, 194–98.

Barriteau, Eudine. *The Political Economy of Gender in the Twentieth-Century Caribbean*. New York: Palgrave Macmillan, 2001.

Barrow, Christine. *Family in the Caribbean: Themes and Perspectives*. Kingston: Ian Randle, 1996.

Basch, Linda, Nina Glick-Schiller, and Cristina Szanton Blanc. *Nations Unbound: Transnational Projects, Postcolonial Predicaments, and Deterritorialized Nation-States*. New York: Routledge, 1994.

Beck, Ulrich. "Cosmopolitan Realism: On the Distinction between Cosmopolitanism in Philosophy and the Social Sciences." *Global Networks* 4, no. 2 (2004): 131–56. doi:10.1111/j.1471-0374.2004.00084.x.

Bejel, Emilio. *Gay Cuban Nation*. Chicago: University of Chicago Press, 2001.

Belfort-Chanol, Aline. *Le bal paré-masqué: Un aspect du carnaval de la Guyane française*. Matoury Cedex: Ibis Rouge Editions, 2000.

Benítez-Rojo, Antonio. *The Repeating Island: The Caribbean and the Postmodern Perspective*. Durham: Duke University Press, 1997.

Bergman, Sara. "*Matikor*, Chutney, Odissi and Bollywood: Gender Negotiations in Indo-Trinidadian Dance." *Caribbean Review of Gender Studies* 2 (2008): 1–28. http://sta.uwi.edu/crgs/september2008/journals/SaraBergman.pdf.

Berlant, Lauren. *Cruel Optimism*. Durham: Duke University Press, 2011.

Béroard, Jocelyne. *Yen ki lanmou*. Note A Bene, 2011, compact disc.

Berrian, Brenda F. *Awakening Spaces: French Caribbean Popular Songs, Music, and Culture*. Chicago: Chicago University Press, 2000.

———. Interview by Siddhartha Mitter. *Afropop Worldwide*, March 2009. Online in two parts at http://www.afropop.org/wp/13573/interview-brenda-berrian-on-the-music-and-culture-of-the-french-caribbean-part-1/ (part 1) and http://www.

afropop.org/wp/13783/interview-brenda-berrian-on-music-and-culture-in-the-french-caribbean-part-2/ (part 2).

———. "Zouk Diva: Interview with Jocelyne Béroard." *MaComère* 2 (1999) 1–11.

Bilby, Kenneth. "A Caribbean Musical Enigma: Barbados." Review of *Destination Barbados* (film), by Ola Balogun. *Caribbean Studies* 36, no. 2 (2008), 236–40. http://www.jstor.org.ez-proxy.brooklyn.cuny.edu:2048/stable/pdfplus/25613190.pdf?acceptTC=true.

Binner, Jane M., and Antony W. Dines. "Marriage, Divorce, and Legal Change: New Evidence from England and Wales." *Economic Inquiry* 39, no. 2 (2001): 298–306.

Binnie, Jon. *Globalization of Sexuality.* Thousand Oaks: Sage, 2004.

Bleys, Rudi. *Images of Ambiente: Homotextuality and Latin American Art, 1810–Today.* New York: Continuum, 2000.

Bobes, Marilyn. "Someone Has to Cry." In Glave, *Our Caribbean*, 57–69.

Boyce Davies, Carole. *Black Women, Writing and Identity: Migrations of the Subject.* New York: Routledge, 1994.

———. "'She Wants the Black Man Post': Sexuality in the Construction of Black Women's Leadership." *Agenda* 25, no. 4 (2011): 121–32. doi:10.1080/10130950.2011.633371.

Boyce Davies, Carole, and Elaine Savory Fido, eds. *Out of the Kuumbla: Caribbean Women and Literature.* Trenton: Africa World, 1994.

Boyce Taylor, Cheryl. *Raw Air.* New York: Fly By Night, 2000.

Brana-Shute, Rosemary. "Neighbourhood Networks and National Politics among Working-Class Afro-Surinamese Women." In *Women and Change in the Caribbean*, edited by Janet Momsen, 132–49. Kingston: Ian Randle, 1993.

Brand, Dionne. *Bread Out of Stone: Recollections, Sex, Recognitions, Race, Dreaming, and Politics.* Toronto: Coach House, 1994.

———. *In Another Place, Not Here.* New York: Grove, 2000. Originally published in 1996 by Knopf Canada, of Toronto. All citations in this book are to the 2000 edition.

———. *No Language Is Neutral.* Toronto: McClelland and Stewart, 1998. Originally published in 1990 by Coach House Press in Toronto. All citations in this book are to the 1998 McClelland and Stewart edition.

Butler, Judith. *Gender Trouble: Feminism and the Subversion of Identity.* New York: Routledge, 2006.

Cabezas, Amalia L. *Economies of Desire: Sex and Tourism in Cuba and the Dominican Republic.* Philadelphia: Temple University Press, 2009.

Campt, Tina. "What's the '*Trans*' and Where's the '*National*' in Transnational Feminist Practice?—A Response," Paper presented at the Feminist Theory and Activism in Global Perspective' Conference, London, September 26, 2009. *Feminist*

Review conference proceedings: http://www.palgrave-journals.com/fr/conf-proceedings/n1s/full/fr201131a.html.

Cave, D. Michelle, and Joan French. "Sexual Choice as Human Right Issue." *Gay, Lesbian, Bisexual, Transgender, and Queer Jamaica.* Blog. June 26, 2010. http://glbtqjamaica.blogspot.com/2010_06_20_archive.html.

Center for Constitutional Rights. "Ugandan LGBT Activists File Case against Anti-Gay U.S. Evangelical in Federal Court." Press release. *Center for Constitutional Rights.* March 14, 2012. http://ccrjustice.org/LGBTUganda/.

Chancy, Myriam J. A. "Subversive Sexualities: Revolutionizing Gendered Identities." *Frontiers: A Journal of Women's Studies* 29, no. 1 (2008): 51–75.

Clarke, Austin. *The Bigger Light.* Toronto: Vintage Canada, 1998.

———. *The Meeting Point.* Toronto: Vintage Canada, 1998.

———. *Storm of Fortune.* Toronto: Vintage Canada, 1998.

Clarke, Edith. *My Mother Who Fathered Me: A Study of the Family in Three Selected Communities in Jamaica.* London: Ruskin House, 1957.

Cliff, Michelle. Interview by Meryl F. Schwarz. *Contemporary Literature* 34, no. 4 (1993): 594–619.

———. *No Telephone to Heaven.* New York: Plume, 1996. Originally published by E. P. Dutton in 1987. All citations in *Island Bodies* are to the 1996 Plume paperback edition.

Clifford, James. "Diasporas." *Cultural Anthropology* 9, no. 3 (1994): 302–38.

Condé, Maryse. *Heremakhonon.* Translated by Richard Philcox. Washington, DC: Three Continents, 1999. Originally published 1976 in French as *Heremakhonon.* Reissued in French as *En attendant le bonheur (Heremakhonon)*, Paris: Seghers, 1988. All citations in this book are to the Philcox translation.

———. "Order, Disorder, Freedom, and the West Indian Writer." *Yale French Studies* 97 (2000): 151–65.

Cooper, Carolyn. *Noises in the Blood: Orality, Gender, and the 'Vulgar' Body of Jamaican Popular Culture.* Durham: Duke University Press, 1995.

Costa, Dora L. "From Mill Town to Board Room: The Rise of Women's Paid Labor." *Journal of Economic Perspectives* 14, no. 4 (2000): 101–22.

Crawford, Charmaine. "'It's a Girl Thing': Problematizing Female Sexuality, Gender and Lesbophobia in Caribbean Culture." In King and Nixon, *Theorizing Homophobias.* http://www.caribbeanhomophobias.org/itsagirlthing.

Crespo-Kebler, Elizabeth. "'The Infamous Crime against Nature': Constructions of Heterosexuality and Lesbian Subversion in Puerto Rico." In Lewis, *The Culture of Gender and Sexuality in the Caribbean*, 190–215.

Crowley, Daniel. "Naming Customs in St. Lucia." *Social and Economic Studies* 5, no. 1 (1956): 87–92.

Cudjoe, Selwyn, ed. *Caribbean Women Writers: Essays from the First International Conference.* Wellesley: Calaloux, 1990.

Cvetkovich, Ann. *An Archive of Feelings: Trauma, Sexuality, and Lesbian Public Cultures.* Durham: Duke University Press, 2003.

Cyrille, Dominique. "Popular Music and Martinican-Creole Identity." *Black Music Research Journal* 22, no. 1 (2002): 65–83.

Dabydeen, David. *The Intended.* London: Secker and Warburg, 1991.

Dalleo, Raphael. *Caribbean Literature and the Public Sphere: From the Plantation to the Postcolonial.* Charlottesville: University of Virginia Press, 2011.

Daly, Stephanie. *The Developing Legal Status of Women in Trinidad and Tobago.* Port of Spain: National Commission on the Status of Women, 1982.

Danticat, Edwidge. *Breath, Eyes, Memory.* 2nd ed. New York: Vintage, 1998.

———. *The Farming of Bones.* New York: Penguin, 1999.

Davis, Natalie. *Society and Culture in Early Modern France: Eight Essays.* Stanford: Stanford University Press, 1975.

Decena, Carlos. *Tacit Subjects: Belonging and Same-Sex Desire among Dominican Immigrant Men.* Durham: Duke University Press, 2011.

Deen, Faizal. *Land without Chocolate.* Hamilton: Wolsak and Wynn, 2000.

Delanty, Gerard. *The Cosmopolitan Imagination: The Renewal of Critical Social Theory.* Cambridge: Cambridge University Press, 2009.

Delgado, Héctor. "From *The Sacred Wild* to the City: Santería in Cuba Today." In *Sacred Possessions: Vodou, Santería, Obeah, and the Caribbean,* edited by Margarite Fernández Olmos and Lizabeth Paravisini-Gebert, 101–21. New Brunswick: Rutgers University Press, 1997.

de Moya, E. Antonio. "Power Games and Totalitarian Masculinity in the Dominican Republic." In Reddock, *Interrogating Caribbean Masculinities,* 89–90.

Derby, Lauren. "The Dictator's Seduction: Gender and State Spectacle during the Trujillo Regime." *Callaloo* 23, no. 3 (2000), 1112–46.

Díaz, Junot. *The Brief Wondrous Life of Oscar Wao.* New York: Riverhead, 2008.

———. "How to Date a Browngirl (Blackgirl, Whitegirl, or Halfie)." In *Drown.* New York: Faber and Faber, 2007. First published 1996 in New York by Riverhead. All citations in this book are from the 2007 paperback edition.

Dixon, Meredith. "Lovers and Children of the Natural Mystic: The Story of Bob Marley, Women and their Children." *The Dread Library,* n.d., http://debate.uvm.edu/dreadlibrary/dixon.html.

Downes, Aviston D. "Boys of the Empire: Elite Masculinity and the Construction of Hegemonic Masculinity in Barbados, 1875–1920." In Reddock, *Interrogating Caribbean Masculinities,* 105–36.

Drayton, Kathleen. "Art, Culture and National Heritage." In *Barbados: Thirty Years of Independence,* edited by Trevor Carmichael, 197–237. Kingston: Ian Randle, 1996.

Duany, Jorge. *Blurred Borders: Transnational Migration between the Hispanic Caribbean and the United States.* Chapel Hill: University of North Carolina Press, 2011.

Edmondson, Belinda. *Caribbean Middlebrow: Leisure Culture and the Middle Class.* Ithaca: Cornell University Press, 2009.

————, ed. *Caribbean Romances: The Politics of Regional Representation.* Charlottesville: University of Virginia Press, 1999.

————. *Making Men: Gender, Literary Authority, and Women's Writing in Caribbean Narrative.* Durham: Duke University Press, 1998.

————. "Public Spectacles: Caribbean Women and the Politics of Public Performance." *Small Axe* 7, no. 1 (2003): 1–16.

Edwards, Walter F. "A Description and Interpretation of the Kwe-Kwe Tradition in Guyana." *Folklore* 93, no. 2 (1982): 181–92.

Elwin, Rosamund, ed. *Tongues on Fire: Caribbean Lesbian Lives and Stories.* Toronto: Women's Press, 1997.

Eriksen, Thomas Hylland. "The Cultural Contexts of Ethnic Differences." *Man* 26, no. 1 (1991): 127–44.

Escoffier, Jeffrey. *American Homo: Community and Perversity.* Berkeley: University of California Press, 1998.

Fairley, Jan. "Dancing Back to Front: Regeton, Sexuality, Gender and Transnationalism in Cuba." *Popular Music* 25, no. 3 (2006): 471–88.

Fanon, Frantz. *Black Skin, White Masks.* Translated by Charles Lam Markmann. New York: Grove, 1967. Originally published in French as *Peau noire, masques blancs,* Paris: Éditions du Seuil, 1952. English citations in this book are taken from the 1967 Grove edition; citations in French are from the 1952 Éditions du Seuil first edition.

Ferguson, Roderick. *Aberrations in Black: Towards a Queer of Color Critique.* Minneapolis: University of Minnesota Press, 2003.

Fisk, Donald M. "American Labor in the 20th Century." *Compensation and Working Conditions.* Department of Labor, Bureau of Labor and Statistics. 2003. http://www.bls.gov/opub/cwc/cm20030124aro2p1.htm.

Foucault, Michel. *History of Sexuality.* Vol. 1: *An Introduction.* Translated by Robert Hurley. New York: Vintage, 1980.

Francis, Donette. *Fictions of Feminine Citizenship: Sexuality and Nation in Contemporary Caribbean Literature.* New York: Palgrave Macmillan, 2010.

Fuss, Diana. "Interior Colonies: Frantz Fanon and the Politics of Identification." *Diacritics* 24, no. 2–3 (1994): 19–42.

Gay, R. "Of Ghosts and Shadows." In *Best Lesbian Erotica 2003,* edited by Cheryl Clarke and Tristan Taormino, 109–21. Berkeley: Cleis, 2003.

Giddings, Paula. *When and Where I Enter: The Impact of Black Women on Race and Sex in America.* New York: Harper Collins, 1984.

Gilroy, Paul. *The Black Atlantic: Modernity and Double-Consciousness.* Cambridge, MA: Harvard University Press, 1993.

Glave, Thomas, ed. *Our Caribbean: A Gathering of Lesbian and Gay Writing from the Antilles.* Durham: Duke University Press, 2008.

——. Introduction to *A Small Gathering of Bones*, by Patricia Powell, vii–x. Boston: Beacon, 2003. Novel first published 1994 by Heinemann.

——. *Whose Song? and Other Stories.* San Francisco: City Lights, 2001.

——. *Words to Our Now: Imagination and Dissent.* Minneapolis: University of Minnesota Press, 2007.

Glissant, Edouard. *Poetics of Relation.* Translated by Betsy Wing. Ann Arbor: University of Michigan Press, 1997. Originally published in French as *Poétique de la Relation*, Paris: Gallimard, 1990.

Godreau, Isar P., Mariolga Reyes Cruz, Mariluz Franco Ortiz, and Sherry Cuadrado. "The Lessons of Slavery, *Mestizaje*, and *Blanqueamiento* in an Elementary school in Puerto Rico." *American Ethnologist* 35, no. 1 (2008): 115–35. doi:10.1111/j.2008.1548-125.00009.x.

Gonzales, Joanna. "Ivy Queen: La Reina de Reggaeton." *The Beat* 23, no. 4 (2004): 32.

Gopinath, Gayatri. *Impossible Desires: Queer Diasporas and South Asian Public Cultures.* Durham: Duke University Press, 2005.

Gordon, Lewis R., T. Denean Sharpley-Whiting, and Renee T. White. Introduction to *Fanon: A Critical Reader*, 1–10. Edited and translated by Lewis R. Gordon, T. Denean Sharpley-Whiting, and Renee T. White. Hoboken: Wiley-Blackwell, 1996.

Gosine, Andil. "Sexual Desires, Rights, and Regulations." *Caribbean Review of Gender Studies* 3 (2009): 1–4. http://sta.uwi.edu/crgs/november2009/journals/Editorial.pdf

Green, Cecilia A. "Between Respectability and Self-Respect: Framing Afro-Caribbean Women's Labor History." *Social and Economic Studies* 55, no. 3 (2006): 1–31.

Greene, Erin. "History of Rainbow Alliance Bahamas." In King and Nixon, *Theorizing Homophobias.* http://www.caribbeanhomophobias.org/node/11.

Grewal, Inderpal. *Transnational America: Feminisms, Diasporas, Neoliberalisms.* Durham: Duke University Press, 2005.

Grewal, Inderpal, and Caren Kaplan. "Global Identities: Theorizing Transnational Studies of Sexuality." *GLQ: A Journal of Lesbian and Gay Studies* 7, no. 4 (2001): 663–79.

Grimes, William. "A Jet-Set Don Juan, Right Up to the Final Exit," review of *The Last Playboy*, by Shawn Levy. *New York Times*, September 16, 2005. http://www.nytimes.com/2005/09/16/books/16book.html.

Groot, Willemien. "Dutch Island Horrified by Same-Sex Marriages." *Radio Nether-*

lands Worldwide, April 23, 2010. http://www.rnw.nl/africa/article/dutch-island-horrified-same-sex-marriages.

Guilbault, Jocelyne. "Music, Politics, and Pleasure: Live Soca in Trinidad." *Small Axe* 14, no. 1 (2010): 16–29.

———. "The Politics of Calypso in a World of Music Industries." In *Popular Music Studies,* edited by David Hesmondhalgh and Keith Negus, 191–204. London: Arnold, 2002.

Guzmán, Manolo. *Gay Hegemony/Latino Homosexualities.* New York: Routledge, 2006.

Halberstam, Judith. *Female Masculinity.* Durham: Duke University Press, 1998.

Hall, Stuart. "Minimal Selves." In *Black British Cultural Studies: A Reader,* edited by Houston A. Baker, Manthia Diawara, and Ruth H. Lindeborg, 114–19. Chicago: University of Chicago Press, 1996.

———. *Questions of Cultural Identity.* Thousand Oaks: Sage, 1996.

Haniff, Nesha. "My Grandmother Worked in the Field: Stereotypes Regarding East Indian Women in the Caribbean: Honorable Mention." In *Matikor: The Politics of Identity for Caribbean Women,* edited by Rosanne Kanhai, 18–31. St. Augustine: UWI School of Continuing Studies, 1995.

Hanson, Vicki. "Correcting 'Corrective Rape.'" Paper presented at 2011 Caribbean HIV Conference, Nassau, Bahamas, November 18–21, 2011. https://www.2011caribbeanhivconference.org/abstract/correcting-corrective-rape.

Harewood, Susan. "Transnational Soca Performances, Gendered Re-Narrations of Caribbean Nationalism." *Social and Economic Studies* 55, no. 1–2 (2006): 25–48.

Harney, Stefano. *Nationalism and Identity: Culture and the Imagination in a Caribbean Diaspora.* London: Zed Books, 1996.

Harris, Max. "Masking the Site: The Fiestas de Santiago Apóstol in Loíza, Puerto Rico." *Journal of American Folklore* 114, no. 453 (2001): 358–69.

Held, David. *Cosmopolitanism: Ideals and Realities.* Malden: Polity, 2010.

Helg, Aline. "Black Men, Racial Stereotyping, and Violence in the U.S. South and Cuba at the Turn of the Century." *Comparative Studies in Society and History* 42, no. 3 (2000): 576–604. doi:0010-4175/00/3412-1362.

Hernández Hiraldo, Samiri, and Mariana Ortega-Brena. "'If God Were Black and from Loíza': Managing Identities in a Puerto Rican Seaside Town." *Latin American Perspectives* 33, no. 1 (2006): 66–82.

Herold, Edward, Rafael Garcia, and Tony DeMoya. "Female Tourists and Beach Boys: Romance or Sex Tourism?" *Annals of Tourism Research* 28, no. 4 (2001): 978–97. doi:S0160-7383(01)00003-2.

Hinds, Alison. "Alison Hinds Speaking about 'Faluma.'" *YouTube* video, 2:34, posted by jouvay.com. August 7, 2008. http://www.youtube.com/watch?v=zdU8_WEnisQ.

———. *Soca Queen.* 1720 Entertainment, 2007, compact disc.

Hirst, Paul Q., and Grahame Thompson. *Globalization in Question: The International Economy and the Possibilities of Governance.* 2nd ed. Cambridge: Polity, 2001.

Ho, Christine G. T. "Caribbean Transnationalism as a Gendered Process." *Latin American Perspectives* 26, no. 5 (1999): 34–54.

Ho, Christine G. T., and Keith Nurse. *Globalisation, Diaspora and Caribbean Popular Culture.* Kingston: Ian Randle, 2005.

Hoefte, Rosemarijn. "A Passage to Suriname? The Migration of Modes of Resistance by Asian Contract Laborers." *International Labor and Working-Class History* 54 (1998): 19–39.

Homel, David. Introduction to *How to Make Love to a Negro*, by Dany Laferrière and translated by David Homel. Toronto: Coach House, 1987.

Horn, Maja. "Queer Caribbean Homecomings: The Collaborative Art Exhibits of Nelson Ricart-Guerrero and Christian Vauzelle." *GLQ: A Journal of Lesbian and Gay Studies* 14, no. 2–3 (2008): 361–81.

Hron, Anthony, Phillip Dayle, Ian McKnight, Robert Carr, and Jamaica AIDS Support. "Report on Persecution of Sexual Minorities in Jamaica." Kingston: Jamaica AIDS Support, May 24, 2003. PDF downloadable at *ASICAL.org*, http://www.asical.org/es/download.php?uid=0&todo=0&leng=es&det=2.

Institute for Multicultural Development. *Factbook: The Position of Muslims in the Netherlands: Facts and Figures 2008.* Utrecht: Forum, 2008.

International Gay and Lesbian Human Rights Commission, and SEROvie. "The Impact of the Earthquake, and Relief and Recovery Programs on Haitian LGBT People." http://www.iglhrc.org/binary-data/ATTACHMENT/file/000/000/504-1.pdf.

Island in the Sun. DVD. Directed by Robert Rossen, 1957. Los Angeles: 20th Century Fox, 2006.

Jiménez, Félix. "(W)rapped in Foil: Glory at Twelve Words a Minute." In Rivera, Marshall, and Pacini Hernández, *Reggaeton*, 229–51.

Kale, Madhavi. *Fragments of Empire: Capital, Slavery, and Indian Indentured Labor Migration in the British Caribbean.* Philadelphia: University of Pennsylvania Press, 1998.

Kanhai, Rosanne. "The Masala Stone Sings: Poetry, Performance, and Film by Indo-Caribbean Women." In Kanhai, *Matikor*, 209–37.

———, ed. *Matikor: The Politics of Identity for Indo-Caribbean Women.* St. Augustine: UWI School of Continuing Studies, 1995.

Kaplan, Caren, Norma Alarcón, and Minoo Moallem, eds. *Between Woman and Nation: Nationalisms, Transnational Feminisms, and the State.* Durham: Duke University Press, 1999.

Kempadoo, Kamala. "Caribbean Sexuality: Mapping the Field." *Caribbean Review of Gender Studies* 3 (2009): 1–24. http://sta.uwi.edu/crgs/november2009/index. asp.

———. *Sexing the Caribbean: Gender, Race, and Sexual Labor.* New York: Routledge, 2004.

———, ed. *Sun, Sex, and Gold: Tourism and Sex Work in the Caribbean.* New York: Rowman and Littlefield, 1999.

Kempadoo, Oonya. *Buxton Spice.* New York: Penguin, 1999.

———. *Tide Running.* Boston: Beacon, 2001.

Kincaid, Jamaica. *Annie John.* New York: Farrar, Straus and Giroux, 1990.

———. *Lucy.* New York: Farrar, Straus and Giroux, 1990.

King, Rosamond S. "Dressing Down: Male Transvestism in Two Caribbean Carnivals." Special issue, "Caribbean Theater and Cultural Performance," *Sargasso* (2004–2005): 25–36.

———. "Jamette Women's Double Cross: Creating an Archive." *Women and Performance: A Journal of Feminist Theory,* 11, no. 1, (1999): 203–10.

———. "Lesbians in English and Spanish Caribbean Literature." Unpublished manuscript, 2011.

———. "New Citizens, New Sexualities—19th Century *Jamettes.*" In Smith, *Sex and the Citizen,* 214–23.

King, Rosamond S., and Angelique V. Nixon, eds. *Theorizing Homophobias in the Caribbean: Complexities of Place, Desire, and Belonging.* 2011. Digital multimedia collection. Launched June 15, 2012. http://www.caribbeanhomophobias.org.

Kutzinski, Vera. *Sugar's Secrets: Race and the Erotics of Cuban Nationalism.* Charlottesville: University of Virginia Press, 1993.

Laferrière, Dany. *How to Make Love to a Negro.* Translated by David Hormel. Toronto: Coach House, 1987. Reprinted in 2010 with full title *How to Make Love to a Negro without Getting Tired,* Vancouver: Douglas and McIntyre. Originally published in French as *Comment faire l'amour avec un nègre sans se fatiguer,* Montreal: VLB, 1985. Unless otherwise noted, citations in *Island Bodies* are to the 1987 Coach House edition.

———. *Vers le sud.* Quebec: Boréal, 2006. Translated by Wayne Grady as *Heading South,* Vancouver: Douglas and McInyre, 2009. See *Vers le sud/Heading South* under *V* for film of same name.

LaFont, Suzanne. "Very Straight Sex: The Development of Sexual Morés in Jamaica." *Journal of Colonialism and Colonial History* 2, no. 3 (2001): 1–25.

La Fountain-Stokes, Lawrence M. *Queer Ricans: Cultures and Sexualities in the Diaspora.* Minneapolis: University of Minnesota Press, 2009.

———. "Trans-locas: Migration, Homosexuality, and Transvestism in Recent Puerto Rican Performance (Freddie Mercado, Javier Cardona, Eduardo Alegría, Jorge

Merced, Arthur Avilés)." Workshop manuscript, Center for the Critical Analysis of Contemporary Culture, Rutgers University, New Brunswick, 2002.

———. *Uñas pintadas de azul/Blue Fingernails*. Tempe: Bilingual Review Press, 2009.

Laguerre, Steve. Interview with Angelique V. Nixon, "LGBT Activism in Haiti through SEROvie." Port-au-Prince, Haiti, July 2011. In King and Nixon, *Theorizing Homophobias*, http://www.caribbeanhomophobias.org.

Lamming, George. *In the Castle of My Skin*. London: Michael Joseph, 1953.

———. *Season of Adventure*. London: Michael Joseph, 1960.

Lancaster, Roger N. "Tolerance and Intolerance in Sexual Cultures in Latin America." In *Passing Lines: Sexuality and Immigration*, edited by Brad Epps, Keja Valens, and Bill Johnson González, 255–74. Cambridge, MA: David Rockefeller Center for Latin American Studies / Harvard University Press, 2005.

Lara, Ana-Maurine. *Erzulie's Skirt*. Washington, DC: Red Bone, 2006.

Larcher, Akim Ade, and Colin Robinson. "Fighting 'Murder Music': Activist Reflections." *Caribbean Review of Gender Studies* 3 (2009): 1–12.

Las fiestas de Santiago Apóstol en Loíza Aldea, July 1949. Film. Directed by Ricardo E. Alegría. San Juan: Centro de Investigaciones Arqueológicos de la Universidad de Puerto Rico, 1949.

Lewis, Linden, ed. *The Culture of Gender and Sexuality in the Caribbean*. Gainesville: University Press of Florida, 2003.

Lorde, Audre. *Sister Outsider: Essays and Speeches*. Freedom, Australia: Crossing, 2007.

Lumsden, Ian. *Machos, Maricones, and Gays: Cuba and Homosexuality*. Philadelphia: Temple University Press, 1996.

The Lunatic. Directed by Lol Crème, 1991. *Google* video, 1.35:03, http://video.google.com/videoplay?docid=-7169180673594460608.

Lundschien, Randy, P. Conner, and David Sparks. *Queering Creole Spiritual Traditions: Lesbian, Gay, Bisexual, and Transgender Participation in African-Inspired Traditions in the Americas*. New York: Routledge, 2004.

Mahabir, Cynthia. "The Rise of Calypso Feminism: Gender and Musical Politics in the Calypso." *Popular Music* 20, no. 3 (2001): 409–30.

Mahlis, Kristen. "Gender and Exile: Jamaica Kincaid's *Lucy*." *Modern Fiction Studies* 44, no. 1 (1998): 164–83.

Manrique, Jaime. "Mayra's Siren Song." *Críticas* (2003). http://www.criticasmagazine.com/article/CA291501.html.

Manuel, Peter. "Chutney and Indo-Trinidadian Cultural Identity." *Popular Music* 17, no. 1 (1998): 21–43.

Mariposas en el andamio (Butterflies in the scaffold). VHS. Directed by Luis Felipe Bernaza and Margaret Gilpin. Charlottesville: Water Bearer, 1998.

Marley. DVD. Directed by Kevin Macdonald. New York: Magnolia Pictures, 2012.

Marley, Bob, and the Wailers. "One Love/People Get Ready." On *Legend: The Best of Bob Marley and the Wailers*. Island Records Ltd., 1984.

Marley, Ziggy, and Kevin Macdonald. Radio interview with John Schaefer, "Bob Marley's Legend." *Soundcheck*. WNYC, April 17, 2012. http://www.wnyc.org/shows/soundcheck/2012/apr/17/.

Mehta, Brinda. *Diasporic Dis(locations): Indo-Caribbean Women Writers Negotiate the "Kala Pani."* Kingston: University of the West Indies Press, 2004.

Meredith, Sharon. "Barbadian *Tuk* Music: Colonial Development and Post-Independent Recontextualization." *British Journal of Ethnomusicology* 12, no. 2 (2003): 81–106.

Meschino, Patricia. "Alison Hinds: Coronating Her Majesty." *Vibe*, February 2008, 68.

Miller, Kei. *The Fear of Stones and Other Stories*. Oxford: Macmillan, 2006.

Minh-ha, Trinh T. "The Totalizing Quest of Meaning." In *Theorizing Documentary*, edited by Michael Renov, 90–107. New York, Routledge: 1993.

Mohammed, Aisha. "Love and Anxiety: Gender Negotiations in Chutney-Soca Lyrics in Trinidad." *Caribbean Review of Gender Studies* 1 (2007): 1–42.

Mohammed, Patricia. "Unmasking Masculinity and Deconstructing Patriarchy: Problems and Possibilities within Feminist Epistemology." In Reddock, *Interrogating Caribbean Masculinities*, 39–67.

Montero, Oscar. "The Queer Theories of Severo Sarduy." In *Between the Self and the Void: Essays in Honor of Severo Sarduy*, edited by Alicia Rivero-Potter, 65–78. Boulder: Society of Spanish and Spanish-American Studies, 1998.

Montesinos, Luis, and Juan Preciado. "Puerto Rico (Estado Libre Asociado de Puerto Rico)." In *International Encyclopedia of Sexuality*, edited by Robert T. Francoeur. New York: Continuum, 2001. Article published 2005. Citations in this book are to the online version at http://www2.hu-berlin.de/sexology/IES/index.html.

Mootoo, Shani. *Cereus Blooms at Night*. New York: Grove, 2009. First published in 1996 by Grove Press. References in this book are to the 2009 Grove paperback edition.

———. *Out on Main Street: And Other Stories*. Vancouver: Press Gang, 2002.

———. *Valmiki's Daughter*. Toronto: House of Anansi, 2010.

Moraga, Cherrie, and Gloria Anzaldúa, eds. *This Bridge Called My Back: Writings by Radical Women of Color*. New York: Kitchen Table / Women of Color Press, 1984.

Moreno Vega, Marta. *The Altar of My Soul: The Living Traditions of Santería*. New York: Ballantine, 2001.

———. "*Espiritismo* in the Puerto Rican community: A New World Recreation with the Elements of Kongo Ancestor Worship." *Journal of Black Studies* 29, no. 3 (1999): 325–53.

Morrison, Toni. *Playing in the Dark: Whiteness and the Literary Imagination.* Cambridge: Harvard University Press, 1992.

Murray, David A. B. *Opacity: Gender, Sexuality, Race, and the 'Problem' of Identity in Martinique.* New York: Peter Lang, 2002.

Naipaul, V. S. *The Mimic Men.* New York: Penguin, 1967.

Namaste, Viviane K. *Invisible Lives: The Erasure of Transsexual and Transgendered People.* Chicago: University of Chicago Press, 2000.

Negron-Muntaner, Frances. "Echoing Stonewall and Other Dilemmas: The Organizational Beginnings of a Gay and Lesbian Agenda in Puerto Rico, 1972–1977 (Part I)." *CENTRO Journal* 4, no. 1 (1991–92), 77–95.

Niranjana, Tejaswini. "'Left to the Imagination': Indian Nationalisms and Female Sexuality in Trinidad." *Public Culture* 11, no. 1 (1999): 223–43.

Nurse, Keith. "Masculinities in Transition: Gender and the Global Problematic." In Reddock, *Interrogating Caribbean Masculinities*, 3–37.

Obejas, Achy. *Days of Awe.* New York: Ballantine, 2002.

———. *Memory Mambo.* Berkeley: Cleis, 1996.

———. *We Came All the Way from Cuba So You Could Dress Like This?* Berkeley: Cleis, 1994.

October, Rose. "Half the Sky Festival: Brooklyn Women in Traditional Performance." Performance with workshop. Half the Sky Festival: Bachelorette Bash, Brooklyn Arts Council, Brooklyn, NY. June 10, 2012.

Of Men and Gods. DVD. Directed by Anne Lescot and Laurence Magloire. Watertown: Documentary Educational Resources, 2002.

Orgullo en Puerto Rico/Pride in Puerto Rico. DVD. Directed by Jorge Oliver and Irma Iranzo Berrocal. San Francisco: Frameline, 2007.

Orsi, Peter. "Cuba Transgender Wedding Shows Shifting Attitudes." *Yahoo News* online, August 13, 2011. http://news.yahoo.com/cuba-transgender-wedding-shows-shifting-attitudes-223709785.html.

Ortiz Cofer, Judith. "The Myth of the Latin Woman." In *Women Writing Resistance: Essays on Latin America and the Caribbean,* edited by Jennifer Browdy de Hernandez, 109–16. Cambridge, MA: South End, 2003.

Pacini Hernández, Deborah. "Dominicans in the Mix: Reflections on Dominican Identity." In Rivera, Marshall, and Pacini Hernández, *Reggaeton,* 135–64.

Painter, George. "The Sensibilities of Our Forefathers: The History of Sodomy Laws in the United States—Virgin Islands." Gay and Lesbian Archives of the Pacific Northwest. 2004. http://www.glapn.org/sodomylaws/sensibilities/virgin_islands.htm.

Paravisini-Gebert, Lizabeth, and Eva Woods Peiró. "'Porfirio Rubirosa': Masculinity, Race, and the Jet-Setting Latin Male." Keynote presentation, Mellon Mays

Undergraduate Conference, Brooklyn College, April 2011. Paper in author's possession.

Peña, Susana. "'Obvious Gays' and the State Gaze: Cuban Gay Visibility and US Immigration Policy during the 1980 Mariel Boatlift." *Journal of the History of Sexuality* 16, no. 3 (2007): 482–514.

Pinto, Samantha. "Why Must All Girls Want to Be Flag Women? Postcolonial Sexualities, National Reception, and Caribbean Soca Performance." *Meridians: Feminism, Race, Transnationalism* 10, no. 1 (2009): 137–63.

Pinto Alicea, Ines. "Sex, Lies, and Stereotypes." *Hispanic* 8, no. 1 (January/February 1995): 20–24.

Portes, Alejandro, Luis Eduardo Guarnizo, and William J. Haller. "Transnational Entrepreneurs: An Alternative Form of Immigrant Economic Adaptation." *American Sociological Review* 67, no. 2 (2002): 278–98.

Pourette, Dolorès. "La figure du makòmè: masque de l'homosexualité masculine dans les mondes guadeloupéens." In Rose Marie Lagrave, Agathe Gestin, Éléonore Lépinard, and Geneviève Pruvost, *Dissemblances: Jeux et enjeux du genre*, Paris: L'Harmattan, 2002, 51–63. Online at *GwadaGays*, http://gaygwada.meilleurforum.com/t270-la-figure-du-makome. All translations of this work are my own.

Powell, Patricia. *The Pagoda*. New York: Mariner Books, 1999.

Puar, Jasbir. *Terrorist Assemblages: Homonationalism in Queer Times*. Durham: Duke University Press, 2007.

Pulis, John W. *Religion, Diaspora and Cultural Identity: A Reader in the Anglophone Caribbean*. New York: Routledge, 1999.

Puri, Shalini. *The Caribbean Postcolonial: Social Equality, Post-Nationalism, and Cultural Hybridity*. New York: Palgrave Macmillan, 2004.

Queen, Ivy. *The Original Rude Girl*. Sony Discos, 1998, compact disc.

———. *Real Album*. Universal Latino, 2004, compact disc.

———. "Yo Quiero Bailar," *The Best of Ivy Queen*. DVD. Perfect Image, 2005.

Quiroga, José. *Tropics of Desire: Interventions from Queer Latino America*. New York: New York University Press, 2000.

Ramírez, Rafael L. *What It Means to Be a Man: Reflections on Puerto Rican Masculinity*. New Brunswick: Rutgers University Press, 1999.

Ramos, Junaita. *Compañeras: Latina Lesbians*. New York: Latina Lesbian Project, 1987.

Rangelova, Radost. "Nationalism, States of Exception, and Caribbean Identities in *Sirena Selena Vestida de Pena* and 'Loca de la Locura.'" *CENTRO Journal* 19 no. 1 (2007): 74–88.

Reddock, Rhoda E., ed. *Interrogating Caribbean Masculinities: Theoretical and Empirical Analyses*. Kingston: University of the West Indies Press, 2004.

Renov, Michael, ed. *Theorizing Documentary.* Introduction by Michael Renov. New York: Routledge, 1993.

Rent a Rasta. Directed by J. Michael Seyfert. La Paz: Yeah But/Not Now Productions, 2006. Full movie online at http://topdocumentaryfilms.com/rent-a-rasta/.

Rihanna. *Loud.* Island Def Jam Music Group, 2011. Compact disc.

Rivera, Raquel Z., Wayne Marshall, and Deborah Pacini Hernández, eds. *Reggaeton.* Durham: Duke University Press, 2009.

Rivera-Valdés, Sonia. *The Forbidden Stories of Marta Veneranda.* New York: Seven Stories, 2001.

Roberts, Glenys. "Revealed: The White Ex-Naval Officer Who Fathered Bob Marley Was a British Captain from Essex." *Daily Mail,* April 18, 2012. http://www.dailymail.co.uk.

Roberts, Peter. "Distinctive Features of *Las Locas*—Black Faces, Brooms, Cans, Tips and Big Behinds." *Sargasso* 2 (2006–7): 31–56.

Robinson, Colin. "Patricia Gone with Millicent: Rescuing the Caribbean's Sexual Imagination from Murder." Unpublished manuscript, 2011.

———. "Toward a Strategy of Imagination." Paper presented at "Queer Islands?" Conference, University of Chicago, April 16, 2005. Paper in author's possession.

———. "The Work of Three-Year CAISO—Reflections at the MidPoint." Activist report on Coalition Advocating for Inclusion of Sexual Orientation in (CAISO), Trinidad and Tobago, published June 2012. In King and Nixon, *Theorizing Homophobias.* http://www.caribbeanhomophobias.org/node/20.

———. "Transforming Patriarchy through Feminist Nationalism: GLBT Explorations of a Global South Sexual Politics in Trinidad and Tobago." PowerPoint presentation given at the Annual Conference of the Caribbean Studies Association, Curaçao, June 2, 2011. PowerPoint in author's possession.

Robinson-Walcott, Kim. *Out of Order! Anthony Winkler and White West Indian Writing.* Kingston: University of the West Indies Press, 2006.

Rodríguez, Juana María. *Queer Latinidad: Identity, Practices, Discursive Spaces.* New York: New York University Press, 2003.

Rodríguez Acosta, Ofelia. *La vida mana.* Madrid: Biblioteca Rubén Darío, 1929.

Roemer, Astrid. *Over de gekte van een vrouw.* Haarlem: de Knipscheer, 1982.

Rohlehr, Gordon. "I Lawa: The Construction of Masculinity in Trinidad and Tobago Calypso." In Reddock, *Interrogating Caribbean Masculinities,* 326–403.

Romain, Guerda. "Before Black Was Beautiful: The Representation of Women in the Haitian Novel." *French Review* 77, no. 1 (1997): 55–65.

Roorda, Eric Paul. "Genocide Next Door: The Good Neighbor Policy, the Trujillo Regime, and the Haitian Massacre of 1937." *Diplomatic History* 20, no. 3 (1996): 301–319.

Safa, Helen Icken. "From Shanty Town to Public Housing: A Comparison of Family Structure in Two Urban Neighborhoods in San Juan, Puerto Rico." *Caribbean Studies* 4, no. 1 (1964): 3–12.

———. *The Myth of the Male Breadwinner: Women and Industrialization in the Caribbean.* Conflict and Social Change Series. Boulder: Westview, 1995.

Saint, Assotto. *Spells of a Voodoo Doll: The Poems, Fiction, Essays, and Plays of Assotto Saint.* New York: Masquerade, 1996.

Saint-Aubin, Arthur Flannigan. "Testeria: The Dis-ease of Black Men in White Supremacist, Patriarchal Culture," *Callaloo* 17, no. 4 (1994): 1054–73.

Salewicz, Chris. *Bob Marley: The Untold Story.* New York: Faber and Faber, 2009.

Salyers Bull, Sheana. "Machismo/Marianismo Attitudes, Employment, Education, and Sexual Behavior among Women in Ecuador and the Dominican Republic." *Journal of Gender, Culture, and Health* 3, no. 1 (1998): 1–27.

Sánchez Taylor, Jacqueline. "Dollars Are a Girl's Best Friend? Female Tourists' Sexual Behaviour in the Caribbean." *Sociology* 35, no. 3 (2001): 749–64.

Santos-Febres, Mayra. *Sirena Selena vestida de pena.* Milan: Mondadori, 2000. Translated into English by Stephen Lytle as *Sirena Selena,* New York: Picador, 2000. Unless otherwise noted, citations in this book are to the Lytle translation.

Sarduy, Severo. *From Cuba with a Song.* Translated by Suzanne J. Levine. Los Angeles: Sun and Moon, 2000.

———. *Written on a Body.* Translated by Carol Maier. Santa Fe: Lumen Books, 1992.

Sassen, Saskia. *Globalization and Its Discontents: Essays on the New Mobility of People and Money.* New York: New Press, 1989.

Saunders, Tanya L. "Grupo OREMI: Black Lesbians and the Struggle for Safe Social Space in Havana." *Souls* 11, no. 2 (2009): 167–85.

Schulman, Sarah. *Ties That Bind: Familial Homophobia and Its Consequences.* New York: New Press, 2012.

Seabrook, John. "The Song Machine: The Hitmakers behind Rihanna." *New Yorker,* March 26, 2012. http://www.newyorker.com/reporting/2012/03/26/120326fa_fact_seabrook.

Seigworth, Gregory J., and Melissa Gregg, eds. *The Affect Theory Reader.* Introduction by Seigworth and Gregg. Durham: Duke University Press, 2010.

Selbert, Patricia. *The House of Six Doors.* Santa Barbara: Publishing by the Seas, 2011.

Selvon, Samuel. *The Lonely Londoners.* New York: Longman, 1999.

Sexual Exiles. DVD. Directed and produced by Irene Sosa. 1999.

Sharpe, Jenny, and Samantha Pinto. "The Sweetest Taboo: Studies of Caribbean Sexualities: A Review Essay." *Signs: A Journal of Women in Culture and Society* 32, no. 11 (2006): 247–74.

Sheller, Mimi. *Consuming the Caribbean: From Arawaks to Zombies.* New York: Routledge, 2003.

Shepherd, Verene. "Constructing Visibility: Indian Women in the Jamaican Segment of the Indian Diaspora." In *Gendered Realities: Essays in Caribbean Feminist Thought*, edited by Patricia Mohammed, 107–28. Kingston: University of the West Indies Press, 2002.

Sifuentes-Jáuregui, Ben. *Transvestism, Masculinity, and Latin American Literature: Genders Share Flesh*. New York: Palgrave, 2002.

Silvera, Makeda. "Man Royals and Sodomites: Some Thoughts on the Invisibility of Afro-Caribbean Lesbians." In Glave, *Our Caribbean*, 368–81.

Skeete, Geraldine. "Representations of Homophobic Violence in Anglophone Caribbean Literature." *Caribbean Review of Gender Studies* 4 (2010): 1–20.

Slater, Miriam K. *The Caribbean Family: Legitimacy in Martinique*. New York: St. Martin's, 1977.

Smith, Faith, ed. *Sex and the Citizen: Interrogating the Caribbean*. Charlottesville: University of Virginia Press, 2011.

Solien de González, Nancie L. "The Consanguineal Household and Matrifocality." *American Anthropologist* 67, no. 6 (1965): 1541–49.

Songs of Freedom. DVD. Directed by Phillip Pike. Toronto: Jahloveboy Productions, 2002.

Sonny Boy. DVD. Directed by Maria Peters. 2010. Amsterdam: Shooting Star Filmcompany BV / A-Film Distribution, 2011.

Starbroek News. "He Wore Blue Velvet . . . ? Seven Fined for Cross-Dressing." February 10, 2009. http://www.stabroeknews.com/2009/archives/02/10/he-wore-blue-velvetseven-fined-for-cross-dressing/print/.

Steckles, Garry. *Bob Marley: A Life*. Northampton: Interlink, 2008.

Steinecke, Julia. "Caribbean Can Be Chilly When It Comes to Welcoming Gays." *Toronto Star*, November 10, 2007. http://www.thestar.com/article/274493—caribbean-can-be-chilly-when-it-comes-to-welcoming-gays.

Stevenson, Betsey, and Justin Wolfers, 2007. "Marriage and Divorce: Changes and Their Driving Forces." *Journal of Economic Perspectives* 21, no. 2 (2007): 27–52.

Swords, Alicia, and Ronald L. Mize. "Beyond Tourist Gazes and Performances: U.S. Consumption of Land and Labor in Puerto Rican and Mexican Destinations." *Latin American Perspectives* 35, no. 3 (2008): 56–57.

Tambiah, Yasmin. "Creating (Im)moral Citizens: Gender, Sexuality and Lawmaking in Trinidad and Tobago, 1986." *Caribbean Review of Gender Studies* 3 (2009): 1–19.

Tate, Shirley. "*Heading South*: Love/Sex, Necropolitics, and Decolonial Romance." *Small Axe* 15, no. 2 (2011): 43–58.

Taylor, Don. *Marley and Me: The Real Bob Marley Story*. New York: Barricade Books, 1995.

Thomas, Deborah A. *Modern Blackness: Nationalism, Globalization, and the Politics of Culture in Jamaica*. Durham: Duke University Press, 2004.

Thorington Springer, Jennifer. "'Roll It Gal': Allison Hinds, Female Empowerment, and Calypso." *Meridians: Feminism, Race, Transnationalism* 8, no. 1 (2007): 93–129.

Tinsley, Omise'eke Natasha. "Black Atlantic, Queer Atlantic: Queer Imaginings of the Middle Passage." *GLQ: A Journal of Lesbian and Gay Studies* 14, no. 2–3 (2008): 191–215.

———. "Summer and the Seven Paths of Yemaya." In *Spirited: Affirming the Soul and Black Gay/Lesbian Identity*, edited by G. Winston James and Lisa C. Moore, 323–33. Washington, DC: Red Bone, 2006.

———. *Thiefing Sugar: Eroticism between Women in Caribbean Literature*. Durham: Duke University Press, 2010.

Tomlinson, Maurice. "Jamaican Law, Homophobia, and HIV." AIDS-Free World. 2011. http://www.aidsfreeworld.org/Our-Issues/Homophobia/Jamaican-Law-Homophobia-and-HIV.aspx.

Tonkin, Boyd. "Anthony C. Winkler: A Playful Pirate of the Caribbean." *Independent* (London), January 5, 2007. http://www.independent.co.uk/arts-entertainment/books/features/anthony-c-winkler-a-playful-pirate-of-the-caribbean-430768.html.

Treviño, Jesús Salvador. "Latino Portrayals in Film and Television." *Jump Cut: A Review of Contemporary Media* 30 (1985): 14–16. http://www.ejumpcut.org/archive/onlinessays/JC30folder/LatinosFilmTvTrevino.html.

Turits, Richard Lee. "A World Destroyed, a Nation Imposed: The 1937 Haitian Massacre in the Dominican Republic." *Hispanic American Historical Review* 82, no. 3 (2002): 589–635.

Umpierre, Luz María. *I'm Still Standing: Treinta años de poesía/Thirty Years of Poetry*. Orlando: Lulu.com, 2011.

United Nations Entity for Gender Equality and the Empowerment of Women (UN Women). *Progress of the World's Women 2011–2012: In Pursuit of Justice*. UN Women. http://progress.unwomen.org/pdfs/EN-Report-Progress.pdf.

United Nations Office on Drugs and Crime (UNODC). *2011 Global Study on Homicide: Trends, Contexts, Data*. Vienna, 2011. http://www.unodc.org/documents/data-and-analysis/statistics/Homicide/Globa_study_on_homicide_2011_web.pdf.

United Nations Office on Drugs and Crime (UNODC), and the Latin America and the Caribbean (LAC) Region of the World Bank. *Crime, Violence, and Development: Trends, Costs, and Policy Options in the Caribbean*. Report 37820. March 2007. http://scm.oas.org/pdfs/2008/CP20887E01.pdf.

van der Zijl, Annejet. *Sonny Boy*. Amsterdam: NIJH and DITMAR, 2004.

Vers le sud/Heading South. DVD. Directed by Lauren Cantet, 2005. Santa Monica: Haut et Court, 2007.

Wahab, Amar. "Mapping West Indian Orientalism: Race, Gender and Representations of Indentured Coolies in the Nineteenth-Century British West Indies." *Journal of Asian American Studies* 10, no. 3 (2007): 283–311.

Walcott, Rinaldo. "Queer Returns: Human Rights, the Anglo-Caribbean and Diaspora Politics." *Caribbean Review of Gender Studies* 3 (2009): 1–19.

Waugh, Alec. *Island in the Sun.* New York: Farrar, Straus and Cudahy, 1955.

Wekker, Gloria. "*Mati*-ism and Black Lesbianism: Two Idealtypical Constructions of Female Homosexuality in Black Communities of the Diaspora." In Glave, *Our Caribbean*, 368–81.

———. "Politics and Passion: A Conversation with Gloria Wekker." Interview by Andil Gosine. *Caribbean Review of Gender Studies* 3 (2009): 1–11.

———. *The Politics of Passion: Women's Sexual Culture in the Afro-Surinamese Diaspora.* New York: Columbia University Press, 2006.

Welter, Barbara. "The Cult of True Womanhood: 1820–1860." *American Quarterly* 18, no. 2 (1966): 151–74.

Wilson, Peter J. *Crab Antics: The Social Anthropology of English-Speaking Negro Societies of the Caribbean.* New Haven: Yale University Press, 1973.

Winkler, Anthony C. *The Lunatic.* New York: Akashic, 1987.

Women's Caucus Strategic Team (Trinidad and Tobago). "Chat XII: Year in Review." PowerPoint presentation given at annual meeting of Women's Caucus Strategic Team, Trinidad, June 15, 2011. PowerPoint in author's possession.

Index

Rosamond S. King is a creative and critical writer, performer, and artist. She is associate professor of English at Brooklyn College. www.rosamondking.com

CPSIA information can be obtained
at www.ICGtesting.com
Printed in the USA
JSHW022005220123
36468JS00002B/173

9 780813 062068